9 10

CANTABRICUS

Cast. de Ortegal
Bares
Espasende
Cose
S. Marta
Carinno
S. Clodio
P. Naval
Landriotte
S. Roman
Ysla S. Cibrian
Sillyro
Viuero
S. Cibrian
C. de Brilo
Burelo
Lagoa
Santiago
Dasoz
Castro de Oro
Rilo
Mures
S. Iusto
Ribadeo
Roupas
Lorẽcana
villanova
Mondonnedo
Rio Maior
Neda
Iuvia
R. Eume
Puentes Deume
Andrade
Betangos
R. Mandeu
Artedo
Luarca
Navia
Asturias
Castropol
Benavente
Abres
Castro de Rey
Sanuso
Santo
Meyra M.
Villalua
Peubla de Navia
Trauada
Quintela
Sobrado M.
Castamenda
Parga
Villa
Vahamanda
Buron
Mellid
Otero de Rey
Castro verde
Fures
Navia de Var[illegible]ca
R. Vlla
Pambre
Ferrera M.
Rio Mino
Lugo
LEON PAIS.
Puebla d'S. Iulian
Fuen Sagrada
Pacos de N
Quinta
Cormorga
Hospital
R. Arnego
Amante
Mesonfrio
Portomarĩ
Sarria
Nogales
S. Roman
Lalin
Taldao
Ruian
Tria Castella
Ferreyra
R. Burbia
Villa pun
Chantada
Nozeda
Villa Soto
Valcacar
Rodeyro
Layosa
Cavedo
Zebreros
Prado
Faua
Villa franca
Osera M.
Carballia
P. Belezar
Puebla d'Brollem
Pacios
P. Paradela
Losada
Cacabelos
Monforte d'Lemnos
Peroxa
Torbo
P. de Lor
Courel
P. de Domingo flores
Iovesende
Cea
Barra
Tierra d'aguiar
Castro de Caldelas
Rubian
Ponferrada
Vilde
Melon M.
Villa
Marin
Ville
Orense
Casa Soa
S. Clodio
Villa Martin
Nobaes
Barco de Villoria
Arnoy
Peytes
Monte Furado
Quelle
P. Minus
Bannos de Molgas
Macede de Tribes
S. Esteuan d'Valdiorras
Buga
Sandas
Alaris
Bollo
Melgazo
Pinor
Buen Iesus
Escuderos
Bentrazes
Villa nueva d'los Infantes
Nozela
da pena
Sotelo
Viana
Puente
Ramirans
P. de los Maderos
Villa de Rey
Vegas de Camba
Porto
Bento
Entrimo
Lobera
Celme
Canizo
Pias
Canda
Mouco
Barra
Gudina
Villa vela
Luvian
Porquera
Mõte Rey Pacos
Requero
ALLIÆ.
Limia fl.
Vald
Salas
Rios
Chaqua souze
Mancalvos
C. d'Rebo

9 10

GALICIA

1997

Design: Alex Vázquez-Palacios
Photography: María Luisa Gil Nieto, Xunta de Galicia.
Photomecanics: G.M.V. color
Printed by: Artes Gráficas Vicus, S.A.L.
c/Segovia, 19. 36205 Vigo.
I.S.B.N.: 84-453-1915-9
Legal deposit: VG-902-1997

GALICIA

1997

XUNTA DE GALICIA

Presentation

The activity of a people during the course of time is a result of its knowledge, culture and spirit of progress. GALICIA 1997 aims to reflect the hard work of the Galician people. With their effort, perseverance and optimism, together with the action of the Government of the Xunta de Galicia, they have created a region which is no longer fragmented but which has achieved the same social and economic standard of living in all areas. The towns and villages on the coast have been communicated with those inland, the clusters of population all over Galicia have been linked together and organized, and the migration of the population has been stabilized.

The result is an agricultural sector which is progressing daily with the improvement and transformation of its structures; high quality livestock; a forestry sector which is regaining its identity without losing sight of its industrial importance; a mining industry with high added value and increasing respect for the environment; an international and highly technical fishing sector with a high exportation rate; an industrial sector which has been reorientated and which uses the latest technology and computer programmes to design its products for the overseas market; a strong building industry with highly qualified human and technical resources; a communications sector which is leading the way among developed countries and which reflects Galicia as a whole; and a modern, fast-acting health system. In short, it is a region which is striding forward with a clear aim: progress and well-being for Galician society.

GALICIA 1997 is a summary of all this. It hopes to portray an optimistic present-day reality and point the way to a future full of hope.

Manuel Fraga Iribarne
President of the Xunta de Galicia

I

TERRITORY

Relief and climate

- Location and extension.
- Geological composition.
- Orography.
- Effects of the relief.
- The soil.
- The coast.
- The climate.
- Effects of the climate.

TERRITORY.
RELIEF AND CLIMATE.

LOCATION AND EXTENSION.

Galicia is situated in the extreme north west of the Iberian peninsula, approximately between the northern latitude parallels 42 and 44, and between the western latitude meridians 7 and 8. It covers 29,424 square kilometres, 5.8% of the total area of Spain. It has a perimeter of 1,919 km, of which 610 are interior and 1,309 are coastal.

GEOLOGICAL COMPOSITION.

Galicia is essentially composed of *granite* and *slate.* These rocks were formed in very deep areas under the crust of the earth, and they were lifted and left exposed as the layers of soil covering them were eroded. In the area now considered Galicia, approximately 1,200 million years ago, there existed taller mountain ranges, perhaps with granite rocks, which bordered a vast sea. Due to erosion, a large amount of sediment gathered on the sea bed, which gradually sunk. Because of strong pressures and internal heat, these sediments were converted into the slate that nowadays forms the soil of the eastern part of Galicia. Subsequent upheavals caused the blocks to fracture, lift and sink. This caused the appearance of the present-day mountain ranges, *rias,* kaolin deposits and holes from which abundant thermal water springs. Gradually, erosion began levelling off the land, giving rise to the central plain that exists today in Galicia.

OROGRAPHY.

Geological history explains the orographical complexity of the Galician relief. The mountain ranges, flatlands, hollows and valleys together form the *Macizo Galaico (Galician mountain ranges).* This relief gradually rises from west to east, with more than half the region reaching an altitude higher than 400 metres. Due to the effects of erosion, there are now generally very rounded forms: old mountains, gentle slopes and numerous alluvial areas. But there are also more or less newly formed areas due to the orographical movements of the Tertiary Age.

The increasing altitude from west to east influences the course of the Galician rivers, since this gradient causes the large rivers, such as the Miño, Ulla and Tambre, to empty into the Antlantic Ocean. Likewise, this general lie of the land in Galicia effects the climatological conditions, as the warming influence of the sea loses its force from coastal to inland areas.

Contours of the Galician relief.

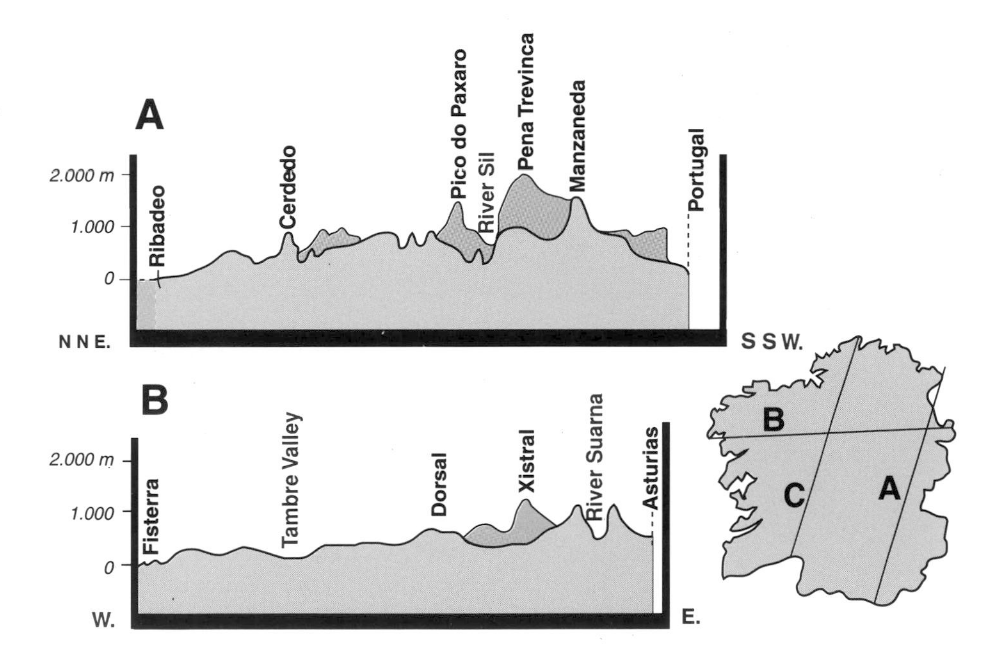

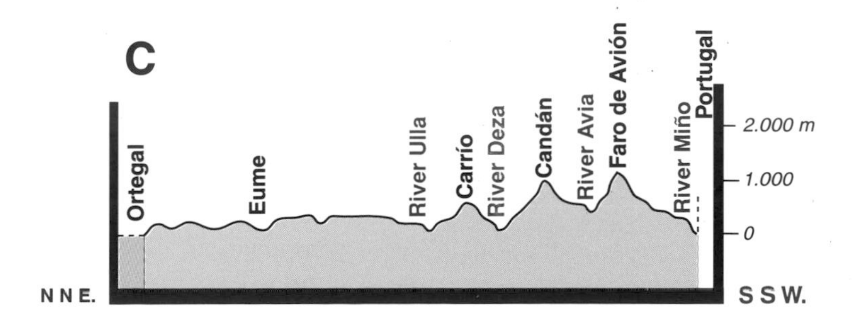

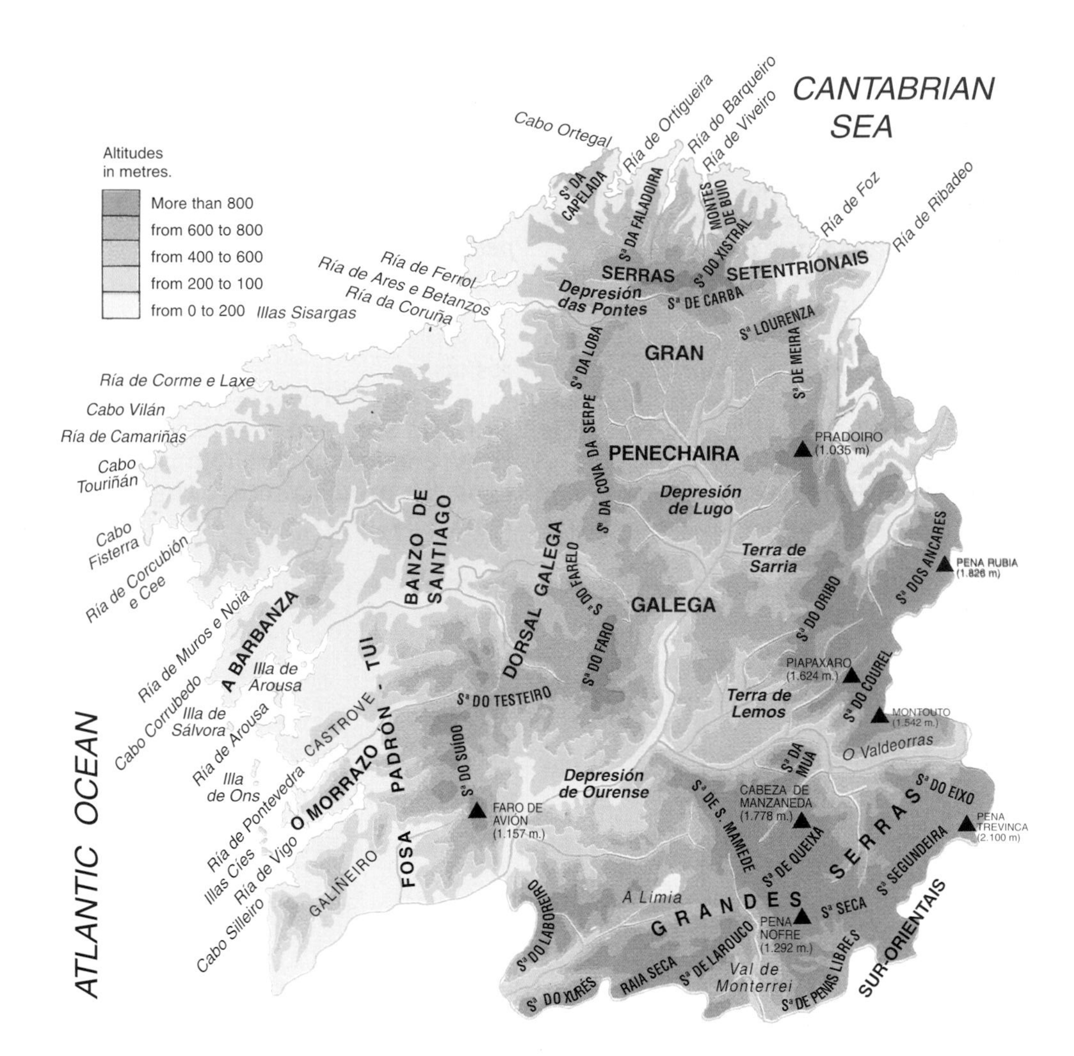

Map of the Galician relief.

The Galician relief is divided into the following classes:

A. *The great central plain:* It has a mean altitude of 500 to 600 metres and is crossed by the river Miño. It contains the depressions of **Lemos, Sarria, Lugo and As Pontes.**

B. *The mountains:* Seemingly, there are not any clearly defined mountain ranges. Even so, we can discern the following groups:

a) *The great southeastern mountain ranges:* Here we find the highest mountains in Galicia. The Sil river divides this group of mountains into two subgroups:

1) *The southern subgroup:* **Cabeza de Manzaneda** (1,778 m) which is the point where various mountain ranges begin and **Pena Trevinca** (2,124 m), the highest peak in Galicia. In this area the alluvial

depressions of **Ourense, A Limia, Monterrei** and **Valdeorras** are located.

2) *The northern area:* Mountain ranges of lower altitude: **O Courel, Os Ancares, Meira...**

b) ***The northern mountain ranges:*** Low ranges that scarcely reach 100 metres. They direct the courses of the short rivers northwards towards the Cantabrian sea, and the tributaries of the river Miño southwards. The highest peak is **Cuadramón** (1,037), the only summit that rises over one thousand metres.

c) ***Dorsal Gallega (The Galician Dorsal mountain ranges):*** Formed by an alignment of mountains in a N-S direction, with altitudes slightly above the 1,000 metre mark. These cause rivers to empty either into the basin of the river Miño, on one side, or the Atlantic rias, on the others. The **Faro de Avión** reaches 1,153 metres.

C. *Escalón de Santiago* and ***Fosa de Padrón-Tui:*** **The Escalón de Santiago** is located between the Dorsal Gallega and the Atlantic, a plateau with an altitude of 200 to 400 metres and the **Fosa de Padrón-Tui,** lying parallel to the coast and separated from it by small mountain ranges situated at right angles between the two, which extend to the sea: **Barbanza, Xiabre, Castrove, Morrazo, Galiñeiro.**

D. ***The lower coastal land:*** Formed by the coastal areas, their mean altitude is below 200 metres.

Mountain landscape.

Valdeorras.

EFFECTS OF THE RELIEF.

The variety of the Galician relief greatly affects the different types of agricultural work. For example, the rugged land, in many cases, prevents the use of modern agricultural machinery. This occurs in the **socalcos,** terraces situated on the hillsides of some sections of the rivers Miño and Sil where vines are cultivated.

Although on steep slopes the ground would sustain meadows, instead there are forests, so as to avoid the negative effects of erosion. In general, we can say that the higher areas of the region are appropriate for woodland development and extensive stock breeding, whereas intermediate areas are used for extensive agriculture with free cattle grazing. In valleys and low lying areas, intensive fruit and vegetable farming gives optimum results.

The most important factor in the settlement of the Galician population is its distribution. However, the general characteristics of the environment (where the population lives) determine the different forms of distribution. The mean altitude, more than one thousand metres, and the interior location of the abrupt, southeastern mountain ranges impose a harsh climate that means that only low lying areas and high valleys where rivers have their source are habitable. On the other hand, in the Rías Baixas the population density is very high because of the gentle forms of relief and the closeness of the sea, which makes the climate warmer.

The intricate Galician orography influences the layout of land communications. In order to lay roads and railway lines, it is often necessary to overcome abrupt differences in height.

When the Galician mountains were broken by the great pressures they were under during some stages of their geological evolution, hot water springs -**caldas or burgas-** and cold water mineral springs appeared. Because of this, Galicia is outstanding in its abundance and wealth of mineral and medicinal waters. It has more than twenty health spas, making it the most important spa region in Spain.

As far as the landscape is concerned, in many parts of Galicia there are frequent **penedos, medas, galiñeiros...** that is to say, granite rocks of different shapes, the result of water and wind erosion.

"Socalcos".

O Ullán region, where the Ulla river meets the sea.

"Penedos".

Landscape at high altitudes.

THE SOIL.

The Galician soil is, in general, permeable and acidic. The most common types of soils are:

- **Tierra parda (Dark grey soil):** Dark grey and highly permeable soil. It lies on slate and other rocks that have a low acid content. This forms most of the soil which is cultivated except that lying at the bottom of valleys.
- **Ranker:** Sandy soil, also very permeable. It lies on steep or moderate gradients and contains many stones. Heather, gorse and woodland are the main types of vegetation growing on this soil.
- **"Veigas":** Dark grey soil found in river valleys. It is rich in humus and is very good for agriculture, although it is mainly used for perennial meadows.

Although less abundant, there are other types of soils:

- **Gley:** Soil that has an excess of water. It can be found in "veigas" and "tierras pardas", and it is normally used for planting fields.
- **Podzol:** Soil which is found in high, cold and damp areas. It is nearly always covered with heather and gorse; if ploughed it can serve as woodland.

In some areas there are **gándaras** and **brañas**, soil that is only slightly permeable, and therefore permanently waterlogged. On this type of soil there is no characteristic vegetation or fauna.

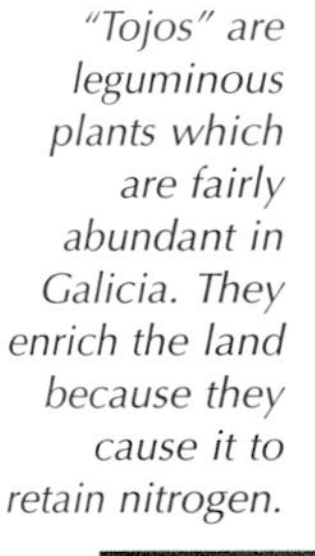

"Tojos" are leguminous plants which are fairly abundant in Galicia. They enrich the land because they cause it to retain nitrogen.

THE COAST.

The Galican coast is bathed by the Bay of Biscay and the Atlantic Ocean. It is the most rugged coastline of the Peninsula and is characterized by *rias,* which are fluvial valleys that have been flooded by the sea. The rias can be classified as:

-*Rias Altas:* Coasts nestling between steep mountains. These are the rias of **Ribadeo, Viveiro, O Barqueiro** and **Ortigueira.**

-*Rias Medias:* The surrounding relief is less abrupt. These are the rias of **Cedeira, Ferrol, Ares-Betanzos, A Coruña, Laxe, Camariñas** and **Corcubión.** The **Costa da Morte** is in the southern stretch of these rias, beaten by the "mare tenebrosum" that terrorised the old world, with its strong and frequent gales. However, between the high cliffs and protected by rivers, there are villages that rob the sea of its riches, amid stories of wrecks and mysterious legends.

-*Rias Baixas:* Gigantic natural harbours and gentle relief. These are the rias of **Muros-Noia, Arousa, Pontevedra** and **Vigo.** In their mouth and interior there are islands, the largest of which is Arousa. It is the only one that is permanently inhabited (5,000 inhabitants) and its economic growth is mainly based on fishing and seafood gathering.

Ria of Viveiro.

The fringes of the Galician coastal mountain ranges reach the sea, giving rise to numerous capes, which are one of the most striking characteristics of the rugged Galician shoreline. Sometimes, the drop to the sea is truly impresive, as occurs in **A Capelada,** near the Ortegal cape, where the cliffs are over 600 metres high and nearly vertical. They are the highest in all the coast of western Europe.

In many stretches of the Galician shoreline there are alternating high, rocky areas with low, sandy areas. The beauty of the Galician coast is clearly shown in beaches like that of **Carnota** –the longest in Galicia-, on the Costa da Morte, or in that of **A Lanzada,** between the bays of Arousa and Pontevedra.

Rias of Ares and Betanzos.

Ria of Arousa, the largest in Galicia.

THE CLIMATE.

The weather in Galicia is, in general, wet and mild, a merge of the oeanic and Mediterranean climates. This is because Galicia is situated exactly in the area of transition between these two climates and lies on the western edge of a continent. So nearly all the coastline has the typical characteristics of an oceanic climate, whilst a large part of the interior has the characteristics of a continental-oceanic climate and the south of Galicia has a Mediterranean climate.

A. Geographical factors.

There are geographical factors that cause this climatological diversity:

The relief mainly influences the distribution of rainfall. The humid S.W. winds from the Atlantic unload most of their humidity in the form of rain as they hit the foothills of the Dorsal Gallega. On their course eastwards, they come accross no other significant mountain barrier until they reach the high southeastern mountains, where they unload virtually all their remaining humidity, largely in the form of snow, entering the Central Iberian Plateau almost moistureless. The area lying between these two mountain ranges receives much less rainfall, making it the driest area of the region. These S.W winds mainly blow from autumn to April, the wettest season of the year.

On the Cantabrian coastal fringe the summers are dominated by N.W winds that often produce permanent cloud cover. In the central plain during winter, there are often cold N.E winds, that blow away the clouds and leave a clear sky.

The warm Gulf current which bathes our shores increases humidity and temperature, with diminishing effect from the coast to the east.

B. Atmospheric factors.

Apart from geographical aspects, the main atmospheric factor that influences weather changes in Galicia is the anticyclone from the Azores, which because of its northerly location in summer, hinders the entry of Atlantic storms from the polar front, that very rarely affect us. In winter months, this anticyclone is located much further south, allowing the storms to reach land, causing abundant rainfall.

From western to eastern Galicia there is a gradual increase in temperature. So the weather gets warmer as we move away from the coast and the number of months with shortage of rainfall also increases.

The crops adapt to the different climatological conditions. A clear example are the vineyards: the low level of humidity in the area of Valdeorras allows the vines to grow almost level with the ground; whereas in the Ribeiro they need to be separated a few centimetres from the soil and in Salnés, and in Condado it is crucial that they are trained up poles.

In Galicia, during most of the year, rainfall is usually greater than the loss of water from the soil through transpiration of plants and evaporation (evapotranspiration or ETP). Nevertheless, in some areas the summers are long and hot, and consequently the ETP rate is above that of precipitation, resulting in a shortage of rainfall. For example, in the Miño and Sil valleys the shortage can be 400 mm and lasts 5 to 6 months.

Some regions have special climates different to those of surrounding areas; in other words, a microclimate. In Galicia, microclimates allow the cultivation of trees and plants typical of Mediterranean and subtropical climates.

EFFECTS OF THE CLIMATE.

In Galicia the soil receives an abundance of water due to the heavy winter rains, but because the ground is very permeable and evaporation rate is high, in summer the soils are arid and crops need additional water.

Galician rivers, although short, have a regular and copious volume of water as a result of the profuse precipitation. The Miño, even though it is one of the shortest of the important rivers in the peninsula, is nevertheless the first in relative volume of water and the fourth in total volume.

The Galician climate supports an abundant vegetation, consisting mainly of deciduous trees: oaks, chestnuts, beeches, alders, birches...In the southern, Atlantic area of Galicia, the climate allows lemon trees, orange trees, and vines to be grown, and in the southern interior you can find olive trees and extensive vineyards, whilst on the Cantabrian coast, meadows and grazing pastures dominate the landscape with important stockbreeding and mixed agriculture.

The climate also clearly influences population density and distribution. In coastal regions, where the climate is mild, population density and distribution are high, whilst in the interior of Galicia where the climate is much harsher, the density and distribution are lower.

The differences in Galician climate cause a great variety in building structures. Houses on the coast are not the same as those in the interior.

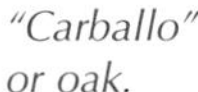

"Carballo" or oak.

Chestnut

Until recently, the Galician forests were mainly made up of oaks ("carballeiras"), chestnut trees ("soutos"), ash and beech groves. These deciduous trees, typical of the oceanic climate, favour the formation of high quality soils and their wood is highly valued.

II

TERRITORY

Hidrography and landscape

- Rivers.
- Slopes and basins.
- Tapping of the rivers.
- Lagoons.
- Landscapes.
- Vegetation.

TERRITORY.
HYDROGRAPHY AND LANDSCAPE.

RIVERS.

It would be very difficult to imagine a Galician landscape without a river or stream, so abundant are they. This is due to many factors, such as the heavy winter rainfall and the abundance of springs and running water.

The main characteristics of Galician rivers are:
Abundant flow, as a consequence of the frequent rains and the lie of the land.

Regular flow. The water of almost all the rivers is originated by rain. This causes their flow to be relatively uniform throughout the year. Nevertheless, at the beginning of spring they reach their highest volume due to rain from Atlantic storms, whilst during the summer their flow is minimal because of the dry months.

The Miño river, passing through Ourense.

Short course, owing to the nearness of the mountains to the sea. The Miño, which is the longest river, is nearly 350 kilometres long.
Rivers confined between banks and with differences in height, because they flow through deep and narrow valleys. And so, in general, they are not navigable, except for the lower section of the rivers Ulla and Miño.

SLOPES AND THE BASINS.

Galician rivers flow into the Cantabrian Sea and the Atlantic Ocean.

Cantabrian coast: Short rivers with varying volume of water, large differences in height and, therefore, strong erosive action. The major rivers are the *Eo* and the *Navia,* which only flows through Galicia near its source.

Atlantic coast:

- -Those that flow into the Atlantic rias: *Eume, Mandeo, Anllóns, Xallas, Tambre, Ulla, Umia, Lérez, Verdugo.*
- -The Miño basin: This covers almost half of Galicia. The main tributary is the river *Sil.* Others are: *Parga, Neira, Avia, Arnoia, Tea.*
- -The Limia basin*:* The *Limia* river, named by the Romans Río del Olvido (River of Oblivion), flows through Galicia during part of its course and then enters Portugal.
- -Tributaries of the river Duero: These are rivers that begin in Galicia and later enter Portugal. The most important is the river *Támega.*

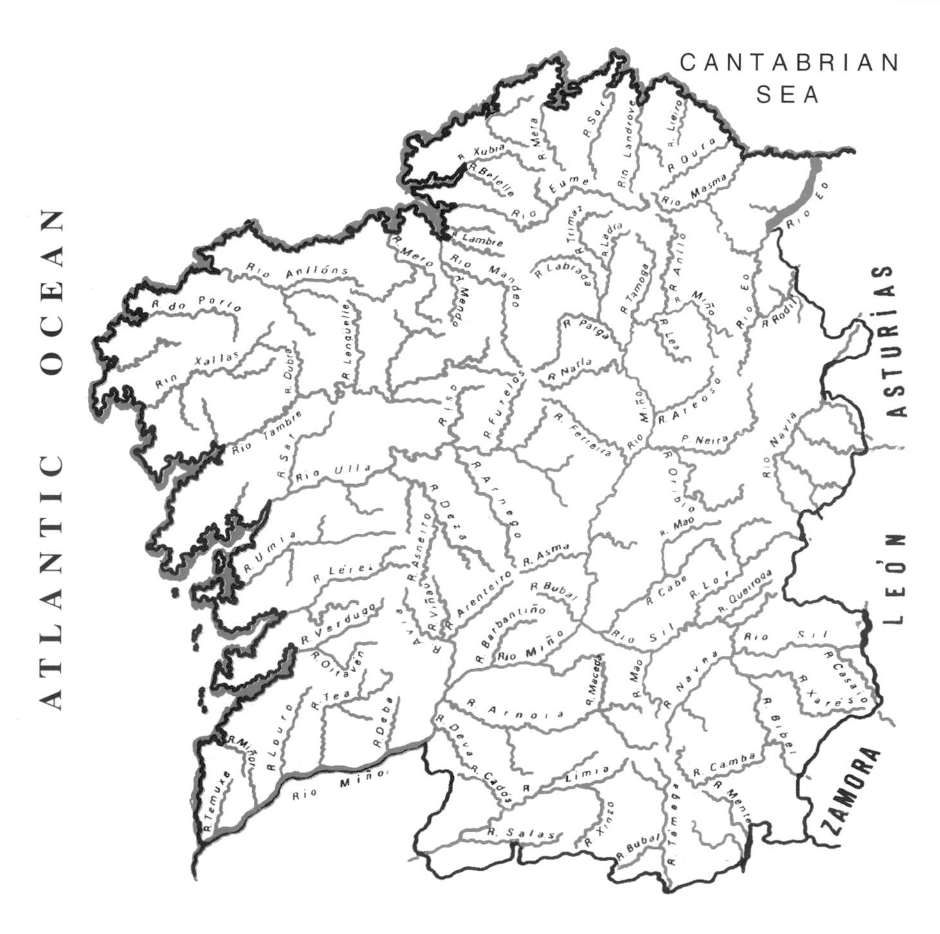

The waterways of Galicia.

TAPPING OF THE RIVERS.

In the numerous Galician rivers sportsmen fish salmon, trout, lampreys, eels and baby eels, salmon trout, shad, etc. This type of fishing is only of some economic importance in the rivers Miño and Ulla.

Many dams were built in Galicia, using the favourable conditions of our rivers – the abrupt differences in height, confined between banks, and with a regular and abundant flow-, which made this an extremely important hydroelectric region.

From long ago, rivers and streams have been used to irrigate pasture land and other crops. Over many years they were also employed in turning the wheels of *molinos* (watermills), that existed in every village. The majority of them are now in disuse.

Galician rivers have environmental conditions which are very favourable for the establishment of fish farms, the reproduction and breeding of the different species, especially trout and salmon.

Mill on the Moeche river, which uses the flow of the Jubia river. Dates from 1872.

LAGOONS.

Galician lagoons are small. In the interior, the main ones are: **Alcaián, Cospeito** and **Fonmiña.** On the coast, these include: **A Frouxeira, Doniños, Baldaio** and **Carregal.**

Coastal lagoons have two types of habitat with a great variety of fauna and flora, due to the mixture of fresh and saltwater. These swamps support an extraordinarily rich diversity of birdlife, primarily migratory species.

Sobrado lagoon.

The salt marsh at Baldaio, in the Costa da Morte, is one of the areas in Galicia with the greatest variety of birds.

LANDSCAPE.

The elements which form the natural environment (types of soils, relief, climate, vegetation...) have, in Galicia, characteristics which are in a certain sense widespread. And so the Galician landscape can be seen as a whole. It is an area of ancient geological formation wrapped in a humid climate, enriched by compact and extensive vegetation and subjected to an age-old and continuous human encroachment. Even so, the great array of orographical and climatological aspects and the numerous man-made features alter the landscape, making it incredibly diverse. The Galician landscape is certainly clearly defined and is different to other geographical regions, yet, at the same time, it is formed by a great variety of specific landscapes, continually contrasting and complementing each other.

The virgin countryside has nearly all disappeared. It only remains in thinly populated areas, such as in some very steep valleys and high mountain ranges.

The countryside which has been affected by man covers almost all the region. It is very diverse due to various natural and human factors:

The "ager" or cultivated land is one of the special characteristics of the Galician landscape. Because of the small size of the fields, the shape and contours of the fields are nearly always irregular.

1. The type of soil:

- *Granite countryside.* This is present in most of the region. It is characterised by its enormous variety: sometimes with gentle and rounded forms; low hills with convex slopes and flattened brows and half-buried worn boulders. Other times it has abrupt forms; rough and wild aspects, with mountain ranges and large rocks that look like ruins on the horizon. This first type of landscape is generally at a high altitude, and the second are areas which have a low mean altitude, where the decomposition of granite has lead to low hills with large stones, rocks and rounded boulders and sudden steep slopes with pebbles and sand.

Granite countryside.

- *Lime countryside.* This exists in some eastern areas of the region. This is a landscape with striated rocks marked by erosion, mountains with narrow passes and valleys with high sides. Rivers meander in confined passages.

- *Clay and slate countryside.* This is found in ancient sedimentary lake basins and marine basins which have been lifted. These are the rolling plains of the plateaus and interior depressions, on occasions split open by running water.

The river Sil, flowing through steep rocky cliffs.

2. The orographical forms:

- *The coast* has as its main characteristic the ever-changing rias, which make it a singular landscape. The varied structure of these wonderful bays, large and small- created by continental forces and marine errosion- form a endlessly contrasting landscape. In it there is every type of form, process and possible combination: inlets, islands, islets, estuaries, beaches, and varying sorts of dunes, platforms of marine abrasion, cliffs and caves, littoral plains, headlands and gigantic peninsulas. The beaches, gentle slopes, and hills lie in progression reaching the extensive and undulating mountains and plains.

The dunes at Corrubedo, on the Barbanza coast, are a curious example of how the wind shapes the land.

The Sisargas Islands, because of their unique fauna, their geographical characteristics and their typography, are the most important reserve of marine birds in the Iberian Peninsula. This is the only place in Spain with a nest building colony of tridactyl seagulls, which come to the coast to reproduce but spend the rest of the time at sea.

-*The valleys,* another of the geographical characteristics of Galicia with a continuous and contrasting landscape. So as to describe them, we can classify them as follows:
Valleys of the mountain ranges, with deep and winding canyons, surrounded by rugged mountains, high peaks and steep gradients marked by streams.
Valleys of the plains, high plains with ample curves; warm and cozy pastoral valleys tinged with tranquil green.
Wide valleys of the low basins, with meandres and ample, gentle slopes, farmed or wooded. Valleys with vegetable gardens and vines, known in some areas as **ribeiros,** where vines mature in the suntraps of the terraces or **socalcos**. In these wide valleys there exists a special type of scenery, the **bocarribeiras**: lands in between the **ribeiro** and the mountains, located on slopes or uneven plains.

Mountain valley.

Lowland valley.

Mountain landscape.

-The mountains, land of 300 to 800 metres in altitude, in which plains, furrowed low mountain ranges and erroded hills alternate. The Galician mountains contain uneven and extensive land, such as the low or high plains, lands with rye and pastoral meadows. In them we can find a few clay plains and lakes of important stockbreeding value, located at the foot of the high mountain ranges.

-The mountain ranges, in which you pass from one mountain to another almost without realising. These have varied scenery, accentuating those of the surrounding mountains.

Mountain range in western Galicia.

3. Human influence:

- *Vegetable gardens and communal land* . The agricultural and stockbreeding structure of the region cause the farmers to live in isolated houses in the middle of their land or in small hamlets not far from their fields. The distribution of crops gave way to the distribution of arable land which makes the intervention of human factors preponderant in the landscape. There is communal land ("enxidos") near every house, small enclosed plots producing fruit, and in the fertile, sunny land are the vegetable gardens ("hortas"), with intensive cultivation of different crops, belonging to individual families.

- *The enclosed land and the* **agras.** Form two typical types of Galician land distribution. The first is an example of the close association between the farming of land and stockbreeding. The fields are encircled by a stone wall, often covered in hurdles, or by a slope of land where trees and bushes have been planted. It is a type of landscape with fields enclosed by hedges, with a woody and green appearance, called a "bocage". The walls, apart from protecting crops from the wind, also defend them from cattle, and so they contrast with woodland, where the animals graze freely. Nowadays, these enclosures are disappearing, because they are obstacles to the exploitation and mechanization of agriculture.

The **Agras.** Large areas of arable land, which in general belongs to various owners. With rare exceptions, they are open fields and are what is left of the old communal way of farming the land, which has now disappeared. This was the rotational cultivation of cereals and the collective use of the pastures in the land subject to the system of rents.

The areas of enclosed land are surprising in the Galician countryside. Small granite or slate walls are used as divisions. Sometimes they divide fields, surround vegetable gardens, show where paths are or simply protect the crops from the wind in some coastal regions.

Prados.

The fields. Fertile and fresh, located in the deepest parts of valleys and at the bottom of slopes. They are generally the result of human action via deforestation and subsequent transport and planting of grasslands.

*The **brañas** and **gándaras.*** Of waterlogged soil, with typical vegetation.

Scrubland, covering considerable areas, desolate because of the deforestation and excessive exploitation by man over many years. On this soil, there is moorland, kermes oaks, gorse, and broom.

*The **forests*** or high woodland, of which there is not a great deal in region, with trees and bushes. In western parts pinewoods dominate due to the replanting that has occured over the last 200 years. In the eastern area, there are still some **fragas** or mixed woods with deciduous trees and some beechwoods that grow on limy soil at an altitude between 700 and 2000 metres. This is the farthest south they grow. In the southeast and in hotter microclimates there are cork oaks and evergreen oaks, trees typical of Mediterranean regions.

The saltus or forest areas characterize the agrictultural landscape in Galicia.

- *Urban landscapes.* These are mainly formed by towns and cities. Nevertheless, rural or agricultural landscapes are in certain ways present in these urban nuclei, especially in towns, giving them a rural touch. On the other hand, certain regions with a high population density and the rias in general have a landscape which is endlessly invaded by countless buildings that give it a semi-urban feel.

The urban landscape of our cities is very diverse due to the different periods through which they have passed. Each period left its mark and in many cases it is easy to spot them in the different sections of the city. There is usually a **casco antiguo** (old centre), with monuments and irregularly layed streets, the **ensanches** (new suburbs), nearly always with a regular and geometric plan. The **barrios** (neighbourhoods), housing on already existing roads, where detached houses are mixed with flats. There are sometimes **polígonos** (estates)**, zonas residenciales** (residential areas)**,** isolated groups of housing, and buildings with no relation to nearby constructions and of varied structure.

The streets in the old parts of Galician towns and cities are characterized by colonnades, balconies, and the use of stone and wood.

VEGETATION.

Galicia is a transitional area between two regions with differing flora, the Eurosiberian and the Mediterranean regions. The first has deciduous woods and the other evergreen woods adapted to a moderately arid climate. Both types are present in this region, and are sometimes mixed together. All in all, present-day vegetation in Galicia has had its location, limits, composition and texture defined by human action.

In times past, the region was largely covered in mixed woods, with oak as the dominant species. In Roman times, the introduction of intensive agriculture produced important changes with the felling and burning of trees so as to increase the land available for crops. Wheat and barley were grown, and the Romans introduced rye, oats, chestnuts and vines. The landscape began to be covered in cultivated land and extensive scrub, as a result of continual felling and burning.

Since the 17th century the Galician forests have suffered devastating deforestation. They were cut down to make charcoal and to supply the shipyards of Ferrol; later, with the arrival of railways, many oak and chestnut woods were destroyed. Recently, the plantation of pines and eucalyptus trees struck another hard blow to the indigenous vegetation.

Today, the majority of Galician woods have been replanted.

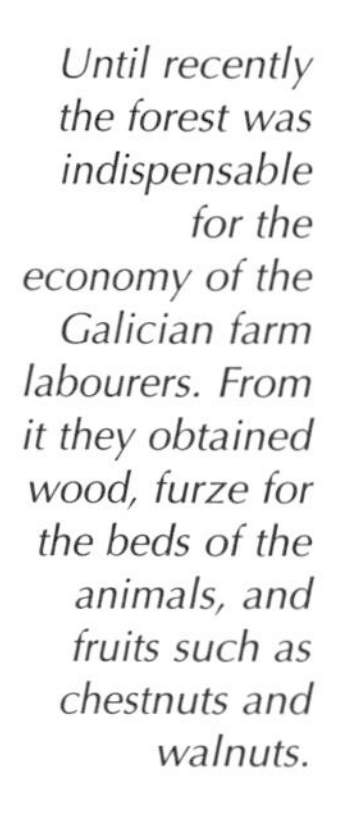

Until recently the forest was indispensable for the economy of the Galician farm labourers. From it they obtained wood, furze for the beds of the animals, and fruits such as chestnuts and walnuts.

Types of vegetation:

-**"Fragas"** or mixed woods. Greatly reduced by the deforestation, they are what is left of the virgin Galician countryside. Small areas are found on land that is inadequate for farming, such as in craggy valleys or on very high mountains. The main species in these indigenous woods are oaks ("carballos") and "rebollo". Less common trees are birches, ash trees and cork oaks. There are also hazel, holly, strawberry, maple and beech trees.

-**"Carballeiras"** or oakwoods. They form the most abundant type of wood in this region, mainly due to human activity. Nowadays, because of the plantation of pines and excessive felling, there are very few carballeiras left.

-**"Soutos"** or chestnut woods. These were a very important tree in this region's history and the staple food of the Galicia. Today they have almost disappeared because of both excessive felling and the "ink disease", now overcome with hybrid species.

-**Pinewoods.** They cover extensive areas in western Galicia. They were introduced from the middle of the 18th century, as the traditional wood supplies began to run out. In the 20th century, massive areas were planted with different sorts of pines.

-**Eucalyptus woods.** They are spreading through the lower areas of Galicia. They were first introduced in the middle of the 14th century.

-**Broom, gorse, moorland and kermes oaks**. These cover more than a quarter of Galician land. **"Xestas"** or broom grow after the felling of "carballeiras"; after cutting back the "xestas" the **"toxos"** or gorse appear. Gorse is burnt leading to the formation of land covered in kermes oaks.

-**Trees lining river banks.** These are the main characteristic in valleys. In central Galicia, black poplars have replaced alders and dominate along the entire length of river banks. There are also willow, ash, birch, hazel and elder trees. As well as reeds, bullrush, watercress, ferns and mint..

A Galician landscape with trees, according to painter Xaime Quessada.

The main features of the Galician vegetation can be roughly divided into three areas:

-*Littoral.* Land that is dominated by replanted pines, some eucalyptus and scrub. The surface covered by deciduous trees is very slight. Half of this area is used for agriculture, urban development and industry. This is the land of maize and other fruit and vegetable crops.

-*Interior.* Land covered in deciduous trees and fields. On higher ground there are the few remaining areas of **fragas** in Galicia. The most common crops are rye and potatoes.

-*Central areas.* Mediterranean species such as evergreen and cork oaks grow here. In higher areas scrub dominates and in lower areas a diverse agriculture has been developed: maize, vines, potatoes... Pine plantations are also quite numerous.

Interior landscape of Galicia.

Vegetable gardens and fruit trees.

Geographical and historical circumstances gave rise to a typical distribution of cultivated lands. The villages are surrounded by small, divided plots with patches of gorse or small woods in between. In fact, there is more woodland than arable land, and it covers more than two thirds of the region. On the other hand, the intensive cultivation in Galicia is perfectly structured into regular spaces of land so as to obtain the highest possible amount of produce. Near the house there are the "eidos" or enclosed areas for the production of vegetables. Next to the village there are "cortiñas", which are also enclosed, for the planting of cereals and fodder crops or green vegetables. Further away from the villages there are the larger, arable farming lands with "agras" for rye and maize, and the "leiras" for wheat and potatoes.

III

POPULATION

- General characteristics.
- Galician emigration.
- Emigration and Statutes.
- Emigration and Economy.
- Human settlement.
- The urban population.

POPULATION.

GENERAL CHARACTERISTICS.

The Galician population has grown since the end of the 18th century.

EVOLUTION OF THE GALICIAN POPULATION						
End of the 18th century	Middle of the 19th century	Beginning of the 20th century	1968	1978	1991	1996
1,150,000	**1,800,000**	**2,000,000**	**2,639,238**	**2,895,469**	**2,731,669**	**2,743,999**

The 1991 census registered a drop in population of 163,000. The last provisional census registered a slight increase in population.

- Current density: 92 inhabitants/km^2.

Characteristics of the current Galician popoulation:

Progressive ageing.
Causes: Very low birth rate.
A decreasing birth rate.
A stable death rate during the last decades.
Consequences: Very slow population growth.
Distribution: Irregular.
Densely populated areas; coastal regions and some interior valleys.
The rest of the region is thinly populated.

This uneven distribution was accentuated by emigration. Almost three quarters of the Galician population lives in the countryside, divided among small but numerous clusters. This distribution pattern is connected to economic and social factors. All in all, because of the expanding industrialization in some areas, there is a continual movement of people from rural to industrial areas, so that the disequilibrium which existed up until now between the urban and rural population is decreasing.

The population density of coastal and interior areas differs. In coastal communities there is an increase in inhabitants, whereas in interior communities exactly the opposite is true. If we compare urban and rural populations, we observe that in the first there is an increase in inhabitants whereas in the second there is a decrease.

The population pyramid of Galicia shows the typical pattern of an ageing population. Firstly, the percentage of people older than 65 is far above 7% which is the point that marks an ageing population. Secondly, the pyramid's base becomes progressively narrower, which shows a continuous decrease in births.

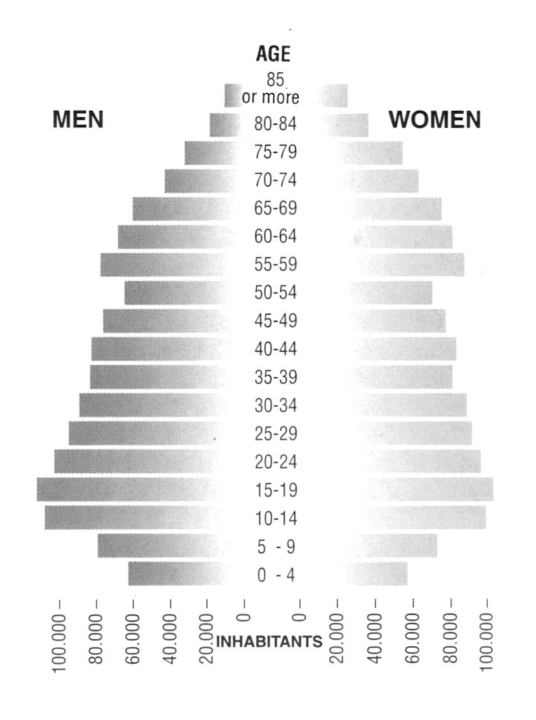

Population pyramid.

The distribution of the active population in Galicia has some special characteristics. In the countryside the high level of emigration of middle aged men resulted in agricultural work being left to women and old people. And so this justifies the high percentage of workers in the agricultural sector in comparison with industrial and service sectors: 30%. The employment rate for men is higher in industrial areas, but is still not enough to assimilate the labour force from rural areas. In other ways too, the employment figures in Galicia are deceptive. According to these, nearly half the population is classed as working in either of the economic sectors. The reality is that a large number of the registered jobs correspond to older people.This elevated number is also due to the percentage of working women, especially in the primary sector; almost 50% of Galician wage earners are women, who work small agricultural family businesses.

GALICIAN EMIGRATION.

Galicians began to emigrate in the 19th century, mainly to Andalucia, the two Castiles and Portugal.

Between 1860 and 1936 the Galician population emigrated to Cuba, Argentina and Brazil. It is estimated that during this period more than half a million people left Galicia.

In the fifties the emigration to Argentina and Venezuela resumed, and at the same time there began a movement from Galicia to Europe –the United Kingdom, France, Germany and Switzerland-, as well as to the more industrial parts of Spain: Catalonia, the Basque country and Madrid. This process stopped at the beginning of the seventies.

When the emigrants arrived in America, cultural and political activities significantly increased, as a continuation of the work being done in Spain in the years preceding the Civil war, and backed by the emigrants already settled in America. Cultural associations were founded in different countries. *The Association of Galician Culture* in Montevideo and *The Association of Galician Culture* in Mexico, among others, became true focal points for the promotion of cultural initiatives. In Buenos Aires *The Argentinian Institute for Galician Culture* and *The Galician Board* were begun. The cultural ouput was extremely extensive: books and magazines, conferences, television and radio programmes...

The publishers founded by the emigrants printed their literary works, investigations, political essays and classics.

These magazines and a few newspapers became the most common form of communication of the Galician associations: *Galeuzka* (Buenos Aires, 1945) *Galicia Emigrante* (Buenos Aires, 1954) and *Vieiros* (Mexico, 1959).

Buenos Aires acted as Galicia's cultural capital. A lot of work was achieved there by important people like Castelao, Blanco Amor, Luis Seoane, Lorenzo Varela, Rafael Dieste and Lois Tobío. Castelao gave a first performance of *Os vellos non deben de namorarse,* the poetry of Curros and Rosalía was reprinted and the publication of the reviews *Nós* and *A Nosa Terra* continued.

On the 3rd of September, 1950, *Sempre en Galiza* was first broadcast on Montevidean radio, transmitted entirely in Galician and still running today. Luis Seoane encouraged the broadcasting of other interesting programmes in Argentina.

In the countries to which they had emigrated, Galicians from the very start formed associations, *irmandades (societies),* centres and Galician houses with the aim of helping each other and so as to keep alive the spirit and culture of their country. They also promoted their children's education. To list a few examples, the schools of Caracas and Buenos Aires, the latter soon to be opened.

Emigration to other regions of Spain occured to a lesser extent. Nowadays, important cultural activities are offered by the many Galician houses and centres throughout Spain.

The fact that Galicia, apart from being a region, is a community which extends all over the world, has its origin, according to data from the "Archivo General de Indias", in the years following the discovery of America; specifically during the succeeding fifty years a considerable number of Galicians emigrated. Many more followed in the next few centuries, specially in the 19th and 20th centuries.

Luis Seoane (1910-1979) was a versatile artist: he was an excellent painter, he made pottery, he was an art critic and he composed plays for the theatre.

EMIGRATION AND STATUTES

With the establishment of the new State of Autonomies, provided for in Chapter VIII of the Constitution, the Statute of Autonomy of Galicia of 1981, in article 7, includes direct and specific references to the Galician community living outside Galicia:

"1. The Galician communities living outside Galicia will be able to request, as such, the recognition of their "Galeguidade"* as a right to participate in and share Galician social and cultural life. A Parliamentary law will regulate, without affecting the State's jurisdiction, the reach and content of this recognition to the aforementioned communities, which in no case will mean the concession of political rights.

2. The Autonomous Community will be able to request of the Spanish State that, in order to facilitate that stated above, it signs the necessary agreements with the States where these communities live".

Article 1.2 of the Statute states that Galicia, as an Autonomous Community, "through its democratic institutions, will assume as an important task the defence and identity of Galicia and of its interest, and the promotion of solidarity among all those who conform the Galician people".

In order to develop the Statute, in 1983 the Law of recognition of Galician nationality which recognises the "Galeguidade" of the communities abroad was passed, which enabled them to take part in the social and cultural life of Galicia.

Galician Centre in Buenos Aires

With the aim of supporting the Galician emigrants, the Galician Government has adopted many measures in the social, cultural and economic fields.

---

*"Galeguidade": the right of Galician Communities living outside Galicia to collaborate and share in the social and cultural life of the Galician people.

EMIGRATION AND ECONOMY.

The industrialization of some countries in western Europe after the Second World War created thousands of jobs. All this labour force was "imported" from less developed countries, among them Spain. Many of the Spanish emigrants were from rural areas and therefore lacked professional industrial qualifications. In the countries where they settled they held the hardest and most strenuous jobs: construction, mining, metallurgy..., precisely those rejected by the domestic population and worst paid.

From the sixties onwards, some developing countries such as Spain found that they had a surplus labour force largely from rural areas. Since this could not be assimilated, a solution was sought by transferring these workers to more developed countries which could give them refuge. In this way an important national problem was solved. Furthermore these emigrants brought back money to their native country. It was thought that this money would lead to the industrialization of the areas where these workers were from, and that in a relatively short period of time there would be no need to emigrate. But this was not the case. Galicia –one of the regions from which most men and women emigrated, who therefore, provided a lot of money- did not become industrialized. This money was spent helping to industrialize other regions of Spain.

So social and economic factors were the main motives in compelling Galicians to emigrate. In the 20th century approximately one million Galicians emigrated. Most of them were peasants or labourers and unskilled workmen from towns and cities. Geographically, the interior areas were the ones which suffered most due to emigration. Middle-aged men and women formed most of this human exodus.

Galician emigrants normally left with the intention of returning, but oftens this was not possible. When the migratory surge lead to America, very few returned. When the destination were the industrialized European countries almost all the emigrants came and still come on holidays to spend a few days with their relatives. But to return on a permanent basis is more difficult.

As a whole, the Galician migratory phenomenon had, because of its intensity, negative effects both for the emigrants and for their families, which in some way influenced the entire society. The contrasting lifestyle of foreign countries, isolation, memories of families and friends, working and living conditions...frequently caused psychological problems in the emigrant, which also effected the family that remained in Galicia and most of the children.

Galician emigrants, in a 19th century engraving.

HUMAN SETTLEMENT.

From the beginning, the existence of small plots of land, paths and countless human settlements formed a special network within the Galician territory. However, economic, social and cultural characteristics varied from one area to another, although everywhere they were basically rural. Central inhabited nuclei grew up, which coordinated all human activity: they are called "villas" (towns). They organize the minimum and necessary services which the small rural communities would not be able to run themselves.

The town is the highest economic and social entity which includes the surrounding *parishes, villages* and *clusters of farms*. The town is made up of a main street and other secondary roads where the public centres are: administration, commercial, and religious centres, among others. Until recently its main function was to be the meeting place where the surplus agricultural products were exchanged among the inhabitants of the area. The daily relationships between rural and urban lifestyles in Galician towns turned them into balanced human settlements.

The origin of many Galician towns and cities dates back to the time of the "castros". The inhabited areas in most of Galicia have therefore always been the same ones. Later, the Romans often made us of the earlier settlements to establish mansions or resting places along the roadways. Because of their strategic situation, some of these mansions were probably the places where taxes were collected, where people were recruited to join the army, and where trading took place. The large country houses were in those times known as *"villae"*.

Betanzos.

In the late middle ages, the documents from this period which mention rural issues also contain the word *villa,* which nowadays comes to mean *aldea (village).* These *villae* were groups of houses situated in the country and surrounded by farmed land and, therefore, due to characteristics of the Galician geography, in areas of varied relief and abundant water. Despite these physical characteristics, they correspond more to a concentrated habitat than to a dispersed one. In the *villae* there were communal customs, which in part have continued to the present day: communal use of woodlands, water for irrigation, use of paths thanks to the so-called "derechos de paso" (rights of way), and communal grazing or **veceiras.**

Therefore, when we talk about a scattered or dispersed population we could think that the isolation of the settlements is their main characteristic. Nothing could be farther from the truth. The groups of villages or hamlets are always joined together within a larger body that includes them all: the parish. Family relationships, customary institutions, and religious practices are connections that make all inhabitants feel neighbours. However, nowadays, some parishes are changing: the subsistance agriculture that formed them no longer exists. Instead there is an agroindustrial system: many inhabitants leave in the morning to work in the nearby factories and return at nightfall to rest, but they scarcely relate with each other. They live in the village but do not take part in its day to day life.

Village

THE URBAN POPULATION.

Throughout the years, the rural class has been predominant in Galicia. Apart from the episcopal centres – Compostela, Mondoñedo, Lugo, Ourense and Tui- and a few coastal groups, most people lived in the countryside. Therefore, the urban population of Galicia has always been low in number compared to the rural population. In the 19th century only 8% of Galicians lived in urban areas.

However, in the 20th century the number of people living in the countryside decreased spectacularly, and on the other hand, the urban population increased.

Evolution of rural/urban populations

	1900	1960	1990
Rural population	90%	76%	30%
Urban population	10%	24%	70%

Causes for the decrease in rural population:
- -Emigration to America and Europe.
- -A movement to the cities.
- -Industrialization lead to changes in agriculture causing a decrease in the demand for manpower.

Santiago de Compostela.

Causes that boost a growth in urban population:

- -The gradual industrialization of urban nuclei which attract manpower.
- -The settlement of returned emigrants in cities and towns.
- -The concentration of the population in the major towns of each area, which offer services that do not exist in country villages: health care, education, leisure activities...

At the beginning of the 20th century urbanization began, as a result of the growth in industrialization. The sudden and intense concentration of industries and services in large nuclei made them attractive to the abundant work force. And so industrial cities such as Ferrol, A Coruña and Vigo grew up, which centralized and dominated their surroundings. On the other hand, phenomenon appeared in these Galician cities which had been unknown until then, such as the differences in social classes. The bourgeousie lived in the main streets and the working class lived in the suburbs and neighbouring areas.

The major activities in a city form its character. For example, the concentration of services in Santiago de Compostela means it can offer services in the administration, religion, education, health care, tourism and culture and, likewise, it is ideal for the organization of meetings and symposiums.

Lugo.

Industrialization also lead to the movement of people from the old parts of cities to new, residential areas. Small shopowners and retired people live in the old parts. Every year there are more abandoned houses, as occurs in Ourense, Lugo and Pontevedra. In the last few years many old centres of towns and cities have been repaired by careful restoration work adapting the buildings to modern use.

Vigo.

Ferrol.

Pontevedra.

A Coruña.

Ourense.

IV

FROM PREHISTORY TO THE MODERN AGE

- The Stone Age and the Metal Age.
  - Petroglyphs.
  - The culture of the "castros" (Celtic dwellings)
- Rome.
- The Sueves.
- The Visigoths.
- The Middle Ages.
  - The Pilgrim Route to Santiago.
  - Gelmírez.
  - Miniature Codices.
  - The Cathedral of Santiago.
  - The independence of Portugal.
  - The "foros" (system of land rents).
  - The Irmandiñas Wars.
- From the Middle Ages to modern society.

FROM PREHISTORY TO THE MODERN AGE.

THE STONE AGE AND THE METAL AGE.

We know of the presence of human beings in the northwestern part of the peninsula during the lower paleolithic age. They gathered their food and hunted, and were therefore nomads. These men formed large groups and together went hunting for deer, roebucks, and horses, that lived in the region at that time. They fished in the rivers and along the coast. They also set up small "workshops" where they made their tools: hand axes, small pickaxes, and scrapers, made mainly from quartz, quartzite and rock crystal. The women mainly gathered fruit and roots. The rest of the jobs were possibly carried out by the community as a whole. The origin of these people is not yet known, but they perhaps arrived in small waves from central Europe and the Mediterranean area.

There were climatic changes during the upper paleolithic and mesolithic ages: the average temperature grew warmer. Gradually, the flora and fauna varied. Small communities of hunters and food gatherers spread into the central parts of the region. Along the coast, the remains of the shells of moluscs, *"cuncheiros",* indicate they fished and ate seafood and shellfish.

The neolithic age begins with the introduction of agriculture. Forests were cut down to create farming lands, and the woodlands were burnt so as to fertilize them. In other words, a sedentary lifestyle began, as is proved by the findings of hand made pottery. Many neolithic instruments were found, made of smooth stone and fine carving: axes, pickaxes, knives, scrapers, arrow heads...These communities prepared the way for the culture of the *mámoas* or the megalithic culture of the northwestern Iberian Peninsula.

The *mámoas* are barrows of earth which cover a megalithic tomb or dolmen. This culture, which had common characteristics with other megalithic peoples in the Mediterranean and Atlantic areas of Europe but also its own specific characteristics, covers approximately from the first half of the third millennium to the years 2000-1800 B.C. They were small communities which spread out all over the region. The dead were buried or incinerated in the dolmens, corridor tombs or cists that were located within the megalithic monuments. Economic activity was relatively intense: there was exchanging of instruments, mining, agriculture -specially cereals-, stockbreeding, hunting, fishing, shellfish gathering, community tasks...and all this needed good social organization, although there were few hierarchic contrasts. These people lived like their predecessors, in huts made of branches.

In the dolmens (*antas* or *vaults*), remains of smooth pottery and neolithic instruments such as axes made of smooth stone were found, indicating that there was intense felling of forests. Remains of painting, engraving and campanulate pottery were also found. The discovery of campanulate glasses and pots mark the beginning of a constant characteristic in Galicia´s history: its position as a "**finisterrae"** (land´s end) means that all cultural tendencies reach it much later than other areas and in a disordered fashion. Sometimes, the mixing of communities, with one which has lived there for a long time mixing with another arriving from elsewhere, occurs gradually. This is why it is not strange to find objects which, judging from their characteristics, must proceed from different eras but which are lying at the same level withing the earth in these archaeological remains. For example, in one same collection of funeral objects in a *mámoa,* paleolithic lithic objects can be found next to neolithic ones.

Dolmen de Dombate, in Bergantiños.

Contacts, specially commercial contacts, with other peoples such as the Tartessians from the south of the Peninsula and later with the Phoenicians made the way into the Bronze Age easier for the communities of prehistoric Galicia, half way through the second millennium B.C. Copper, tin and gold were mined. Avieno says that the inhabitants of these lands, from the age of megalithic culture, were known by the name of **oestrymnions.** This is how he describes them:

"A tall cape rises up here
(which in old times was called oestrymnis).
The summit, high up and rocky,
leans towards the gentle Noto. [1].
At the foot of this mount its inhabitants see Oestrymnico,
where the Oestrymnicas islands lie,
with their richness of tin and lead;
their inhabitants are strong and fearless people,
skillfull traders.
Their ships ply these seas which they know well.
They sail over waters full of monsters.
Their ships are not made of pinewood or quoits,
nor do they use other ships -do not fear-,
they make them joining strips of leather,
to ride over the salty sea.
From there to the sacred island (that was its name in olden times)
there is two days´ sailing.
This island rises up over the waters,
covered in green, where the hibernans [2] live.
Close by is the island of the Albions.
The Tartessians traded with the Oestrymnions as did the inhabitants of Carthage, and the neighbours of the columns of Hercules also sailed these seas".

Island of Ons, which is possibly where the Oestrymnican Islands were.

(1) Noto: South Wind.
(2) Hibernia: modern day Ireland.

THE PETROGLYPHS.

The Oestrymnians mentioned by Avieno were probably an ethnic group who had their origins in the Cro-Magnon "race" during paleolithic times. During the neolithic age, waves of peoples from the Mediterranean arrived, bringing with them the campanulate megalithic culture, and at the end of the Bronze Age peoples from Atlantic Europe settled here.

The oldest *petroglyphs* or *insculptures,* open-air rupestrian engravings, date from eneolithic times or the beginning of the Metal Age. They are highly varied: there are geometrical forms (combinations of circles, spirals, squares, reticulated forms, labyrinths, swastikas, and zigzags), shapes of animals (deer, serpents, horses...), anthropomorphous shapes, arms and instruments, hunting scenes and scenes of livestock grazing...

There is much of this type of rupestrian art all over Galicia, but it is specially common in the "Rías Baixas" (the southern rias of Galicia). These engravings probably had a religious function.

Petroglyph.

THE CULTURE OF THE "CASTROS"*.

The Bronze Age gives way to the Iron Age. Celtic peoples from Constantinople and others who come from the Tajo valleys, the Mediterranean and other far away Atlantic areas such as Brittany and Ireland settle in the northwestern area of the Peninsula. Settlements, social relations, the economy, customs and beliefs all changed. The culture of the *mámoas* changed to the *castreña* culture, the culture of the *castros,* which were the typical Celtic dwellings. This culture survived until the Middle Ages and in some aspects up until a few decades ago, as can be seen by the *pallozas* or round stone dwellings used until fairly recently in the high mountains in western Galicia.

The castros were fortified settlements in which the peoples who had built them lived permanently or where they took refuge with their livestock and their riches in times of war. These settlements were made up of one or more areas, nearly always round or oval in shape, surrounded by barricades, embankments, trenches and walls. Inside, the houses were generally round.

The *castreños* reared animals, specially cows, pigs, sheep, goats and horses. The men hunted wild boars and deer and often fought. War was, in fact, a frequent activity in the *castreña* society. This can be proved by the fortifications in the castros, the artistic representations of battles, the amount of arms found and the writings of classical contemporary authors.

The women and slaves grew vegetables and cereals in small patches of land, from which they obtained beer, flour and flax. On the coast they fished and gathered shellfish, and they extracted tin, iron, lead and gold from mines.

The basic unit of organization was the patriarchal *family,* which was a unit for production and consumption. In hierarchichal order, next came the *clan,* which had its own territory and lived in the castros. In the clan there were two leaderships: a collegiate leadership (the old people) and a personal leadership (the war chief). These clans formed part of a superior unit: the *"populi"* or *tribes.* Each populi had a government formed by chiefs and magistrates, and their influence spread over a larger or smaller territory according to their capacity for battle.

We do not know a great deal about the beliefs of the *castreños,* but we do know they adored the sun, the moon, mountains, springs, rivers and trees. The castros do not contain any temples, idols or funeral areas.

---

* Fortified celtic settlements.

Finally, an important characteristic of the *castreña* culture was their skill as gold and silversmiths, which has its origins in the Bronze Age. But the smiths of the castros created their own style and they transmitted it to their successors up until the modern day.

Castro de Baroña. Ria of Muros and Noia.

The jewellery they mostly made were *torques* (ancient necklaces), armbands, pendant earrings and diadems. They also made smaller necklaces, rings, combs, glasses...They are all magnificently decorated jewels which have been worked using various techniques: chiselling, embossing, filigree, engraving and granulation. The patterns in general are geometrical, although there are also iconographic representations, as in the diadem of Ribadeo, which represents a scene including knights, ordinary people, and animals.

Castreña jewellery had different functions: it served as decorations, symbols of the honour of the fighters, perhaps as money for trading and even as offerings to the gods.

ROME.

The times of Augustus brought the final conquest of the peoples in the north of the Iberian Peninsula: *Galaicos* (Galicians)*, astures* (Asturians) and *cántabros* (Cantabrians). The Romans gained rule over them with the *Cantabrian Wars,* from the year 29 to the year 19 B.C. The last and most legendary resistance against the invaders happened on *mount Medulio,* where the *castreño* inhabitants, surrounded, committed collective suicide and burnt everything they owned.

The Romans were interested in conquering *Gallaecia,* as they called it, because of the riches of its mines: tin, copper, silver, and gold were all minerals they exploited extensively.

Once the territory was pacified, *Romanization* took place: in other words, there was a gradual change in the *castreño´s* way of life towards the economic, social and political structures of the Romans. However, in many districts and during a fairly long time, the *castreño* and the Roman culture coexisted and influenced each other.

The conquered lands were incorporated in the province of Hispania Citerior. Augustus quartered three legions in the western territories of the peninsula and organized them into three juridical convents (bracarense, asturicense and lucense), with capitals in *Bracara Augusta* (Braga), *Asturica Augusta (*Astorga) and *Lucus Augusti* (Lugo). Modern day Galicia covers the Lugo convent, the northern part of the Braga convent and part of the Asturias convent.

Urban life as Romans understood it did not exist in Gallaecia, except for a few urban centres created by the conquerors. This explains why Romanization did not affect the basic organization of the population. The *Galaicos* still based their economy on stockbreeding and horticultural agriculture, and maintained the land as communal property. But, little by little, a rural sedentary population began to grow up and crops and various species were planted: vines, fig trees, chestnuts and olive trees. New techniques came into use, such as ploughing, fallowing and irrigating the land.

In Gallaecia the Roman system of organization of the rural population and land use was slow to arrive: the *villae,* agricultural farmhouses belonging to just one owner, with the *palatium (pazo* or manor house), the owner´s house. There were also *vici* and *paci* (villages) inhabited by smaller landowners, who freely worked their lands and lived off their products.

Except for the Roman clusters of population, the pre Roman rules about property, production and exchange were generally maintained, although they were influenced by the Roman economy. And so, while the *Galaicos* had land as communal property, the Romans introduced the concept of *private property.* Both forms coexisted and continue to do so today.

One of the great transformations of the land came with the building of terrestrial routes: the *roadways.* This system of roads, which linked the capitals with the three juridical convents, was based on three great routes of communication, interlinked by secondary roads. They were the XVIII route (*Vía Nova)* which linked Bracara with Asturica, the XIX route which went from Bracara to Bergido (*Castro de Ventosa)* and the XX route (*Per loca maritima)* which left Tude *(Tui)* and lead to Lucus Augusti. The communications centre of the three was in *Bergidum* (Bierzo), an important mining area.

Romanization gradually changed the age-old cultural habits of the *castreño* culture. The merging of the dominant Roman culture with the surviving indigenous cultural characteristics is called ***Galaico-Roman culture.*** Walls, bridges, funeral monuments, mosaics, and pottery are all artistic examples of this time. The brigatine lighthouse Tower of Hercules, the impressive city walls of Lugo, the tunnel of Montefurado and the bridge over the Bibei river are examples of power and technical skill.

Roman bridge over the Bibei river.

Latin became the written language and gradually took the place of the autochthonous languages. The pre Roman religion was full of divinities and rites, but the syncretism of the Roman religion caused it to assimilate the indigenous divinities and, instead, it worshipped the emperor, the symbol of Romanization.

However, Christianism broke up the social norms of the Romans and the cohesion of the family by introducing new values: manual work, the exaltation of poverty, preventing worship for the emperor...Christianism was introduced in Gallaecia much later than in other areas. The first Christian communities appear in the 3rd century, in Astorga and León. However, in the 4th century the *priscilian movement* contributes to the spreading and settling of Christianity in Gallaecia. ***Priscilian*** was the leader of a religious and social movement of rural origin, typical of areas with little Roman influence, as opposed to official Christianism, which was more deeply rooted in Romanized urban areas. It was largely a conflict between the great landowners, many of them clergymen, and the peasants under their rule. It sprung up in Lusitania, but its principal followers were bishops and priests in Gallaecia. The priscilian doctrines spread all over the western part of the peninsula, causing conflicts and a split within part of the hispanic Church. They were declared heretics, the priscilianists were persecuted and Priscilian was decapitated in Treveris, and considered a martyr by his followers. The movement survived for centuries in the rural areas. Its ascetic tendencies were enormously influential in the later monastic development.

Roman art. Statue of Adai. Lugo Museum.

Roadway monument. Pol.

THE SUEVES.

In the year 409 bands of Sueves, Vandals and Alans, who had been in the Galias for some years, crossed to Hispania. They must have made a violent arrival, taking hold of food and livestock. The *galaicos* resisted in the most protected castros. The emperor Honorio made an agreement with the Visigoths to throw them out. In the year 416, the Visigoths crossed the Pyrenees and managed to defeat the Alans and the Vandals, but not the *Sueves,* who resisted and consolidated a monarchy in the northwest, the first in all the Peninsula. The Campus Gallaecia of that time spread from the Cantabrian sea to the Duero river and from the Atlantic to Cauca (Segovia) and Numancia.

The Sueves were Germanic and came from the Rhine and Elba regions. About 30,000 of them arrived and soon dominated Gallaecia, although they fought with the indigenous population for years. Gradually the Sueves were accepted by the population and they soon changed their arms for ploughs. They changed from fighters to farmers.

The most glorious period of the Sueve kingdom was that of the monarch Theodomiro (559-570), who organized the kingdom, dividing it into diocese and counties. On Saint Martin Dumiense´s orders, monasteries and churches were built, centres of study and work were set up, councils were created and steps were taken towards the unity of *Galaicos* and Sueves.

The Sueves created a rural aristocracy with castles and palaces. This was when ecclesiastical organization into parishes was consolidated. Many names of rivers, places and people today have Sueve origin.

The Sueve king Theodomiro and bishops Martin, Andrew and Lucrecius at the I Council of Braga. Year 561.

THE VISIGOTHS.

In the year 585 the Visigoths conquered the Sueve kingdom. But Gallaecia was never totally Sueve nor Visigoth. Religion, language and culture barely changed. Only the system of taxes changed. Two different legislations coexisted, one for the Galaico-Romans and another for the Germanic people. Nevertheless, they both contributed and there was progress in urban, commercial, industrial and agricultural fields. Writing and the arts flourished, with figures such as Idacio, Paulo Orosio, St Martin Dumiense and St Francisco of Braga. Art flourished mostly in Visigothic architecture.

Santa Comba de Bande. 8th century. One of the buildings which boasts the most pure Visigothic architecture.

In the church of St Antoíño de Toque there are remains of Visigothic art.

THE MIDDLE AGES.

The Sueves and the Visigoths, who dominated Gallaecia during the 5th, 6th and 7th centuries, maintained the social and cultural organization of the Roman Empire. With the arrival of the Muslims, as in the rest of the Iberian Peninsula, a new historical period began with deep repercussions all over Europe.

During eight centuries the Reconquest, with its periods of peace and war, conditioned the efforts of the rulers. In western Europe, a society divided into classes prevailed, and feudalism was the basis of the political, social and economic system of organization. The Church played an essential role, not just in the spiritual field but also in politics.

Asturian kings painted on Tomb A of the Cathedral of Santiago.

From the 8th century Galicia depended on the Asturian monarchy, which set up *villae* (villas), agricultural settlements which were permanently lived in. Goth nobles became the owners of great areas of land and, together with the clergy, became privileged landowners.
The nobles, bishops and abbots were owners of large estates which the serfs took care of. The castle was the centre of feudal life: those who were not privileged, that is to say the serfs, worked for the landowner in a state of servitude. Half way through the Middle Ages there was a period of development, during which the population in villages grew, production increased and so did the farm lands. The urban centres also grew, while the woodlands and forests diminished. New clusters of population appeared. The working of the land grew more intense during the 12th and 13th centuries. The system of leaving the land fallow with three year rotations was reduced, and technical improvements were introduced, such as the use of tools, the mouldboard plough or the watermill. In the lower Middle Ages the cultivated surface area was increased and more intense systems for working the land were introduced. Farm equipment was improved, the number of vineyards grew and the system of leaving the land fallow in the cultivation of cereal crops disappeared.

Pambre Castle.

THE PILGRIM ROUTE TO SANTIAGO.

In the 9th century, during the Reconquest, the remains of *Santiago el Mayor (St James the Greater)* and his disciples Atanasius and Theodore were discovered in Galicia. Tradition has it that the monk Pelagio saw lights near the monastery of Saint Félix of Solovio. The bishop of Iria Flavia, *Theodomiro,* began excavations and found a necropolis with remains that were attributed to the Apostle and his disciples.

The Asturian king *Alfonso II the Chaste* began the construction of a mausoleum. With Alfonso III a second church was built and Alfonso VI, in the 11th century, began to build the Romanesque cathedral which stands today in Compostela.

The news of the discovery of the tomb spread rapidly, boosted by the kings of Asturias and León and by the monks of the religious order of Cluny, who from the 10th century promoted the *pilgrimages* to the sanctuary of St James.

Throughout the Middle Ages, the pilgrims from other areas of the Iberian Peninsula, France, Italy, Germany, Flanders and the northern countries became cultural and commercial intermediaries. *Gontescalco,* bishop of Puy (France), is said to be the first pilgrim who reached the tomb of the Apostle; it was the year 950.

The pilgrimages influenced many aspects of spiritual and material life in the lands through which they passed. The Order of Cluny introduced *Gregorian Reform,* enforcing Roman liturgy instead of Hispanic-Visigothic liturgy. In art, the Way of St James became an open window towards Europe and an entrance towards the Greek culture which was preserved by the Muslims. *Romanesque art* spread over much of the Peninsula.

Cultural centres sprung up, such as the *cathedral schools* of Santiago and Palencia. In the 12th century works on astronomy, mathematics, astrology, alchemy and philosophy were translated into Latin. There were travelling artists who left the mark of their art in many places. *Minstrels* and *troubadours* recited *romances* and the Pilgrim Route itself inspired many literary works.

The settling of foreigners and the development of commerce made the towns and cities grow enormously, and caused the appearance of the *burgos* (boroughs). Aswell as traders, craftsmen, money changers and artists settled in them. There was also an important influence on agriculture, with the exchanging of knowledge on fruits and methods of cultivation. Hospitals, taverns, monasteries and bridges were built. Finally, it is worth mentioning the drawing up of laws for the resolution of conflicts, and the boosting of diplomatic relations between the Spanish kings and the monarchs of other European nations.

Puerta Santa (Holy Door) of the Cathedral of Santiago. It only opens during Holy Years; in other words, when the festivity of the Apostle falls on a Sunday.

Medieval pilgrims. Miniature from the Cantigas de Santa María.

GELMÍREZ.

At the end of the 11th century, Santiago de Compostela became an extraordinarily important religious centre, and together with Rome and Jerusalem formed the trilogy of the Holy Cities of Christianity.

At that time, *Diego Gelmírez* was named bishop of Compostela. He was a great promoter of the pilgrimages of St James. This political and combative bishop took an active part in the political struggles of his time and was enormously active in all areas. He organized the ecclesiastical administration, promoted study and began a great number of buildings in the city. In the face of the maritime attacks on Galicia on the part of Moors and Normans who from time to time devastated the region, he ordered the building of a squadron, one of the first in the Christian kingdoms of the Iberian Peninsula. With the aim of making Compostela greater, he succeeded in gaining from *Pope Calixtus II* the condition of metropolis for the diocese of Santiago.

Codex Calixtinus. Cathedral of Santiago de Compostela.

In the times of Gelmírez much important European literature about Santiago and the cult to Santiago was produced. One of the most noteworthy works is the *Codex Calixtinus* or the *Liber Sancti Jacobi,* which contains the miracles of the Apostle, an extremely important guide for pilgrims and a description of the city of Compostela. The Codex Calixtinus is a manuscript with beautiful miniature illustrations which is kept in the Archive of the Cathedral of Santiago. Its author or compiler is said to have been the French priest *Aimeric Picaud.*

MINIATURE CODICES.

From the time of Gelmírez, Galician culture enters a period of splendour and Galician is the language chosen for literary compositions in the rest of the Peninsula. This is the case of the most important literary monument in the history of Galicia and perhaps one of the most important works of universal literature: the miniature codex *Cantigas de Santa María* (The ballads of Saint Mary) by Alfonso X the Wise. During these centuries of the Middle Ages other miniature codices were composed. We make special mention of the *Tomb A* (Cathedral of Santiago) and the *Diurnal* or the *Book of Hours* of *Fernando I* (University of Santiago).

Cantigas de Santa María. Library of El Escorial.

THE CATHEDRAL OF SANTIAGO.

In the 11th century, floods of pilgrims were flowing into Compostela. A great temple was needed to comfortably house the people who visited the tomb of the Apostle from all the countries of Europe. The building of the cathedral began when Diego Peláez was bishop and Alfonso VI was King. In 1075 the building of the altar began, which was consecrated by bishop Gelmírez in 1105. The Codex Calixtinus tells us that the work was completed in the year 1122. Almost half a century of labour resulted in an architectural treasure, to which another jewel of a sculpture would be added later: the *Pórtico de la Gloria* or Door of Glory, a work by the genius *Maestro Mateo.*

The Santiago cathedral is a Latin cross cathedral with three naves in the aisle and three in the transept. It has an ambulatory with five chapels and a barrel vault, aswell as a triforium or gallery.

The Romanesque style used in Santiago had enormous influence. All over Galicia there are Romanesque churches and chapels, as the expression of a style which became deeply rooted in this region and survived for centuries, living side by side with the new Gothic style of the lower Middle Ages.

Interior of the Cathedral of Santiago.

Pórtico de la Gloria.

THE INDEPENDENCE OF PORTUGAL.

During the 9th and 10th centuries Galicia had kings who reigned for short periods of time. At the end of the 11th century, the Galician nobility tried to turn our region into its own kingdom, making it independent of the Astur-leonés monarchy. Civil wars and political disputes finally brought about the separation of Portugal, during a slow process in the 12th century. With the independence of Portugal, Galicia lost importance as a political body because its expansion towards the south was prevented. It maintained its condition of kingdom without a king and was governed in name of the king of Castile-León by a superior governor.

Gelmírez. Tomb of Toxosoutos. National historical archive. Madrid.

Queen Doña Urraca. Tomb A. Archive of the Cathedral of Santiago.

Fernando I. Miniature of Tomb A in the Cathedral of Santiago.

Diurnal or Book of Hours of Fernando I. University of Santiago. Fructuoso, author of the Codex, hands it over to King Fernando I.

THE "FOROS" (SYSTEM OF LAND RENTS).

During the Middle Ages the majority of farm lands were owned by the monasteries, although sometimes the feudal nobles also had lands. The monks and the nobles started to come to agreements with the peasants. Sometimes they lent their lands out to farm labourers in exchange for a certain rent, and the peasants were declared their masters´ subjects: this was the system of "foros".

Generally the contracts were long ones. Sometimes they were even permanent: in other words, they passed from fathers to sons. Later on, this duration was limited to six and three generations.

The rent paid by the peasants to the nobles or monasteries varied. It could be fixed or proportional, and could be paid in money or in kind. Normally it was paid in kind and was proportional. In general, the peasant or *concessionary* had to pay the owner of the lands a third of the fruit harvest and half the harvest of the vines every year.

In the 15th century, the historical, political, economic and social conditions changed and influenced the organization of agricultural activity. The Castilian monarchy, with the Catholic Kings, gained rule over Galicia. The Galician nobles left and went to Court, the power of the Church increased, and a new social group appeared: the *hidalgos.* These were noblemen from the lower classes *(escuderos)*, professionals of the administration (*escribanos* and *regidores),* and members of the secular clergy (*párrocos*). From then on, the clergy and also part of the class of hidalgos were the owners of most of the "foros" contracts.

The conditions of the "foros" changed. They were reduced to a duration of three generations, and therefore became temporal contracts. This meant that the owners of the land or *foristas* could renew the contracts or *cartas forales,* or once the contract was finished they could spoliate the *foreros.*

There was usually a fixed rent which had to be paid in its totality each year, even in the case of bad harvests, natural calamities (such as floods, frosts, or hail) or social problems (wars or epidemics).

With time, the "foros" system spread all over Galicia. According to some historians, nine tenths of the cultivated lands in Galicia were subject to this system of rents.

THE "IRMANDIÑAS"* WARS.

The end of the lower Middle Ages saw the transition to an urban society in Galicia, which was formed due to the spread of commerce and because of difficulties in the agricultural sector. In many cases, fields were abandoned and productivity diminished. This meant hunger and destitution, specially for the lower classes.

In the 14th century, the nobility, which was still highly privileged and hungry for more power, opposed the Church and the people. The bougeoisie and the lower clergymen incited the peasants to rise up against the nobles. Numerous social conflicts and uprisings brought about the ***Guerras Irmandiñas*** or "Irmandiñas" Wars, in which the labourers and the city and town people rebelled against the feudal noblemen.

The first Irmandiña War (1431) was against the *House of Andrade*, but the irmandiños did not manage to make the nobles give in, because they were backed by Castile. The second Irmandiña War (1467) spread all over Galicia; the people fought against the nobles of *Lemos, Moscoso* and *Andrade*. The irmandiños destroyed many castles, but finally the nobles dominated the situation. Specially noteworthy in this battle was *Pedro Álvarez de Soutomaior*, "Pedro Madruga", who for the first time in Galicia used gunpowder in the army.

After the Irmandiñas Wars, the Galician aristocracy was strengthened and carried out harsh repressive measures against the losers, forcing them to build a great many fortresses. However, this situation of privilege did not last long for the nobles. For some time now, with the development of the cities and commerce and the social ascent of traders, the nobles had had to increase their expenditure in order to maintain a higher lifestyle than the rest of the population. But their income from the land did not increase, and this brought them to economic ruin. Their economic loss was echoed by a loss in military power, because of the introduction of armies permanently at the service of the monarchies. As a consequence, the nobility also lost all its political power.

FROM THE MIDDLE AGES TO MODERN SOCIETY.

At the end of the Middle Ages the kingdom of Castile-León was the most powerful of the Peninsula. The Civil War brought about the death of the Castilian king Enrique IV, with the victory of the followers of Isabel, who was married to Fernando, heir to the crown of Aragón. This meant the union of the monarchies of Casile-León and Aragon personified in their kings, Fernando and Isabel: the *Catholic Kings*.

During the civil battles for the crown of Castile, the Galician nobles who were in favour of Doña Juana were defeated. Pedro Álvarez de

* Brotherhood.

Soutomaior fled to Portugal and *Pedro Pardo de Cela,* known as "El Mariscal", was executed in 1483. And this was the end of the nobles´ resistance to royal power. Many nobles went to the Court, where they gained high ranking positions: others took part in the sovereign wars. They only came to Galicia from time to time to charge their rents.

With the Catholic Kings a new political period began. The pilars of the medieval monarchies disappeared and gave way to a centralized monarchy. In order to gain definite control over the nobles and total rule over the old kingdom of Galicia, Isabel and Ferdinand adopted the following measures:

- They divided the Galician kingdom into *5 provinces: Mondoñedo, Lugo, Santiago de Compostela, Tui and Ourense.*
- They created a *Military Headquarters,* governed by a nobleman who was not Galician.
- They also created:
    - The *Royal Audience,* in order to force the carrying-out of the royal justice as stated in the General Ordinances (Ordinance of Alcalá of 1348, and the Royal Ordinances of Castile of 1484).
    - The *Councils of Brotherhood* to enforce law and order, gain resources to complete the Reconquest of the Peninsula, and represent the Galician Brotherhood in the General Councils of Brotherhood which maintained yearly meetings in different cities in Castile.

Fortress of Mens-Malpica. Costa da Morte (Coast of Death).

V

FROM THE MODERN AGE TO TODAY

- The Modern Age.
- The Old Régime.
- Agriculture.
- Fishing.
- Industry.
- Commerce.
- The leamed generation.
- The Baroque.
- The nineteenth century.
- The alienation process.
- Provincialism.
- The literary "Rexurdimento" or Renaissance.
- Galicia overseas.
- Regionalism.
- Agrarianism.
- Nationalism.
- Policial evolution.
- Autonomy.

FROM THE MODERN AGE TO TODAY.

THE MODERN AGE.

The economic, social and political transformations during the last years of the Middle Ages lead to a new political era in Europe. The *Humanism* of the period is characterized by new conceptions about art, literature and science, by secular thought which gave priority to the human being and to nature, by a yearning for freedom, and by the boosting of possibilities for creative skills and investigation. During the 15th and 16th centuries, authoritarian monarchies were consolidated, cities grew up, commerce developed and *capitalism* was born. All these changes formed part of the *Renaissance.*

In Galicia, the new cultural tendencies were adopted by people like *Alonso III de Fonseca,* who founded a *College-University* based on the *Old Study* which had started up in 1495 as a place of study for poor students. Arts, Theology, Law and Science were taught in the College, which had study rooms, classrooms, a library, a dining hall and bedrooms. This was the beginning of centuries of existence for the University of Compostela.

Palace of Fonseca. Santiago de Compostela.

The cultural rebirth can also be seen in Renaissance buildings such as the College of Fonseca, which we have already mentioned.

THE OLD REGIME.

Social and economic evolution during the Modern Age was slow. Galician society was made up of *nobles,* who, although few, ruled over lands of which they were not the owners; *clergymen,* who belonged to a Church which had been highly strengthened since the 16th century, and which sent much of the rent it earned from its lands out of Galicia; *hidalgos* or noblemen, descendants of noble families which had come down in the world, who lived in the *pazos* (Galician country manors); *peasants* who represented 80% of the population, ranging from day labourers to farmers who owned small farms; *sailors, merchants* and *craftsmen,* who were fewer in number than the peasants.

The clergy and the nobles rented out their lands to the hidalgos. They, in their turn, lent them to the peasants, after raising the rent. This is how the hidalgos kept half the rents of the land without owning any property and without working. The clergy received money from land rents, tithes and charity. Thanks to their riches they built impressive monasteries and churches, and amassed valuable works of art.

From 1500 to 1800 the Galician population as a whole grew considerably. By the end of the 18th century Galicia had a far higher population density than the average in the peninsula. In 1787 there were 1.340.000 inhabitants, more than an eighth of the Spanish population. This growth in the population forced many people to emigrate, temporally or permanently, during the second half of the 18th century.

Basilica of Santa María de Pontevedra (16th century). Parish church which belonged to the Union of Navigators, one of the jewels of the Rennaissance in Galicia.

AGRICULTURE.

Agriculture was the basis of the economy. The increase in population forced an increase in production. As a consequence, woods were cleared, new production units were created similar to the medieval "vilanovas", chestnut woods were turned into vineyards, and maize and potato started to be grown, which revolutionized the economy.

The increase in agricultural production barely improved the standard of living of the peasants. The land rents and the tithes left the farmers with less than half their crops. It is hardly surprising that during these centuries there were permanent conflicts in the rural areas.

FISHING.

Fishing was a basic activity along the Galician coast. However, not much was fished because of the rudimentary tackle used. The *cerco* (a type of net) was the most widely used method, for fishing sardines. In the middle of the 18th century Catalan merchants arrived in Galicia with new techniques for fishing and tinning fish. The Catalans tried to industrialize the fishing sector and took charge of all the fish caught, buying it from the sailors and setting up salting factories. This sector was boosted again at the beginning of the 19th century, and nowadays it is the basis of the Galician tinning industry.

The improvements in production and tinning gave way to the exportation of sardines, specially to Catalonia. But the traditional fishing methods used along our coasts could not compete with those of the Catalans. This is why the Galician sailors, backed by the clergy and the hidalgos, rose up against the Catalan immigrants so as to forbid the use of the *xábega*, a type of fishing tackle which they had introduced.

INDUSTRY.

Up until the middle of the 19th century there existed in Galicia a textile industry based on handmade articles. The merchants ordered woven or burlap materials from the women in the villages, which they exported to America. This craft disappeared gradually from the second half of the 19th century onwards.

Half way through the 18th century the first factories were set up in Galicia. Don Raimundo Ibáñez founded a cast iron factory in *Sargadelos* in 1796. In 1804 he built a pottery factory next to it, which is working again nowadays.

COMMERCE.

Galician commerce was underdeveloped during these centuries, because the bad state of the thoroughfares made relations between districts difficult. The radius of influence of the fairs was very small. Ribeiro wine was sold in great quantities; until the 16th century it was exported to the northern cities of Spain and to some countries in Europe. In the 18th century the exportation ceased and Santiago de Compostela was the main centre where it was consumed.

Livestock was sold in Castile and Portugal. In the areas of Viveiro and Ribadeo flax was imported. The fabric left via the ports of Viveiro, Ribadeo and A Coruña headed for America and other ports in Europe.

THE LEARNED GENERATION.

The learned Galicians, worried about the problems of the country, tried to find solutions to improve the situation of agriculture, fishing, industry and commerce. On numerous occasions they turned to the Crown with studies on the commerce of livestock, navigation on the Miño river, thoroughfares and the *xábega* (fishing tackle used by the Catalans).
They founded academies and societies such as the *Academy of Agriculture of the Kingdom of Galicia, Economic Societies of the Friends of the Country,* or the *Royal Maritime Consulate.*

Among these learned men, specially worthy of mention are *Benito Jerónimo Feijoo, Martín Sarmiento, José Cornide Saavedra, Lucas Labrada, Pedro Antonio Sánchez* and *Juan Francisco de Castro.*

Modern pottery figure from Sargadelos.

THE BAROQUE.

As had happened with the Romanesque, the Baroque triumphed all over Galicia and superimposed later styles in time and in space. The most important example of Baroque architecture is the *Obradoiro facade* of the Cathedral of Santiago. It was begun in 1789 under the orders of Fernando Casas y Novoa, and it stands as an arch of triumph to receive pilgrims and to protect the Pórtico de la Gloria (Door of Glory of the Cathedral) without dimming the light around it.

Other outstanding examples of baroque architecture are the facades of the monasteries of Oseira, Sobrado dos Monxes, Celanova and San Martiño Pinario. There are also many Baroque alterpieces and belfries in churches situated all over the region.

The Obradoiro facade.

THE 19th CENTURY.

During the War of Independence a British army, under the command of general John Moore, came from Portugal to help the Spanish. When he was defeated by the French in Castile, he fled to Galicia in January of 1809. The British were followed by the French under the command of Soult, who caught them up near A Coruña. In the *battle of Elviña* Moore died; the British, who suffered many casualties, were able to board ships and flee.

The French troops occupied our region, but the Galicians fought against the invaders. Everybody took part in this fight: soldiers, hidalgos, priests, farmers and students. The civilians formed gangs -*alarmas*- which constantly harassed the French detachments. A popular army was set up -*División del Miño*- and the students from Santiago formed the *Literary Batallion.*

In this conflict the most important events were the reconquest of Vigo and the *Battle of Pontesampaio,* from the 7th to the 9th of June, 1809, where the Galicians under the command of Morillo definitively defeated the French.

Politically speaking, in Galicia the majority of the clergy, the nobility and part of the bourgeoisie were absolutists. The merchants, craftsmen, the professional people and the hidalgos generally supported liberal ideas. Farmers and sailors did not become involved in political issues. The liberals conspired on repeated occasions against the absolutist régime. In 1815, general Porlier, the hero of the War of Independence, rose up in A Coruña. This revolt failed, as did others afterwards.

The Carlist groups of Santiago, Chantada, Sobrado, A Fonsagrada and Tui intervened in the first Carlist war. With the defeat of the Carlists, Liberalism was consolidated.

Cathedral-fortress of Tui.

THE ALIENATION PROCESS.

In the times of Isabel II, when the minister Mendizábal ordered the secularization of the religious orders and the alienation and selling of their posessions, in Galicia practically all lands belonged to the clergy. But these lands were not sold, seeing as they were rented out, and instead the rents themselves were sold. The farmers continued to work the lands and pay rents to their new owners, mostly merchants and city people.

The consequence of the alienation process was that more than 7,000 clergymen were left in precarious conditions; that the bourgeoisie became the owner of most of the land and gained great power; and, finally, that the artistic and cultural heritage was greatly damaged. Buildings were abandoned and archives, libraries and works of art were lost.

At the same time, the state of the economy included an agricultural sector which was backward and was still based on the rent system. The main industries were the tinning industries in the Rías Baixas, the shipyards in Vigo and Ferrol, the tobacco factory in A Coruña and the pottery factory in Sargadelos. The railway was built in Galicia much later than in other regions and countries. The first section (Santiago de Compostela-Carril) dates back to 1873.

Monastery of Sobrado dos Monxes, which suffered the effects of the alienation process.

PROVINCIALISM.

At the time of the War of Independence, the fact that Galicia was different from other Spanish regions began to be discovered: it was different in its history, its geography, its language, and its customs. Between 1840 and 1846 a cultural movement called *provincialism* began, promoted by an intelectual minority. The provincialists became aware of Galicia´s different characteristics and of its backwardness. They wanted to gain political autonomy in order to solve the region´s problems.

In 1846 colonel *Solís* made a declaration in Lugo against the central Government. This revolt spread rapidly all over Galicia. The provincialists supported the rebellious military and the Superior County Council of Galicia was created. The rebellion did not last long. Solís was defeated near Santiago and shot at Carral together with another eleven officials.

Plaza del Campo. Lugo.

THE LITERARY "REXURDIMENTO" OR RENAISSANCE.

During the first half of the 19th century a literary movement sprung up in Galicia which aimed to dignify the Galician language: the *Rexurdimento.* The rebirth of Galician as a literary language, which was started up by the *forerunners* -Añón, Pintos, Faraldo...- was confirmed with the publication in 1863 of the *Cantares Gallegos (Galician Songs)* by *Rosalía de Castro,* who together with *Manuel Curros Enríquez* and *Eduardo Pondal* formed the three most important writers of the Rexurdimento. Benito Vicetto and Manuel Murguía were specially important in the search for Galicia´s historical roots.

In the 20th century various groups were born who studied the problems of the region and contributed to the exaltation of Galician language and literature, for example: *Solidariedade Galega (Galician Solidarity),* la *Real Academia Galega (Galician Royal Academy),* promoted by emigrants in Cuba, the *Irmandades da Fala (Society for the Defense of the Galician Language),* who founded the nationalist newspaper *A Nosa Terra (Our country),* the review *Nós,* and the *Seminario de Estudos Galegos (Seminary of Galician Studies),* which promoted the study and investigation of Galician culture.

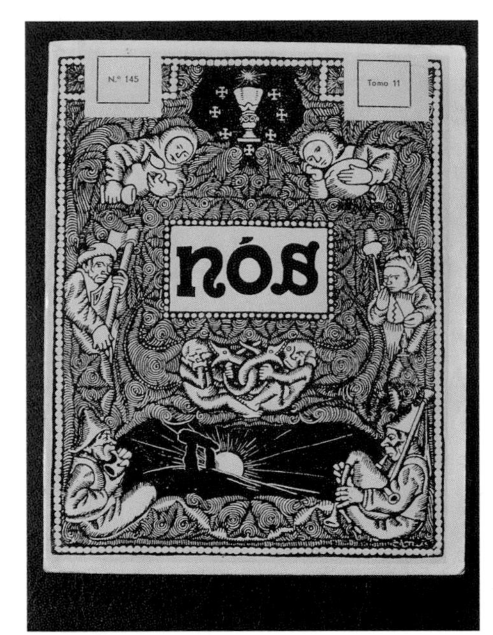

"Nós" review.

Galician Centre in Havana.

GALICIA OVERSEAS.

Many centuries ago, thousands of Galicians began to emigrate because the agricultural sector was so chronically backward and there were scarcely no industries. At the beginning they emigrated to Portugal and Andalucia and they went to the harvests in Castile each summer. From the middle of the 19th century onwards they travelled overseas: to Cuba, Argentina, Brazil, Uruguay, Venezuela...

The emigrants founded various societies with the aim of helping each other and mantaining the bonds with Galicia. They built hospitals and schools and published newspapers and books in Galician. They also sent money for the building of schools and thoroughfares in Galicia. The most important Galician societies overseas were the *Galician centres* of Havana, Buenos Aires and Montevideo.

REGIONALISM.

Politically orientated movements were born at the same time as the Galician cultural movements. The *federalists* wanted an autonomous Galicia within a federal State. They made their Galician nationalist ideas popular among farmers and sailors. In 1883 they wrote up a *Project for the Constitution of the Future Galician State.* Later on, the *regionalists* argued in favour of a decentralized organization of the State, too. *Alfredo Brañas,* a teacher and politician, was a great theoretician of regionalism in Spain. His ideas influenced the Basque and Catalan regionalists. In his book *Regionalism* he puts forward the idea that the State should become decentralized and should concede political power to the various Spanish regions.

Market, on a 19th century print.

AGRARIANISM.

The beginning of the 20th century gave rise to a social movement which fought to improve the conditions of the farmers: *Agrarianism.* The agrarianists wanted to abolish the system of rents, finish with the caciquism which was so enrooted in the country, and improve agriculture. Basilio Alvarez, a priest from Ourense, was its main promoter.

Otero Pedrayo.

NATIONALISM.

Galician *Nationalism* grew up within the *Irmandades da Fala. Antón Villar Ponte* published a manifesto proposing a Galician government with strong powers, the coofficiality of Galician and Castilian and the federal organization of the Iberian peninsula. The ideologist of nationalism was *Vicente Risco,* who in 1920 published the *Theory of Galician Nationalism.* With the coming of the Republic, many nationalists joined the ORGA (Galician Autonomous Republican Organization) and other parties.

In 1931, in Pontevedra, the *Partido Galeguista (Galician Nationalist Party)* was created, which included nearly all nationalists. It aimed to achieve a Statute of Autonomy for Galicia. The main promoters were *Castelao, Alexandre Bóveda, Otero Pedrayo* and *Vicente Risco.* The Statute was presented for the approval of the Galician municipalities in 1932, but was not to be approved by the plebiscite of the Galician people until June 28th, 1936. It was passed by a wide margin, and Castelao presented it before the Assembly of the Republic on the 15th of July of the same year. However the Civil War interrupted the process of definite approval by the Assembly.

Alexandre Bóveda.

POLITICAL EVOLUTION.

The postwar years were a period of recovery from the harsh conflict, after the first few moments of international isolation.

The Galician communities overseas took in exiles and organized activities in defense of the Galician culture. In 1950, after the death of Castelao in Buenos Aires, the Galician Nationalist Party was dissolved. In that year the *Galaxia* publishing house was created, mantaining and spreading nationalist ideology among the new generations.

From the sixties onwards, student demonstrations and strikes took place in demand of freedom and democratic rights, and the workers, for their part, organized themselves into trades unions and also staged demonstrations and strikes. From 1964, secret political parties were organized to fight for democratic freedom, and in 1966 the Law of the Press and Publishing abolished the censorship which had existed previously.

Once Franco died, after a short period of transition, the Spanish Constitution was passed in 1978, which opened the doors to a new democratic era. The first years were difficult, but the State of the autonomies was consolidated and Galicia, a historic community, passed the Statute of Autonomy by referendum in 1981. The *Galician Parliament* has legislative power and the *Xunta de Galicia (Autonomous Government of Galicia)* is the government of the region.

The Galician Parliament.

VI

A LANGUAGE FOR A REGION

- Galician, a Romance language and a European language.
- Galicia, Galician and the Pilgrim Route to Santiago.
- History of Galician language and literature
  1. Birth-Splendour.
  2. Decline.
  3. "Rexurdimento" or Renaissance.
- Galician today.
- Galician in the public Administration.
- Galician in education.
- Media and cultural production.

A LANGUAGE FOR A COUNTRY

Galician is the language of Galicia.
Statute of Autonomy.

GALICIAN, A ROMANCE LANGUAGE AND A EUROPEAN LANGUAGE.

A language is the way in which each community interprets and expresses its reality and its culture.

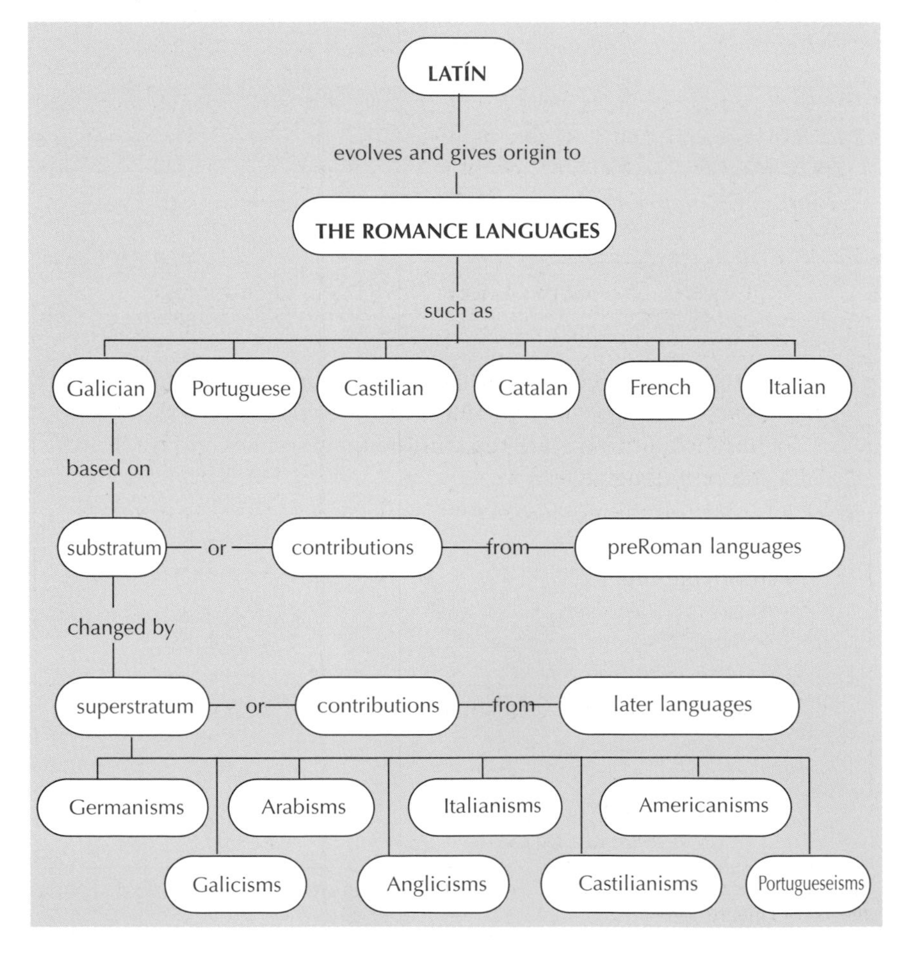

Due to historical circumstances, Galician becomes a minority language in the 15th century, giving way to Castilian, the official language of all the territories that make up Spain.

This discriminatory situation continues until 1981, the year in which the Statute of Autonomy recognises Galician as the language of Galicia. Galician survived during those four centuries thanks to farmers, fishermen and craftsmen, who continued to use it in their day to day relations.

WORLD		EUROPE	
LANGUAGES	**STATES**	**MONOLINGUAL COUNTRIES**	
4,000	200	Portugal Iceland Albania	Liechenstein San Marino Vatican City

There are very many languages that suffer the consequences of discrimination, sharing a territory with other official languages.

The European Council showed its concern in the fifties about cultural and linguistic diversity. At the beginning of the eighties investigations were carried out on the situation of minority languages, and in 1992 the *European Charter of Minority and Regional Languages* was passed.

European Charter of Minority and Regional Languages.

It defends the following principles:

- The linguistic plurality of Europe is of enormous cultural wealth.
- The minority languages are living through a complicated situation.
- The public authorities are responsible for defending the position of minority languages.
- In order to promote and save minority languages it is essential to use them:
  - In private life.
  - In public life.
  - In social life.
  - In economic life.
- The only way to end linguistic discrimination is to use minority languages:
  - In education.
  - In administration.
  - In the system of justice.

Spain plays an active part in this philosophy since it entered the European Community on the 1st of January, 1986.

Territories with linguistic normalization programmes		Field.
Galicia	Switzerland	Education.
Cataloni	Estonia	Mass media
Euskadi	Belgium	Administratión.
Brittany	Flandes	
Wales	Israel	
Friesland	India	
Ireland	Canada.	

The European Union gives economic support to activities and projects that promote the progress of minority languages.

GALICIA, GALICIAN AND THE PILGRIM ROUTE TO SANTIAGO.

The medieval splendour of Galician is not unrelated to the pilgrimages to Santiago de Compostela. The Pilgrim Route to Santiago linked Galicia to other cultures and gave it prestige in the Christian Europe of the time. In the 9th century the remains of the Apostle St James the Great (Santiago) were found and shortly afterwards the pilgrimages to Compostela began. The Pilgrim Routes to Santiago go by land, from Central Europe, France and Portugal, and by sea, to the ports of A Coruña and Ferrol and to the rias of Noia-Muros, Arousa and Vigo.

The pilgrimages reached their climax in the 11th, 12th and 13th centuries, thanks to the Archbishop of Compostela, Diego Gelmírez, and to popes Calixtus II and his successor Alexander III, who instituted the Santiago Holy Year by means of the bull *Regis Aeterni*. It conceded the grace of the Jubilee to those who visited the tomb of the Apostle when the 25th of July fell on a Sunday.

During the Lower Middle Ages, hospitals, cities and monasteries grew up along the Way of St James, offering rest at the end of each stage in the journey. The Cluniacs payed an important social role and they spread Provencal lyrical poetry and the French arts.

People of many nationalities and ranks pilgrimed to Compostela: Bretons, the Irish, Greeks, Germans, Lombards and specially the French; and nobles, serfs or religious men, which favoured cultural exchange.

Compostela became an important centre of population, and was visited by sculptors, architects, painters, and miniaturists, who all left examples of their art in the cathedral.

Compostela became a central theme in lyrical poetry, developing its own -*Cantigas de Amigo (Ballads of the Friend)*- and also influencing Occitan learned poetry -*Cantigas de Amor (Ballads of Love)*-. The Pilgrim Route to Santiago also influenced prose, with works such as *Miragres de Santiago (Miracles of Santiago)*, a version of the *Liber Sancti Jacobi*, which spread news of the pilgrim way. The Galician language became enriched with French and Provencal vocabulary: *frade (monk), forasteiro (stranger), trobar (to sing)...*

The Codex Calixtinus, in the Santiago cathedral, is a guide for pilgrims which describes each stage of the journey along the Pilgrim Route from France.

> *The Pilgrim Route to Santiago, a sociological, cultural and religious phenomenon, which was the cause and consequence of important historial events, is still a living phenomenon today.*

Miniature of the Codex Calixtinus.

The Apostle St James, as a pilgrim.

STAGES		
Name	**Chronology**	**Description**
1. Birth-Splendour..	9th-15th centuries	Galician-Portuguese lyrical literature.
2. Decline.	15th-18th centuries	Spoken language. Dark Ages.
3. "Rexurdimento" o or Renaissance.	19th-20th centuries	Great writers.

1. Birth-Splendour.

From the 9th century Galician is spoken as a different language from Latin. During the 10th, 11th and 12th centuries Galician was the only spoken language in the region. In the 12th century it was co-official with Latin for notarial documents, edicts, and lawsuits, although Latin was the universal language of culture.

Cantigas de Santa María. They were composed in the Court of Alfonso X the Wise, who directed the process and also took part in the writing. They are an example of the prestige achieved by Galician as a literary language, at the end of the 13th century.

First known documents:

Literary:

"Ora faz ost´o Senhor de Navarra". Satirical ballad by Joam Soares de Paiva. Written aproximately in the year 1200.

Non literary:

"Noticia do Torto", of 1211.

"Testamento de Afonso II de Portugal", of 1214.

Galician becomes the language of lyricism par excellence throughout the Peninsula, except in Catalonia. It is an international language because it is used by Galician, Portuguese, Castilian, Sicilian, and Occitan writers, aswell as writers of the royal and noble courts such as Santiago, Toledo, Coímbra or Lisbon.

Profane lyrical works include the *Cantigas de Amigo,* the *Cantigas de Amor* and the *Cantigas de Escarnio e maldicir (Ballads of Mockery and Scorn).*

The *Cantigas de Santa María (Ballads of Saint Mary),* a work which praises the Virgin, are an example of religious lyricism. They are the most important example of medieval poetry in the Peninsula on the theme of the Virgin Mary.

Medieval literary prose arrives late on the scene, and is scarce. The cultural centres at that time were the monasteries and the monastic schools, where ecclesiastical Latin was used. All in all, from the end of the 13th century the most widespread themes in medieval Europe had a version in Galician.

Medieval Galician literature	
Profane lyricism	Cantigas de amigo. Cantigas de amor. Cantigas de escarnio e maldicir.
Religious lyricism	Cantigas de Santa María.
Prose	Texts about King Arthur. The History of Troy. Chronicle of Troy. Miragres de Santiago. Some translations.

2. Decline.

After the period of glory, Galician and Galician literature begin the 14th century in obvious decline.

Causes for the decline of Galician

- The Galician nobility is defeated after supporting the losers in the dynastical struggles for the Crown of Castile, and foreigners take its place.
- A foreign nobility, uncompromising with Galician culture and language, settles in Galicia.
- There is no middle class capable of defending its own interests and those of the country.
- The Galician Church loses autonomy.

Galician, which becomes differentiated from Portuguese from the middle of the 14th century, begins a period of three centuries of decline: the 16th, 17th and 18th centuries, during which it disappears from public life and from written documents and takes refuge in the private relations of farmers, sailors and craftsmen. There is no written, learned literature. An oral, popular literature develops. From the 15th century, as a result of the policy of the Catholic Kings, Castilian is imposed as the language of the Administration, the Church, and the rich and powerful, and as the language of culture and social prestige.

Castilian and Portuguese enter a process of fixation and codification and therefore become languages of culture, while Galician becomes slightly fragmented. Galician literature is, therefore, left out of the Renaissance and the Baroque. However, popular literature survives in the form of lullabies, blind men´s ballads, carnavals, riddles, legends, romances, stories, farces, tongue twisters...

The learned generation.

The end of the long period known as the Dark Ages becomes enlightened by the learned generation, a group of people who are concerned about the development of Galicia and put forward innovative proposals in favour of economic, social and cultural life.

Specially noteworthy is the learned Benedictine Fray Martín Sarmiento, who in the 18th century defended the use of Galician in education, administration and the Church; that is to say, he defended the language of Galicians and its standardization.

3. "Rexurdimento" or Renaissance.

The 19th century is a period of literary, cultural, political and historical recovery.

Rosalía de Castro. To conmemorate the centenary of the publication of the Cantares Gallegos, the Day of Galician Literature is celebrated each year since 1963. It serves to pay homage to a writer who is no longer living and to exalt Galician culture.

LANDMARKS

1809: First Galician texts against the French invasion.

40-50: *Provincialism*. Spoke out against the marginalization of the region. Valued all things Galician.

Regionalisms: Defended Galician.

1861: Floral Games in A Coruña.

1862: *Album of Charity*: First anthology.

1863: Publication of *"Cantares Gallegos", (Galician Songs)*, by Rosalía de Castro.

1864: Short Galician-Castilian Grammar, by Francisco Mirás.

1876: *O Tío Marcos da Portela*, newspaper, by Valentín Lamas Carvajal.

1880: Publication of

- *Follas Novas (New Leaves)*, by Rosalía de Castro.
- *Aires da Miña Terra (Airs from my country)*, by Curros Enríquez.
- *Saudades Gallegas (Galician nostalgia)*, by Valentín Lamas Carvajal.
- *Maxina ou a filla espúrea (Maxina or the illegitimate daughter)*, by Marcial Valladares.

1886-1888: Monolingual press appears:

- *O Galicismo*, in Pontevedra.
- *A Monteira*, in Lugo.
- *As Burgas*, in Ourense.

1889: *Catecismo do Labrego (Peasant´s catechism)*, by Valentín Lamas Carvajal.

1894: *A Tecedeira de Bonaval (The weaver of Bonaval)*, by Antonio López Ferreiro.

1895: *O Castelo de Pambre (Pambre Castle)*, by Antonio López Ferreiro.

LANDMARKS

1905: *O niño de pombas (The nest of doves)*, by Antonio López Ferreiro.
Creation of the Royal Galician Academy.

1916: *Irmandadas da Fala (Society for the Defence of the Galician Language)*. A Coruña. Later in Ferrol, Ourense, Betanzos, Santiago...

A Nosa Terra (Our Country), the Irmandades da Fala´s newspaper.
Members: Villar Ponte, Losada Diéguez, Vicente Risco, Ramón Cabanillas...
They worked for the normalization of Galician.
They promoted the founding of various publishers:
- *Celtiga*, in Ferrol.
- *Lar*, in A Coruña.
- *Alborada*, in Pontevedra.

1919: National Conservatory of Galician Art, which would soon become the Galician Dramatic School.

1920: *Grupo Nós*: Generation formed by Vicente Risco, Otero Pedrayo, López Cuevillas, Castelao...They aim to normalize, universalize and bring Galician culture up to date.
Revista Nós (Nós Review): In contact with European trends.

1923: Seminar of Galician Studies. Created by Fermín Bouza Brey, Filgueira Valverde, Lois Tobío, Ricardo Carballo Calero, Antonio Fraguas, Xaquín Lorenzo...

1925: Generation of the Year 25: Manuel Antonio, Amado Carballo, Bouza Brey.

1931: Creation of the Galician Nationalist Party.
The Statute of Autonomy of Galicia is passed.
Prewar Theatre Plays: Alvaro Cunqueiro, Eduardo Blanco Amor, Carballo Calero, Pura and Dora Vázquez.

1936: The Civil War begins, and so does a period of hardship for the non official languages of Spain.

1939: End of the Civil War: beginning of the exile of intelectuals to Argentina, Venezuela, Mexico, Cuba...
Postwar poetry: Aquilino Iglesia Alvariño, Xosé María Díaz Castro, Xosé María Alvarez Blázquez, Eduardo Moreiras.
Galician literature in exile:
- Poetry: Emilio Pita, Luis Seoane, Lorenzo Varela.
- Prose: Ramón de Valenzuela Otero, Silvio Santiago.
- Plays: Manuel Varela Buxán.

1946-47: Benito Soto colection of poetry.
Bibliófilos Galegos Publishing House.
La Noche (The Night), a weekly bilingual supplement and Santiago newspaper.

1950: Creation of Galaxia Publishers.
Founders: Otero Pedrayo, Ramón Piñeiro, Francisco Fernández del Riego...
Review of Galician Economy.
Atlántida, culture and arts review
Grial, review of theoretical essays
1950-1997: *Lyricism is reborn*: Miguel González Garcés, María Mariño Carou, Pura Vázquez, Antón Tovar, Luz Pozo Garza, Cuña Novás, Manuel María, Uxío Novoneyra, Xohana Torres, Bernardino Graña, García Bodaño, Méndez Ferrín, Arcadio López Casanova, Celso Emilio Ferreiro, Xesús Rábade, Darío Xohán Cabana, Xosé Vázquez Pintor, Alfonso Pexegueiro, Ramiro Fonte, Manuel Rivas.
Renovation of prose: Blanco Amor, Alvaro Cunqueiro, Anxel Fole, Gonzalo R.Mourullo, Camilo Suárez-Llanos, X.L.Méndez Ferrín, Carlos Casares, Xohana Torres, Xosé Neira Vilas, Xavier Alcalá, Paco Martín, Xosé Fernández Ferreiro, Alfredo Conde, Xosé Manuel Martínez Oca, Anxel Adolfo Rei Ballesteros, Tucho Calvo, Víctor Freixanes, Xesús Rábade.
Theatre: Daniel Cortezón, Manuel María, Xohana Torres, Isaac Díaz Pardo, Bernardino Graña, Xosé L. Franco Grande.
From 1973 onwards: Manuel Lourenzo, Euloxio Ruibal, Roberto Vidal Bolaño.
New Galician publishers are created:
- Edicións Xerais.
- Edicións Sotelo Blanco.
- Ir indo...

1971: Creation of the Institute of Galician Language.
1982: Orthographic and Morphological Rules of the Galician Language.

Institute of Galician Language.

GALICIAN TODAY.

Galician, in spite of being a minority language in the plurilingual Spanish State and in Europe, enjoys a fairly wide use because it is deeply rooted in the people. The Sociolinguistic Map of Galicia, drawn up by the Royal Galician Academy, and of which the first volume was published in 1994, offers optimistic data:

ABILITY IN THE FOUR LANGUAGE SKILLS IN GALICIA

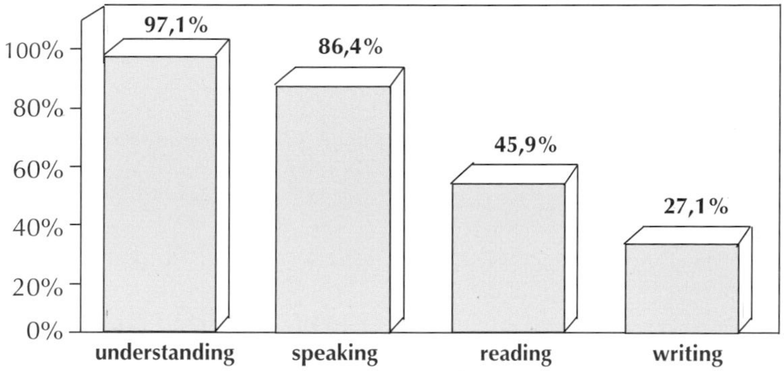

100%
80%
60%
40%
20%
0%
97,1% understanding
86,4% speaking
45,9% reading
27,1% writing

The percentage is lower in writing, which cannot be learned spontaneously and which was not taught until recently.

Galician is used above all in the rural areas. However, people who live in the cities, many of whom have come from the country, have a high degree of ability in Galician.

The language of Galicia should regain social prestige with its official status, and due to its introduction in the media, in the administration and in education.

Only 7.7% of the inhabitants of Galicia do not use Galician and the majority of these were not born in the autonomous community.

GALICIAN IN THE PUBLIC ADMINISTRATION.

Galicia´s own autonomous administration uses Galician as a means of communication.

The Head Office of Linguistic Policy, which belongs to the Department of Education and Universities, makes the use of Galician in the public administration more dynamic.

Bodies/activities

- Offices of Linguistic Normalization in the county delegations of education.
- Beginners´ and advanced courses for civil servants.
- Publication of forms, application forms, letters and circulars, office signs, and vocabularies in Galician.
- Galician language exams for civil servants.
- Publicity campaigns:
  · *Fálalle galego (Speak Galician to him/her).* 1984.
  · *O galego é útil (Galician is useful).* 1987.
  · *Mellor en galego (Better in Galician).* 1989.
- Normalization activities in various town halls.
- Galician School for Public Administration.
- Partial use of Galician in the Justice administration.
  Campaign: *¡En galego, é de xustiza! (In Galician, it´s only just!)*

GALICIAN IN EDUCATION

The Law of Linguistic Normalization, passed in 1983, states that teaching Galician language and literature is obligatory at all levels of pre university education.

Activities

- A Linguistic Normalization team in each school.
- Beginners´, advanced and specialized Galician courses for teachers.
- Publication of text books and teaching material for teachers.
- Funds for parent associations for courses and programmes for the promotion of Galician.

Galician universities

Statutes: Galician is an official language, together with Castilian.
Campaign: *En galego, estamos no mundo (In Galician, we are in the world)*

University of Santiago.
- 1984: Translation service.
- 1988: Linguistic Normalization service.
- Campain: *¡En galego o que ti queiras! (In Galician, whatever you like!)*

University of A Coruña. 1989.
- Office for promoting the use of the Galician language.

University of Vigo. 1990.
- Linguistic Normalization service.

Universities in other parts of Spain and the world	
Teach Galician **35 universities**	
Universities of:	Number
Spain:	8
Europe:	16
America:	10
Australia:	1

- *Centre of Linguistic and Literary Studies Ramón Piñeiro.*
  3 years of work.
  21 publications.
  36 scholarship holders.
  18 projects of investigation.

MEDIA AND CULTURAL PRODUCTION.

The presence of Galician is scarce.

- Radio and television.
  Creation of the Company of Galician Radio and Television.
    Galician Radio.
    Galician Television.

- Written press and publications.

The only daily newspaper in Galician is:
O Correo Galego
Other publications in Galician are:
A Nosa Terra.
Revista Galega de Educación.
A Trabe de Ouro.
Cadernos da Lingua.
Análise empresarial.
Irimia.
Encrucillada.
Luzes de Galicia.
Olibos.
Revista Galega do Ensino.
Dorna.
Revista de Literatura.

VII

AUTONOMOUS ADMINISTRATION. I.

- Autonomous institutions.
- Galician Parliament.
- Galician Government.
- Administration of local bodies.
- High Court of Galicia.

AUTONOMOUS ADMINISTRATION. I.

Galicia achieves its autonomy as a historical community.

AUTONOMOUS INSTITUTIONS

Historical communities are considered to be those which at some moment of their modern history enjoyed full autonomy or have been in the process of attaining it definitively, and they therefore enjoy a special jurisdiction.

The organization of the autonomy is based on the following institutions:

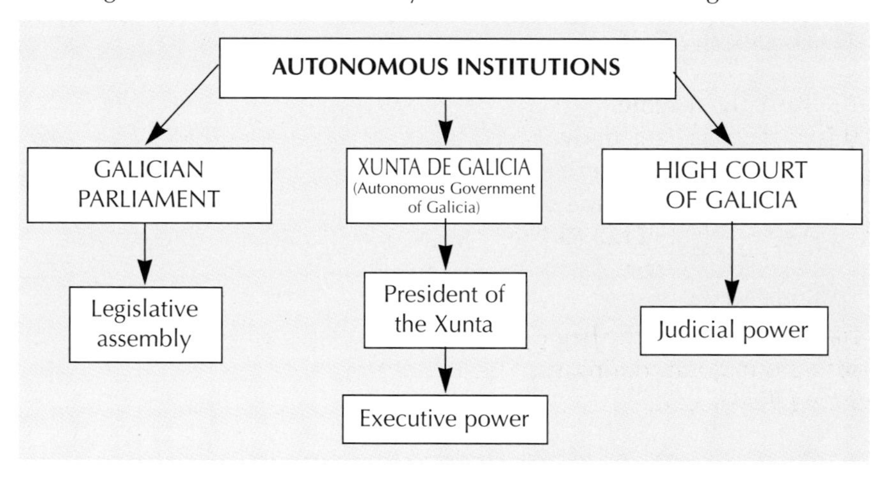

PARLIAMENT OF GALICIA

It is elected by universal suffrage and by a system of proportional representation which assures the presence of representatives from the different areas of Galicia.

The *Parliament* is the legislative power in the Autonomous Community and it controls the executive actions of the Xunta. It is made up of 75 Members of Parliament (MPs) voted in by universal suffrage -an equal, free, direct and secret vote- for a period of four years. Parliamentary meetings take place in *plenary sessions* and *committees.*

The **permanent committees** deal with the following areas:
1. Institutional, general administration, justice and interior.
2. Territorial planning, public works, environment and services.
3. Economy, public finance and the budget.
4. Education and culture.
5. Health, social policy and employment.
6. Industry, energy, commerce and tourism.
7. Agriculture, food, stockbreeding and forests.
8. Fishing and seafood production.

Floor of the Galician Parliament.

There are also permanent committees for the Regulation of Parliament, the Statute of the MPs, and Petitions, aswell as those which must be constituted by statutory provisions. The Parliament is in Santiago de Compostela.

The Parliament Table.

This is a collegiate body which approves all documents and makes decisions about the internal functioning of the Parliament, according to the Regulation. It is made up of:
- The President of the Parliament.
- Two vicepresidents.
- Two secretaries.

They are named at the beginning of each legislature. They must achieve absolute majority during the first round of votes, and simple majority during the second.

Functions:
- Interprets the Regulation of Parliament.
- Makes decisions and takes action when needed for the organization of its work mechanisms and for its internal regulations.
- Approves the Parliament´s expenditure.
- Assesses texts and documents, and decides whether they are to be processed.
- Programmes the general lines of action in Parliament.
- Sets the dates for plenary sessions and committees.
- Coordinates the various parliamentary bodies.

The Parliament Table meetings take place behind closed doors.

The President of Parliament.
The President represents the Parliament. He assures it is working properly, directs the debates and keeps them in order, and orders the payment of expenses. He must abide by the Regulation and make sure it is abided by. He directs and coordinates the activites of the Table.

He is elected during the session when the Parliament is formed; this requires absolute majority during the first round of votes and simple majority among those who in the first round obtained the highest number of votes.

Board of Spokespeople.
The Board of Spokespeople is made up of the parliamentary groups´ spokesmen.

It must voice its opinion on the criteria which need to be established to set the order of the debates and the activities of Parliament. It must also decide which committees are to deal with which legislative texts; that is to say, Law proposals and Government bills.

It is compulsory to hear the Board of Spokespeople´s opinion on some of the Table´s duties, such as the programming of the Parliament´s general lines of action, setting the dates for the activities of the plenary and the committes in each sitting, and coordinating the work of the parliamentary bodies.

Popular Initiative.
In order that Parliament may consider a question which has not been proposed by the Government nor by a parliamentary group, it is necessary to present a proposal, an initiative backed by 1,500 signatures.

Parliamentary groups.
At least five MPs are needed to form a parliamentary group.

When, during a legislature, a group is reduced to a minimum less than half the minimum number, it is automatically dissolved. When a new sitting begins, if the party or coalition whom they represent has died out, these MPs may form a parliamentary group just once.

A parliamentary group can be made up of members of a certain party or coalition, but also of associates, who can join the group in practice even though they were elected as part of another group before.

Parliamentary groups take part in committees, in the Permanent Delegation, in the plenary and in the convocations. They are the motor of parliamentary activity.

Mixed Group.
Political parties which do not have a minimum of five MPs to form their own group must necessarily form part of the Mixed Group.

Formation of the Galician Parliament after the legislative elections on October 19th, 1997.

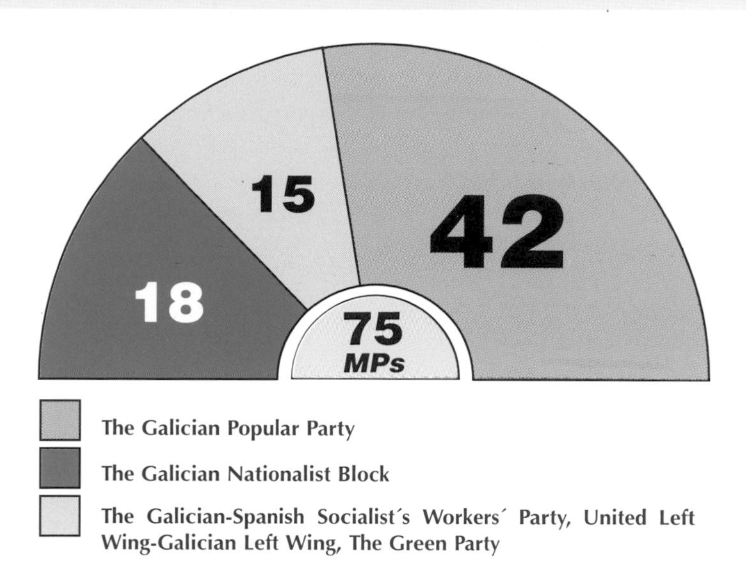

THE XUNTA DE GALICIA: GOVERNMENT OF THE AUTONOMOUS COMMUNITY

The *Xunta* is the collegiate body which, directed by the President, runs the general policy and administration of the Autonomous Community. In order to do so, it has legislative powers, executive powers and power to set out the rules according to the Statute of Autonomy and the law.

The Xunta de Galicia has the following duties:

- Establishing the guidelines and carrying out the government programme.
- Preparing the budget of the autonomous community and handing it in to Parliament for its approval.
- Passing Government bills to send them to Parliament or, as the case may be, deciding their withdrawal.
- Enacting legislative decrees if the Parliament has expressly delegated it to do so.
- Giving or denying its consent for Parliament to process Law proposals for increasing credits or decreasing revenue, according to the terms established in the Regulation of Parliament.
- Approving the planning and execution of the laws of Galicia, and

also State laws when Galicia has the power to carry them out, as stated by the Statute of Autonomy or by delegation or transfer.

- When needed, approving the required measures in order to carry out the international treaties and conventions and the rulings and guidelines they entail, when referring to matters which are attributed to the autonomous community.
- Approving and sending to Parliament the proposals for cooperation agreements with other autonomous communities for their ratification or approval, as the case may be.
- Deciding to lodge claims of unconstitutionality and taking part in cases of unconstitutionality which affect Galicia, aswell as appealing to the Constitutional Tribunal in conflicts of responsibilities. Deliberating on questions of confidence which the President of the Xunta proposes to pass on to Parliament, and dissolving Parliament, which the President can decree.
- Resolving administrative complaints in those cases provided for by the law.
- Resolving by way of decree conflicts of jurisdiction between the different departments of the Xunta.
- Appointing and dismissing, following the suggestions of respective ministers, members of the Galician public Administration who have equal or higher status than directors of the head offices, and whichever others are seen fit by the law.
- Creating, changing and abolishing the Delegate Committees of the Xunta.
- Determining the superior organic structure of the Vicepresidency or Vicepresidencies and the Departments of the Xunta de Galicia.
- Appointing the autonomous community´s representatives in the State´s economic bodies, financial institutions and public companies. Similarly, supervising the management of the public services and of the public bodies and companies of the autonomous community, and administering its patrimony.
- Coordinating the activities of the County Councils in all that directly affects the general interest of the autonomous community, and deciding on the transference or delegation of functions to them. Parliament must be informed of these decisions.

Administrative offices at San Caetano. This is where most of the departments are. Santiago de Compostela.

- Being aware of the Parliament´s resolutions and carrying out, if need be, the resulting measures.
- All other responsibilities attributed to it by any legal or reglamentary disposition and, in general, deliberating on those issues which must be resolved by decree or which, due to their importance and repercussions on the life of the Autonomous Community, demand an analisis on the part of the Xunta.

Presidency.
The *President of the Xunta of Galicia,* who shall be elected by the Galician Parliament among its members, is the supreme representative of the Autonomous Community and the ordinary representative of the State in Galicia, and he/she directs and coordinates the action of the Xunta or Government.

Due to his position he has a right to:
- The preeminence corresponding to the supreme representation of the Autonomous Community and the ordinary representation of the State in Galicia.
- Recieving whetever honours are established by the law in force and are decided by the Autonomous Community.
- Being addressed as His Excellency.
- Using the Galician Flag as a standard.

He shall not carry out any representative functions except those in the Parliamentary mandate, nor any other public function which does nor arise from his position, nor any commercial or professional activity nor any other which will undermine his independence and the dignity of his position.

The political responsibility of the President of the Xunta before Parliament is that established in the Statute of Autonomy, in the Regulation of Parliament and in Law 1/1983 of February 22nd.

As supreme representative of the Autonomous Community, he must represent it in its relations with other State institutions; sign agreements of cooperation with other autonomous communities; call elections to the Galician Parliament after its dissolution; enact, in the name of the King, the laws of Galicia aswell as, if need be, the legislative decrees, and order their publication in the Official Diary of Galicia.

The President, under his own exclusive responsibility and after deliberating with the Consello de la Xunta (Government Council), can dissolve Parliament by way of a decree which will state the date of the elections. This can not occur before one year has passed since the last time the Parliament was dissolved.

As ordinary representative of the State in Galicia, the President of the Xunta shall mantain relations with the Delegation of the Spanish Government in order to achieve a more efficient coordination of the State´s activities in Galicia and those of the Autonomous Community; and he shall order the publication in the Official Diary of Galicia of the appointment of the President of the High Court of Galicia; and the publication of Galicia´s laws and legislative decrees in the Official State Bulletin.

To assure the direction and coordination of the activities of the Xunta de Galicia, the President must:

- Create, change or abolish by way of Decree the vicepresidency or vicepresidencies if they exist and the departments, aswell as appointing and dismissing the vicepresidentes and ministers.
- Call, preside, suspend and end the meetings of the Council and of the delegate committees, and direct their deliberations.
- Direct and coordinate the action of the Government and asure its continuity.
- Ensure that the Xunta´s instructions are carried out, and promote or coordinate the carrying-out of the agreements of the Council and of its delegate committees.
- Ensure that the various departments are coordinated.
- Coordinate the Xunta´s legislative programme and the laying out of general norms.
- Entrust a vicepresident or a minister to take responsibility over an office or a department or of Presidency itself, in the case of absence, illness or inability of the President.
- Ask Parliament for its support, after deliberation with the Council.
- Present Government bills before Parliament either in person or by delegating a member of Government for this purpose.
- Ensure that Parliament gets all information and documentation it asks of the Xunta.
- Request the celebration of a plenary session in Parliament.
- Request a general debate in Parliament.
- Inform Parliament when claims of inconstitutionality and conflicts of duties have been lodged before the Constitutional Tribunal, and when the Xunta has agreed to

Palace of Raxoi. Emblematic building which houses the Presidency of the Xunta, Santiago Town Hall and the Council of Galician Culture.

Council of Galician

Galician Institute of Housing and Land.

represent Galicia in the claims and issues of inconstitutionality that affect Galicia.
- Perform all functions and attributes that correspond to him according to the current dispositions.

Departments: "consellerías".
The departments are the organic bodies which form the structure of the Xunta de Galicia.

Each department is headed by a minister, who has double responsibility: political responsability as a member of the Government, and administrative responsibility as the head of the corresponding department.

In order to carry out their aims and objectives more efficiently, the departments are structured into hierarchic internal organs. The members with most responsibilities are the secretary generals and the general directors, belonging either to the departments or to autonomous organisms.

As heads of department, the ministers have the following duties:
- They represent their department.
- They propose to the Council of the Xunta the appointment and dismissal of members with high ranking positions within their departments when a Decree is needed to do so.
- They take the initiative to direct and inspect all services of the department and carry out other duties which which they are assigned within the autonomous bodies dependant on their departments.
- They present to the Council, for its approval, a proposal for the structure and organization of their departments.
- They propose all Government bills or decrees which refer to the responsibilites of their department to the Council.
- They have the power to implement the rules in all matters related to their department.
- They resolve the administrative claims lodged against the bodies and authorities within their department, except when the law confers this responsibility to another body.
- They control the expenditure of the services of their department which are not under the responsibility of the Council, within the limits of the budget accorded, and they control the corresponding orders of payment on the part of the financial services responsible.
- They sign in the name of the Xunta the contracts which refer to issues of their department.
- They resolve conflicts of jurisdiction between the authorities within their department.
- And they carry out all other duties stated in the current legislation.

The departments are situated in Santiago de Compostela.

GALICIAN GOVERNMENT

President of the Xunta de Galicia	Manuel Fraga Iribarne
Minister of the President's Office and Public Administration	Dositeo Rodríguez Rodríguez
Minister of the Treasury	José Antonio Orza Fernández
Minister of Territorial Policy, Public Works and Housing	José Cuiña Crespo
Minister of Education and University Regulation	Celso Currás Fernández
Minister of Industry and Trade	Antonio Couceiro Méndez
Minister of Agriculture, Stockbreeding and Food Policy	Castor Gago Álvarez
Minister of Culture, Social Communication and Tourism	Jesús Pérez Varela
Minister of Health and Social Services	José María Hernández Cochón
Minister of Fishing, Shellfish and Aquiculture	Amancio Landín Jaráiz
Minister of Law, the Interior and Labour Relations	Jesús Carlos Palmou Lorenzo
Minister of Family and Employment Promotion, Women and Youth	Manuela López Besteiro
Minister of the Environment	José Carlos Álamo Jiménez

Galician Centre of Contemporary Art. Santiago de Compostela.

LOCAL TERRITORIAL ADMINISTRATION.

The Spanish Constitution states that the territorial organization of the State must be structured in autonomous communites, provinces and municipal districts.

The legal framework.

The Statute of Autonomy of Galicia refers to the traditional local structures of organization: the parish and the region (an area larger than the municipal district).

At the same time, the law which regulates the system of local bodies states in article 3:

1. - The local territorial bodies are:
   a) The municipal district.
   b) The province.
   c) The Island, in the Balearic and Canaries archipalgoes.
2. - The following also enjoy the status of local bodies:
   a) Those which are smaller than the municipal district, instituted or recognised by the autonomous communities, according to article 45 of this law and the corresponding statutes of autonomy.
   b) The metropolitan areas.
   c) The associations of municipal districts.

Local bodies which are smaller in surface area than the municipal district.

The local bodies which are smaller in surface area than the municipal district are regulated by the laws on the system of local bodies of the autonomous communities, in order to decentralize the administration within the separate clusters of population, which keep their traditional names: hamlets, parishes, villages, neighbourhoods, communities, boroughs, localities, and others.

The **village mayor** has the same duties as those provided by the law for normal town mayors, but limited to the administration of his area. The **Assembly of Neighbours**, the responsibilities of the plenary, although some agreements must be ratified by the Town Hall.

In Galicia´s case, the Statute of Autonomy stresses the role of the **parishes** as local bodies in themselves, although their system of organization and exact role will be established in a future law to be passed in the Galician Parliament. It will set out their statutes, consider them local territorial bodies, and grant them autonomy to administer their own interests.

The Galician bill for the system of local bodies

A Government bill to regulate the system of local bodies in Galicia will leave the treatment of the region and the parish, as basic local territorial bodies for the organization of the Galician territory, to more specific laws, according to the Statute of Autonomy. However, it does tackle issues as important as the creation of groups of municipal districts or the changes in their boundaries, aswell as the coordination of the Provincial Councils.

Map of the 315 municipal districts of Galicia.

HIGH COURT OF GALICIA.

The High Court is the highest body of the system of justice in Galicia, without affecting the jurisdiction for which the Supreme High Court (in Madrid) is responsible.

The Justice administration is carried out in Galicia through the ordinary lawcourts, the provincial courts and the High Court.

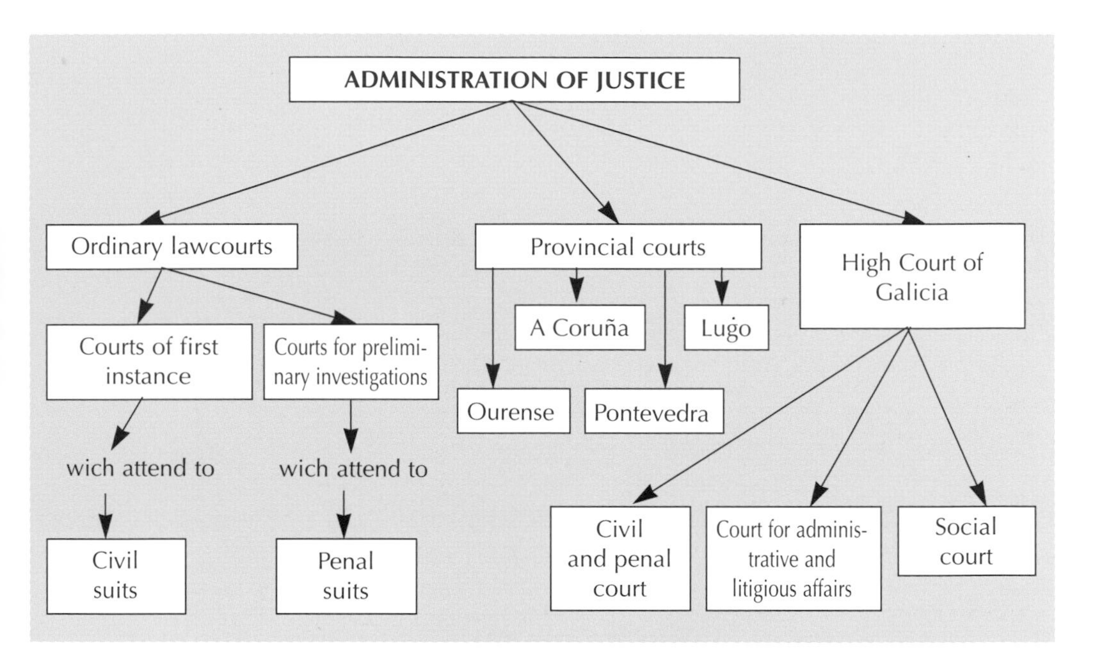

High Court of Galicia. A Coruña.

Article 21 of the Statute of Autonomy considers the Galician High Court as the highest jurisdictional body within the organization of the system of justice in Galicia, and where all procedural instances come to an end, according to the terms laid out in article 152 of the Constitution and in the Statute of Galicia.

The organization of the High Court includes a Court of Government, presided over by the president of the High Court, and formed by the presidents of all the courts.

Court for Civil and Penal suits.
This court is presided over by the President of the High Court and also includes four magistrates.

The President of this court and of the High Court itself is appointed by the King, at the proposal of the General Law Council, for a period of five years. The candidates must be magistrates with ten years´ service in this category and twenty years in the profession, and they must also have special knowledge of Galician civil law and the Galician language. The president is considered magistrate of the Supreme High Court and is the representative of the legislative power in Galicia.

This court deals with the following civil and penal orders:

- **Civil order**: Parliament is responsible for conserving Galicia´s Civil Law, which it can also change and develop to adapt it to the living reality of Galicia. The legislative jurisdiction of the autonomous Parliament in this speciality includes issues that range from determining the sources of the law itself and deciding their order of importance, to the economic organization of the family, servitude and other royal rights, use of the rivers, use of waters and mines, the management of rural and urbanistic property, hereditary succession and the methods of distributing it, contracts and specialities including those specified in the laws on roads, the law of the land, and the law which governs woodland owned by communities of neighbours.
  The High Court of Galicia must be informed of and resolve high court appeals and appeals of revision relating to Galician Civil Law

- **Penal order**: The court deals with the penal suits which the Statute of Autonomy reserves for the High Court. The members of the Galician Parliament and of the Xunta, during their mandate, can be prosecuted for punishable acts committed within Galician territory by the High Court, while those offences comitted by these members outside Galicia are handled by the penal court of the Supreme High Court.

The High Court of Galicia also deals with lawsuits against judges, magistrates, and members of the Department of the Public Prosecutor for committing offences when on duty in the autonomous community, except when this responsibility is attributed to the Supreme High Court.

This court also has the power to lodge appeals against the decisions of juries, which it can also present as high court appeals before the Supreme High Court in Madrid.

Court for administrative and litigious affairs
Deals with administrative and litigious appeals against:
- Orders and dispositions of the bodies of the State administration which are not attributed to them, or which by law are attributed to other bodies of this jurisdictional order.
- Administrative orders and dispositions of the Government Council of the Autonomous Community, of its president and its ministers.
- Acts related to personnel and administrative affairs, dictated by the governmental bodies of the Galician Parliament and its members.

It also deals with:
- Litigious and electoral appeals against agreements made by the Electoral Board.
- In second instance, the appeals provided for by the law which are lodged against the decisions of the tribunals for administrative and litigious affairs in the Autonomous Community.
- And finally, questions of jurisdiction between the tribunals for administrative and litigious affairs located within the Autonomous Community.

Social court.
This court deals in sole instance with labour issues which go beyond the responsibilities of the social tribunals and are within Galicia´s jurisdiction, and with appeals lodged against the sentences passed by the social tribunals in Galicia, aswell as with questions of jurisdiction between these tribunals.

High court appeals against sentences passed in sole instance by the Social Court can be lodged in the Fourth Court of the Supreme High Court.

It is possible to lodge appeals against sentences which this court passes in second instance by way of appeal against those passed by the social tribunals, in cases when these sentences differ from others passed before on the same issues by other lawcourts, so as to assure that the same principles apply to the same cases. These appeals can be lodged within Galicia and also in other courts including the Supreme High Court itself, with effects on the issue questioned but not on the results.

Judicial demarcation of Galicia.

ARZÚA: Judicial District.

**The municipal district of Padrenda belongs to Bande Judicial Discrict.*

Within the last two years, the Galician community has gained responsibility over the services and the civil servants of the Justice administration in Galicia. Together with the responsibility over the services of the public prosecutor´s office which it will assume in 1998, Galicia will reach the highest possible level of responsibility it can legally have in this field. Galicia has therefore become one of the Spanish autonomous communities with most capacity to provide the judicial administration with the resources it needs.

Once it gained responsibility over services and personnel in January of 1996, the Department of Justice, Home Affairs and Labour Relations designed the Plan of Judicial Infrastructures, which was approved by the Autonomous Government in the year 1997. This Plan will provide all the Galician judicial bodies with the best buildings and with the necessary space to cover their needs during the next 25 years. It will also allow all the services of the Justice administration to be joined together in the same building. There is an anticipated investment of almost 5,000 million pesetas for the years 1996 to 1999, inclusive.

This programme for the building and rehabilitation of courts, tribunals and offices has meant that the new building for the Provincial Court of A Coruña is already being used, as are the courts of Pontevedra, Ortigueira, Ribeira, Sarria and Ribadavia. The rehabilitation of the buildings of the High Court of Galicia, the lawcourts of Vigo, Lugo, Ferrol, Ourense and the Provincial Court of Pontevedra are in the planning stage, and the construction of the annex building of the tribunals of A Coruña is under way.

Now that Galicia has gained responsibility over the Justice administration personnel, which it achieved in January of 1997, it is able to rationalize the staff according to the needs of the Autonomous Community.

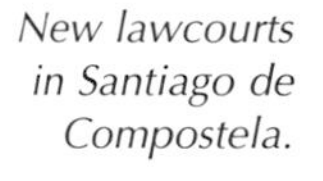

New lawcourts in Santiago de Compostela.

New lawcourts in Pontevedra.

Provincial Court of A Coruña.

VIII

AUTONOMOUS ADMINISTRATION. II.

- Jurisdiction of the Autonomous Community of Galicia.
- Jurisdiction of the Spanish State.
- Control of the autonomous administration.
  - Regional Audit Office.
  - Ombudsman.
  - High Court.
  - Constitutional Tribunal.
- Other administrative bodies.
  - Decentralization of the autonomous administration.
- Territorial bodies.
- Consultive bodies.
  - Advisory Council.
  - Galician Economic and Social Council.
  - Galician Council for Labour Relations.
  - Galician Educational Council.
  - Council of Galician Culture.
- Galicia-Europe Foundation.
- House of Galicia in Madrid.

AUTONOMOUS ADMINISTRATION. II.

The autonomy recognized in generic form in article 137 of the Constitution to enable the various territorial bodies to administer their own interests is specified by the designation of their respective areas of responsibility.

JURISDICTION OF THE AUTONOMOUS COMMUNITY OF GALICIA

The jurisdiction of the Autonomous Community of Galicia includes:

- Organising the institutions of self-government.
- Changing the boundaries of the municipal districts within its territory.
- Territorial, urbanistic and housing planning.
- The public works of interest for Galicia within its own territory.
- Railway tracks and roads running entirely within Galicia, and also all transport delivered by these means or cable transport.
- Fishing ports, pleasure harbours and airports, and, in general, all those which do not carry out commercial activities.
- Agriculture and stockbreeding according to the general planning of the economy.
- Forests and their use.
- Administering the protection of the environment.
- Carrying out the projects, the construction and the tapping of water resources, canals and irrigation channels of interest for Galicia, aswell as mineral and thermal waters.
- Fishing in interior waters, shellfish and seafood production and cultivation, hunting and river fishing.
- Fairs in Galicia.
- Promoting the economic development of Galicia within the objectives marked by the national economic policy.
- Handicrafts.
- Museums, libraries and conservatories of interest for Galicia.
- Heritage monuments of interest for Galicia.
- Promoting culture, investigation and, if this is the case, the teaching of the Galician language.

- Promotion and planning of tourism within the Galician territory.
- Promoting sport and a productive use of free time.
- Social welfare.
- Health and hygiene.
- Surveillance and protection of buildings and plants. Coordination and other aspects of management of the local police according to terms stated in the organic law.
- Administering the law and managing the public corporations which represent economic and professional interests.
- The cooperatives and mutual benefit societies which are not included in the Social Security, with respect for commercial legislation.
- Public entertainment, without affecting the state´s jurisdiction on public security.
- Maritime transport which occurs exclusively between the Galician ports or from one part to another of Galicia, without connection with other ports or parts of other regions.
- Carrying out the State legislation on associations.

JURISDICTION OF THE SPANISH STATE

The Spanish State, taking into account the responsibilities which have been transfered to the government of Galicia, reserves exclusive jurisdiction on issues which are considered of global interest. These issues can be summed up as follows:

- Procedural legislation, without affecting the necessary specialities derived from the particularities of substantive law in Galicia.
- Carrying out mercantile, penal and penitential legislation.
- Labour legislation, without affecting the carrying-out of this legislation by the organisms of the autonomous community.
- Civil legislation, without affecting the conservation, modification and execution by Galicia of its own civil law.
- Intelectual and industrial property.
- The bases for the planning of credits, banks and insurance.
- Weights and measures.
- Coordinating the general planning of economic activity.
- General coordination of scientific and technical investigation.
- General coordination of health and legislation on pharmaceutical products.
- Basic legislation and economic régime of the Social Security, without affecting the carrying-out of its services by Galicia.
- Common administrative procedure, without affecting the specialities deriving from Galicia´s own organization; and legislation on obligatory expropriation, the basic legislation on contracts and administrative concessions and the system of responsability of all public administrations.
- Seafishing, although in this case Galicia is responsible for the planning of the sector.

- Basic legislation on protection of the environment, without affecting Galicia´s power to establish extra rules for protection. Basic legislation on forests, the tapping of the forests and livestock.
- The mining and energy legislation.
- Basic legislation on the press, radio and television, and, in general, all media, without affecting Galicia´s responsibility for its development and action.
- Museums, libraries and state-owned archives, without affecting the running of them by Galicia.
- Public security.
- Basic legislation for the development of education.

In Spain, the Government is based on the general State Adminstration. In Galicia, the State Administration is structured within various bodies which as a whole are called the Peripheral State Administration. It is coordinated in Galicia by the Government Delegation, which is based in A Coruña and has Government Subdelegations in each province.

CONTROL OF THE AUTONOMOUS ADMINISTRATION

The activity carried out by the Autonomous Administration is controlled by:

- Regional Audit Office
- Ombudsman
- High Court: Court for administrative and litigious affairs
- Constitutional Tribunal

Regional Audit Office

The Statute of Autonomy regulates the external control of the management of Galicia´s budget using the *Consello de Contas de Galicia* or Galician Regional Audit Office, based in Santiago de Compostela.

Organization:

Its organization and function is regulated by the law, which establishes the guarantees, rules and procedure to assure that the accounts of the Autonomous Community are handed in, and that they are submitted for approval by Parliament.

Jurisdiction:
The Galician Regional Audit Office, being the body which supervises the accounts and the management of economic and financial issues and the accountancy, will carry out its affairs according to the programmes of expenditure and income of the public sector of the Autonomous Community.

Area of responsibility:
Its area of responsibility includes the Autonomous Administration and its autonomous bodies, local administrations and their autonomous bodies, the public companies which depend on these two administrations, and the fishermen´s associations, chambers of property, agricultural chambers, chambers of commerce, industry and navegation, and other similar bodies.

Bodies of the Regional Audit Office:
The Plenary is composed of five counsellors designated for a period of six years by Parliament, resulting from the majority of the vote of three fifth of its members. It is presided by the chief counsellor, who is assisted by the secretary general.

The president of the Xunta names the chief counsellor, who must be one of the five members, according to the proposal of the Plenary, and for a period of three years. His post runs out when his mandate has come to an end, when he resigns, due to permanent invalidity or when he loses his capacity as chief counsellor.

Ombudsman

Apart from the ordinary channels which citizens can use to defend their rights, there is another important institution in Galicia which ensures that the citizens´ fundamental rights are respected: the *Defender of the People* or *Ombudsman*, which was created by the Galician Parliament by law on the 6th of June, 1984.

The Ombudsman is a high commissioner of Parliament who, within the Galician territory, defends the fundamental rights of the people included in Chapter I of the Constitution, and those included in the preliminary chapter of the Statute of Autonomy of Galicia.

The Ombudsman can begin any investigation, ex officio or at somebody´s request, into actions or resolutions of the Galician public administration, and can extend it to the activities carried out by the departments of the Xunta and any administrative authority, civil servant or agent who is at the service of the Administration. He can also supervise the activities of the public companies or those which depend of the Galician Administration, in order to guarantee a respect of the aforementioned rights.

In order to do so, communication between the citizen and the Ombudsman of Galicia is straightforward and lacking in burocratic obstacles. Any person or legal entity with a legitimate interest, including individual members of Parliament and the parliamentary committees involved in the defence of rights and public liberties, can send his or her complaint to the Ombudsman by post. However, the administrative authorities cannot present complaints within the field of their jurisdiction.

The Ombudsman cannot become involved with individual complaints which are in the lawcourts awaiting sentence. This does not prevent him from investigating general complaints formulated in these individual protests, nor from assuring that the Administration resolves the complaints presented before it in the appropriate time and way.

While these investigations are being carried out, all public bodies have the legal obligation to cooperate, in all that refers to answering whatever is required of them and providing all data required.

Once the investigation has been carried out there is a resolution, of which the interested party will be informed in its totality. The Ombudsman cannot adopt coercive resolutions nor invalidate any of the Administration´s actions, but he can suggest that the public Administration changes the criteria used in the actions which have been investigated, or, when he is convinced that the strict carrying-out of a rule can cause the citizens to undergo unfair situations, he can also suggest to the Galician Parliament or to the Administration to modify it. A large part of the efficient actions of the Ombudsman consist of solving citizens´ problems related to proceedings with the Administration.

Offices of the Ombudsman. Santiago de Compostela.

All activities carried out by the Ombudsman are presented afterwards before the Galician Parliament in an annual report, which reveals the shortcomings detected in the Administration.

Galician High Court.
The court for administrative and litigious affairs controls the action of the Autonomous Community and its legislation.

Constitutional Tribunal.
The Constitutional Tribunal controls the actions carried out by the bodies of the Autonomous Community of Galicia in all that refers to the constitutionality of its statutory rules under the force of law.

OTHER ADMINISTRATIVE BODIES.

Autonomous decentralization.
The Xunta lays the foundations for a gradual decentralization of functions.

In each province there is a **provincial delegation** for each department of the Xunta which includes all its bodies and services. The provincial delegates depend, organically and functionally, on the corresponding minister.

Because of their special characteristics, the departments of Economy and Finance, and of Fishing, Shellfish and Aquiculture are organised into territorial delegations.

CONSULTIVE BODIES

Galician Advisory Council.
This is the highest juridical and technical advisory body of the Xunta.

It facilitates the action of the Administration, which can count on its own advisory body.

The *Galician Advisory Council,* based in Santiago de Compostela, enjoys full organic and functional autonomy, which guarantees its objetivity and independence. Once the Advisory Council has given its opinion on an issue, this issue cannot be sent on for more opinions to any other organism or body of the Autonomous Community.

It is regulated by law, and it is composed of five regional ministers named by order of the president of the Xunta for a maximum period of six years. They can be reelected just once. One of these ministers will be elected president, and he or she will represent the Council to all purposes. He will be assisted by a non-voting secretary general who belongs to the body of lawyers of the Council itself.

In the following cases it is obligatory to consult the Council:

- Projects for reforming the Statute of Autonomy of Galicia.
- The projects of delegated legislation which are referred to in article 10.1 of the Statute of Autonomy of Galicia.
- Cooperation agreements with other autonomous communities.
- The issuing of bylaws while executing laws, and the modification of bylaws.
- Conflicts on the jurisdiction of the various departments of the Xunta and among other high bodies and institutions of the Autonmous Community.
- Administrative appeals of revision.
- Revision, ex officio or by petition of the interested party, of the administrative actions according to the form stipulated in the Law of the juridical legislation of public administrations and the common administrative procedure.
- Invalidation, interpretation, modification and annulment of administrative concessions whatever their objective may be, where the aplicable rules say so.
- Complaints lodged against the Autonomous Community by way of compensation for damages and loss.
- Creation or elimination of municipal districts, and the modification of municipal districts.
- Dismissal of its members.
- In general, all cases stated by a specific legislation.

Palace of Amarante, which houses the Advisory Council and the Social and Economic Council of Galicia. Santiago de Compostela.

Economic and Social Council of Galicia.

The Economic and Social Council of Galicia was created by the Xunta to consult socioeconomic matters. It is provided for in the Constitution and in the Statute of Autonomy, in order to facilitate the participation of everyone in political, economic, social and cultural life.

It is a means of fulfilling the desire of the economic and social agents that their opinions and suggestions be taken into account when the Xunta makes its decisions, and a means of meeting the Government´s desire to channel the participation of society in this way.

In this body, many socioprofessional organisms are represented, without affecting the field of action reserved for the Council for Labour Relations.

The Economic and Social Council is regulated in law number 6/1995 in three aspects:

- It is obligatory for the Xunta to consult it when ruling in matters of special economic and social importance.
- It is optional to consult it on the Xunta´s request or that of its members.
- It can also be consulted upon one´s own initiative, via studies or reports or proposals for normative reform.

The Council can also voice its opinion on the execution of important social and economic plans.

The Council is made up of 35 members:

- A president.
- Eleven members designated by the most representative trades unions, in proportion to their representation.
- Eleven members designated by the organizations of employers, in proportion to their representation.
- Eleven members distributed in the following manner: four representatives of the agricultural sector, two representatives of the maritime-fishing sector, two representatives of the users and consumers, and three representatives of the Galician universities.
- One secretary general.

It does not include Government representatives in order to guarantee its independence when forming and voicing its criteria.

It is also worth mentioning that the Economic and Social Council can become a forum for debate, in order to discuss specific problems which affect Galicia´s strategic sectors and agree on a determined line of action.

A technical cabinet made up of experts aims to guarantee the tecnical quality of its reports. The experts must be specially prepared and have recognised experience in socioeconomic affairs, and must carry out their work with independence.

Galician Council for Labour Relations

The Galician Council for Labour Relations is a collegiate body ascribed to the Department of Justice, Home Affairs and Labour Relations, and it works on labour policy. It is formed above all by the Galician trades unions and organizations of employers, according to the requirements of representation stipulated by the law. The Administration does not form part of this Council, following the principle of not interfering in the autonomy and neutrality of the parties, but its president is named by the president of the Xunta.

The Council is obliged to voice its opinion on all the Government´s legislative projects on labour policy and it is a permanent forum of debate and dialogue for the Galician social agents.

The Council also carries out important studies on various issues related to the social reality of Galicia, and promotes debates by organizing seminars and specific forums.

The Council administers the proceedings handled by the Galician Interprofessional Agreement on Extrajudicial Proceedings for the Solution of Labour Conflicts (AGA), as entrusted by the trades unions and employers´ organizations who signed it.

Galician Educational Council.
The Galician Educational Council, regulated by law 3/1986, is the highest advisory and participational body for the sectors involved in the general planning of education, and it advises on the bills or the regulations proposed or enacted by the Xunta within the Autonomous Community.

Council of Galician Culture.
The Council of Galician Culture, provided in article 32 of the Statute of Galicia, is responsible for the obligations and faculties of the Autonomous Community for the defence and promotion of the cultural values of the Galician people.

It is a collegiate councelling and advisory body, with capacity for initiative, investigation and organization. It has legal status and is made up of representatives of cultural life and distinguished persons.

The Council of Galician Culture consists of:

- The president, who is elected by the Council by secret ballot, and named by a Government decree.
- The vicepresident or vicepresidents, who are elected by secret ballot among the members of the Council.
- The secretary, who is elected by secret ballot among the members of the Council.
- The minister of Culture and Communication.

House-museum of Rosalía de Castro. Padrón.

Faculty of Journalism. University of Santiago.

Museum of the Galician People. Santiago de Compostela.

Padre Sarmiento Institute. Santiago de Compostela.

- One representative of the Royal Galician Academy; one representative of the Galician Academy of Jurisprudence and Legislation; two representatives of the Galician universities, elected among its teachers; one representative of the Padre Sarmiento Institute of Galician Studies; one representative of the Seminar of Galician Studies; one representative of the Academy of Sciences; one representative of the Institute of the Galician Language; one representative of the Institute of Studies on St James; one representative of the Galician museums; one representative of the Society Rosalía de Castro; two representatives of the foundations of interest for Galicia, elected by secret ballot by the Council.
- Ten distinguished persons from the field of culture, elected by secret ballot by the Council.

GALICIA-EUROPE FOUNDATION.

The Galicia-Europe Foundation is a private, non profitmaking institution, created in order to promote all activities which will help Galicia increase its links with Europe.

Objectives:

- To increase the formation and information of Galician society in issues related to Europe and its institutions.
- To channel questions of interest for Galicia in Europe.

It includes various public and private Galician entities and it is open to other institutions representative of Galician economic and cultural life with the same objectives.

Its representative, governmental and administrative body is the *Board,* presided by the president of the Xunta and composed of representatives of various entities which make up the Foundation. The Board trusted the directorship of the Foundation to the Department of Relations with the European Union and Foreign Affairs, in order to coordinate the activities of the various Galician sectors with Europe in a more efficient manner.

Since its creation, in 1988, the Galicia-Europe Foundation has offered a wide range of information and advice through its offices in Santiago de Compostela and Brussels. It has offered assistance and has solved problems for the members of the Foundation and all public and private organisms who asked for help in relation to a wide range of issues concerning the European Union.

In order to increase the knowledge of Galician society in European affairs, the Foundation has carried out various activities:

- Organizing and subsidising courses and seminars to explain and debate specific aspects of European matters of special importance to Galicia.
- Financing grants for increasing studies on Europe in prestigious European universities. These grants are for students and researchers who want to complete their university degrees with postgraduate courses in these universities.
- Financing grants for graduates who wish for work experience in European organisms in Brussels.
- Organizing work experience for people connected with the organisms which are members of the Foundation Board, which is carried out in Brussels and is aimed at gaining a knowledge of the organization and functioning of the European institutions, or organizing periods of study and research on European issues.

All these activities are complemented with publications such as:

- *The Galicia-Europe Bulletin,* a monthly magazine written by the Galicia-Europe Foundation, the University of Santiago´s Centre for European Documentation, and the Galician Confederation of Employers´ "Eurowindow". It is widely distributed among Galician society.
- The *Euro-Galicia Rapid Bulletin,* a magazine which is published every two weeks, aimed specially at people connected with the organisms which are members of the Foundation Board.
- The book *Europe,* which includes articles and information on European issues, and which is periodically brought up to date.
- The colections ***Monographs, Galicia-CEE Rendezvous, European Norms and Essential Texts on the European Unions,*** on different issues.

THE HOUSE OF GALICIA IN MADRID.

The *House of Galicia in Madrid,* which was inaugurated in 1992, is aimed at spreading the culture, the economy, and in general the activities and projects of the Xunta in the capital of Spain.

It is situated in a well built 1920s building between the Prado Museum and the Retiro Park.

The House of Galicia organizes the following activities, among others:

Institutional activities: This body acts as the institutional representation of the Xunta in the capital of Spain. The president and the most important members of the Autonomous Administration aswell as other Galician autothorities have offices there to work in during their official visits to Madrid.

Spreading of culture: The House of Galicia in Madrid aims to display the work of the Galician plastic artists, those who are recognised and also new hopes, so that it becomes increasingly well-known out of Galicia. Painting, sculpture, photography, and handicrafts exhibitions, lectures, presentations of books, round tables or music recitals form part of the cultural activities which the House of Galicia offers almost on a daily basis.

Economic and management promotion: Galician companies from different sectors present their products to the press and to professionals in the House of Galicia. Sales promotions are also organized, and these activities are increasingly beneficial within the current process of the internationalization of the economy.

Other activities organized include lectures on economy, management congresses, presentation of fairs and exhibitions, fashion promotions,

The House of Galicia in

exhibitions of Galician products, work meetings and food and wine tasting sessions.

The House also organizes professional presentations of products and sales promotions to boost the most important exportation industries of Galicia: fashion, preserves, jewellery, slate, granite, handicrafts, audiovisual products, furniture, food, wines and liqueurs.

It also serves as a forum for meetings between company managers who want to trade, invest or cooperate between themselves and with other companies in Spain and abroad.

Private entities ask to use the rooms in the House for activities in which Galicia is present: meetings, signing of agreements, or congresses on economy.

Tourism information office: Potential visitors to Galicia have an information office in the House of Galicia with leaflets and documents about where to stay, communications and places of interest. The office also takes part in promotion activities, with travel agents and transport companies.

Since it was inaugurated the activities of the House of Galicia have been on the increase. The number of activities and the flow of visitors are growing.

Almost a million people have visited the House and taken part in its activities in its five years of existence.

IX

MODERNIZATION OF GALICIA'S AUTONOMOUS ADMINISTRATION SINGLE ADMINISTRATION

- Administrative reform.
  - Regulation of public function.
  - Regulated codification.
- System of administrative procedure management.
- System of administrative information and citizen services.
- Training of public sector employees.
- Evaluating the performance of administrative units.
- Single administration.

MODERNIZATION OF GALICIA'S AUTONOMOUS ADMINISTRATION. SINGLE ADMINISTRATION.

ADMINISTRATIVE REFORM.

The disappearance of a central-state system and its substitution by a new decentralized State has led to the appearance in Spain of autonomous communities as new centres of power and political decision-making. This political decentralization has been accompanied by an administrative decentralization, which resulted in new public administrations, executive branches of these new regional powers.

These new administrations inherited at the outset both the positive and negative characteristics of the centralized Administration.

The Autonomous Administration of Galicia, having consolidated its organization and attained an important level of power, began in 1990 an administrative reform programme in order to achieve greater efficiency and better citizen services.

In order to attain these objectives the following procedures have been implemented:

a) Regularization of Galicia's Public Function.
b) Regulated codification.
c) Establishment of System of Administrative Procedure Management (SGPA).
d) Creation of System of Administrative Information and Citizen Services.
e) Training of public-sector employees.
f) Evaluating the performance of administrative units.

Such a complex and extensive operation required a specific organizational system composed of the following organs:

- Central Commission of Administrative Rationalization, which assumed the strategic direction of the project.
- Provincial commissions of administrative rationalization.
- General Services Inspectorate.

Their operations are complemented by those entrusted to the:
- Director-General's Office of Organization and Computer Systems.
- Director-General's Office of Public Function.
- Galician School of Public Administration.

The *General Services Inspectorate* is uniquely configured as a central organ promoting administrative reform with a singular setup and global jurisdiction throughout the entire Autonomous Community, whose responsibilities may be grouped into two kinds of functions:

a) The classical function of supervising the enforcement of current legislation and which specifically involves the following operations:
- Administering the incompatibilities of the Xunta de Galicia's high-ranking positions.
- Schedule control.
- Complaints and appeals regarding the functioning of both the Xunta de Galicia's centres, establishments and services and the conduct of the Xunta de Galicia's public-sector employees.
- Creation of the Xunta de Galicia's General Archive.

b) The modern function of operating as an internal consultancy helping to improve the Autonomous Administration's functioning, acting as the driving and promotion organ of all administrative activity.

The aforementioned objectives may be summarized as follows:

1.- Regularization of the public function.

Having transferred the human and material resources required in order to implement the autonomous government and established a corresponding legal framework, it was necessary to regulate the Galician public function, which was carried out by means of the following operations:
- Approval of the Public Function Law of Galicia.
- Approval of the development regulations: integration of civil servants into the Autonomous Community of Galicia's Administration, administrative situations, filling job vacancies, professional promotion and internal promotion, personnel selection and disciplinary code.
- Drawing up of lists of the Xunta de Galicia's jobs.
- Announcing and resolving transfer applications among civil servants.
- Offering public-sector employment and announcing applications/competitive examinations in order to attain the status of Xunta de Galicia civil servants.

2.- Regulated codification.

This aspect of the reform consists of:

- Analyzing all current legislation applicable to each area of the Autonomous Administration's operations.
- Reducing, classifying and systematizing such legislation in order to provide administrators with a reduced set of regulations, with all the stipulations to be applied day by day.

SYSTEM OF ADMINISTRATIVE PROCEDURE MANAGEMENT (SGPA).

The Xunta de Galicia has a very advanced technological platform at its disposal. The *Xunta de Galicia's Administrative Network* consists in 75 data and application servers that service 139 local networks connecting more than 2,000 personal computers, all of which is interconnected by means of a private telecommunications network that includes a maximum of 1,400 X-25 and RDSI accesses.

This platforms forms the basis of the horizontal applications of administrative management that have been established: System of Administrative Procedure Management, System of Subsidy Management, System of General Information, Corporative Electronic Mail and Corporative Access to the Internet, which make it possible to know at any time the volume and particular status of each of the different processes that a citizen may bring before the administration.

The comprehensive mechanization of this administrative activity has enabled the establishment of a general information system that makes it possible to obtain information about what may be requested, how to do so and where by means of the Network of *Citizen Information Offices*. The information system enables citizens to know the particular status of their administrative process by means of a personal code that is given to them each time they begin any procedure.

This information is available by means of Internet at the Xunta de Galicia's official Website, in different languages, the address of which is WWW.xunta.es.

The platform's flexibility will enable the future integration of other applications and the system plans of the different government departments; at the end of this process the computerization will be global and all of the Xunta de Galicia's administrative operations will be carried out in computerized fashion.

System benefits.

a) Citizens may know at any time the situation of their administrative processes.

b) The system's high degree of flexibility enables the immediate inclusion of new procedures or the modification of existing ones.
c) Procedures are streamlined, since the system prints the documents that each process generates.
d) There is more legal security, since all the documents are revised by the persons in charge of the different units and by the *General Services Inspectorate.*
e) Information about the real workload of each administrative unit, which helps to suitably gauge the staff by means of the redistribution of existing personnel.

SYSTEM OF ADMINISTRATIVE INFORMATION AND CITIZEN SERVICES.

The *System of Administrative Information and Citizen Services* is part of the operations included in the *Xunta de Galicia's Administrative Reform.*

Its administration is fully integrated within the *General Services Inspectorate.*

The system consists of three basic elements:
- 1. The *Administrative Information and Citizen Services Telephone* (902-120012) installed in the *Head Office for Operational Communications of Galicia (CEGOP).*
- 2. The network of Administrative Information and Citizen Services offices.
- 3. The administrative information and citizen services points (PIC) situated in Santiago de Compostela, A Coruña, Lugo, Ourense, Pontevedra, Ferrol, Vigo and Lalín, in which citizens themselves may directly look up information.

All of these system elements are connected by network and have at least one computer and its corresponding printer, by means of which the following three applications are available:
- The *Xunta de Galicia's General Information.*
- The *Citizens' Guide*, which contains a summary of the procedures at the request of the interested party, including the name of the administrative procedure, its code, its objective, application requirements, documents to be presented and the telephone numbers and addresses of the services in charge of administering them.
- The *Process Consultation*, by means of which citizens may immediately know, using computerized means, the situation of any application that they may have presented to the Xunta de Galicia.

Immediate Reply Service (SERI).

The Immediate Reply Service consists of citizen services offices situated in each government department. In the SERI more than 40 administrative operations may be carried out in streamlined fashion, which helps to process the citizens' administrative procedures.

Some administrative procedures that may be carried out in the SERI

President's Office and Public Administration Department.
Galician Register of Non-Governmental Cooperation and Development Organizations. Register of sports entities. Register of Civil Protection volunteer groups. Register of entities collaborating with Civil Protection. Register of non-regulated tourist businesses and activities. Stamping of tourist establishment price lists.

Department of Territorial Policy, Public Works and Housing.
Authorization of private road transport. Authorization of road transport (merchandise and passengers). Authorization of ambulance vehicles. Authorization of funeral vehicles.

Department of Education and University Regulation.
Exemption of the Galician language subject in Primary and Secondary Education.

Department of Industry and Commerce.
Authorization of interior water installations. Authorization of low-voltage installations (types B and C).

Department of Agriculture, Stockbreeding and Forestry.
Registration of agricultural machinery. Animal health registration of farms and related installations. Register of livestock transportation vehicles. Issuing of hunting/fishing licences.

Department of Health and Social Services.
Technical-health certification of health service vehicles.

Department of Fishing, Shellfish and Agriculture.
Licences for shellfish fishing on foot. Issuing of recreational sea fishing.

Department of Justice, Home Affairs and Labour Relations.
Authorization of use of recreational and gambling machines. Issuing of professional documentation to bingo hall and casino employees.

TRAINING OF PUBLIC-SECTOR EMPLOYEES.

The Autonomous Community of Galicia has as its disposal the *Galician School of Public Administration (EGAP)*, an autonomous organism linked to the President's Office and Public Administration Office. Its goal is the training of public-sector employees.

Objectives of the EGAP:

- Selecting, training and advanced training of personnel at the service of Galicia's Public Administration.
- Linguistic regulation of the public function.
- Researching, undertaking and publishing of studies in the field of the Administration and Galician public-sector law.
- Collaboration with other similar organisms.

The programming of courses and seminars is decentralized and interdisciplinary.

The annual programming of courses includes classical technical subjects (budget administration, administrative procedure, computer science) and others aimed at contributing to the reforming and modernizing of the Galician Administration (courses of Galician administrative language, of citizen services, etc).

The need to know the best training programmes is behind the presence of the EGAP in the most important forums: the International Association of Public Administration Studies, the European Group of Public Administration, the International Association of Administrative Sciences, the Training Section of the European Council's Permanent Council of Local Authorities, and the Local and Regional Training Centre.

The EGAP carries out a policy of exchanging specialists and sending Galician grant holders to the Royal Institute of Public Administration (England), the École Nationale d'Administration (France) or the Scuola della Pública Administrazione (Italy). It also collaborates with different Portuguese institutions: the EGAP, the Escola de Gestâo da Universidade do Minho or Coímbra's CEFA.

There is also regular collaboration with other Spanish administration schools: Canary Islands Institute of Public Administration, Catalan School of Public Administration or the Institute of Territorial and Urbanistic Studies. It also has close links with the National Institute of Public Administration and France's École Nationale d'Administration. The EGAP was the venue of the first course that this prestigious French school held abroad.

The regulations regarding the EGAP's organization and functioning reflect its research centre nature in the subjects of public administration and statutory law. One of the school's most important functions is therefore the promotion of studies about Galicia's administrative peculiarities.

The school runs research and working parties, dedicated to investigation in areas such as Galician administrative language or public ethics. The centre of local studies channels the investigation centred on the operational areas of local entities.

The EGAP is a basic and useful reference point for everyone interested in Administration matters. Its library is a documentation centre with the latest technologies and attends to the information requests of different sources. More and more national and foreign researchers, lawyers, former students, journalists and other professionals are using the school due to the growing importance of its bibliographic and documental resources.

As far as its own activities allow, the EGAP frequently offers its installations for the celebration of courses, congresses, seminars and meetings. It thereby fulfills its desire to be a specialized training centre and also a debating forum dealing with matters of interest for Galician society.

Galician School of Public Administration (EGAP). Santiago de Compostela.

SINGLE ADMINISTRATION.

The proposal of the *Single Administration,* formulated by Mr Manuel Fraga Iribarne, defends the redefining of the State's peripheral administration, so that the Autonomous Administration may normally assume in its territory the management functions of public policies, including those drawn up by the State.

This proposal, inspired by the principle of subsidiarity, overcomes duplications and overlapping by promoting the principle of autonomy and decentralization, mentioned in Article 103 of the Constitution.

The Single Administration model is based on the acknowledging of a double executive function for the Autonomous Communities:

- An autonomous function, corresponding to their own jurisdictional field.
- A delegate function, regarding execution functions transferred from or delegated by the State.

The main objective of Article 150.2 of Spain's 1978 Constitution (whose general and indefinite nature is the fundamental basis supporting the Single Administration proposal) is the transfer or delegation of specific administration faculties, not complete affairs and authority, linked to exclusive power, as long as "entitlement", "substantial decision-making powers" and final responsibility are guaranteed, in any case, as belonging to the State by means of the control mechanisms established by the *"ad hoc"* Organic Law.

Germany's autonomous federalism has resolved the matter of the functions of applying the *Bund* laws by assigning their entitlement as a general rule to the *Länder* as entities in charge, in practice, of implementing federal laws. The Spanish system is different but enables the reinforcement of the Single Administration by means of the technique of transfer or delegation organic laws.

It implies transferring or delegating to autonomous communities functions corresponding to matters of state entitlement and, therefore, their functionality lies in the scope of the so-called execution jurisdiction.

Determining the nucleus of matters that the State should reserve for itself is the main point under discussion. Trying to abstractly determine the limits of this irreducible nucleus will not be possible without a prior analysis and study of each matter.

In first place, there can be no transfer or delegation of all those matters in which the State, reserving its entitlement, decision-making power and responsibility, cannot guarantee or assure a uniform and homogeneous practical result in the different parts of Spanish territory. It is generally understood that exclusive jurisdictions defined as absolute (nationality, immigration, international affairs, defence, law administration, monetary system, etc) are not suited to transfer or delegation since they are clearly linked to the State's oneness and sovereignty. On the other hand, the organic law in question would apply to those exclusive jurisdictions defined as relative (foreign health, general interest ports, airspace control, aircraft registration, public works, etc).

The Single Administration is an application of the principle of cooperation in sharing jurisdiction that requires the constitution of the Autonomous State, implying that each problem will be resolved by seeking the most efficient level for its solution, all of which aims at making better use of the available resources and improving the services that the public Administration offers society.

The consolidation of the autonomous State requires taking into account all the administrative consequences of a decentralized political framework, promoting the adaption of structures and procedures to the needs and opportunities derived from the complex structure of the State designed by the Constitution, which represents a challenge of legitimizing public activities, as far as it enables the fulfilling of the citizens' demands for more and better services at a lower cost.

Aircraft registration is an example of relative exclusive jurisdiction.

Of singular transcendency with regard to the Single Administration's application is the approval of the Law of Organization and Functioning of the State's General Administration (LOFAGE), which, according to its own authors, represents precisely a most special application of the said doctrine to the State's peripheral administration, by means of its rationalization and reduction, since the bringing together of the state territorial administration under the figure of the Government's subdelegates and the dependence of the delegate will add coherence to the bureaucratic machinery and will facilitate relations with the autonomous administrations.

The LOFAGE will include the elimination or restructuring of organs whose subsistence is unnecessary in view of the transfer of jurisdictions to the autonomous communities and the town councils, as well as the promotion of the figure of the State's present delegates, who will carry out all the functions and will be the highest representation of the State Administration in each Community.

X

REGIONAL DEVELOPMENT POLICY

- Natural regions.
- Galicia's Regional Development Plan.
- Organization of the Regional Development Plan.
- Planning, coordination, promotion and technical management organs.

REGIONAL DEVELOPMENT POLICY.

NATURAL REGIONS.

In recent years there have been attempts to establish the basis of a territorialization or division of the country, following criteria or factors such as topography, altitude, demography, population density, habitat, land use, road network, commercial activity...

Obviously, the conception of *natural region* is out-dated although relief, climate, vegetation and human settlement, ways of life... explained during centuries the unequal extension covered by each region, transitional areas and the dominance of valleys or mountains. Nevertheless, it is still possible to draw up a map of the main natural regions.

So let us have a look at some examples reflecting variety and contrasts:

- The *Rías Baixas,* with an oceanic climate but some Mediterranean characteristics, is the most densely populated part of Galicia. It is also one of the most urbanized and industrialized areas.
- On the other hand, the *Eastern Regions,* with a typical mountain climate including frequent winter snowfalls, is the most sparsely populated part of Galicia with the largest distances between population centres. Likewise, it is a mainly agricultural and stockbreeding area where autochthonous forests are still to be found.
- *As Mariñas,* which is a densely populated area with a mild climate, has one of Galicia's largest concentrations of industry and its economic strength is a magnet that attracts a lot of people.
- *Terra Cha,* which is sparsely populated with a more continental climate, has a low degree of industrialization.
- In *Terra de Montes* there is a mixture of scrubland and farmland, which indicates its low level of commercial activity.
- In *O Rosal* the landscape, with a high degree of human settlement, reflects a maximum level of agricultural land use, which demonstrates a clear commercial orientation of its produce.

- In *A Ulla,* with a mild climate and early springs, the landscape, sprinkled with houses and ancestral homes, is full of fruit trees, meadows and other fruit and vegetable productions. On the other hand, in *As Frieiras* the harsh climate offers a bleak outlook with forests and pasture land only inhabited by the odd small village.

The diversity of agricultural and livestock productions is therefore a constant Galician characteristic. In the *Central Regions* the transitional climate between the oceanic coastline and the more continental interior, the altitude and the tableland relief favour pasture land, which explains the region's high degree of stockbreeding. In the *Miño Valleys* the microclimates of the steep riverbanks facilitate the existence of crops that need a lot of sunshine such as grape vines.

Galicia's inhabitants adapted to the different conditions (climate, soil, topography...) they encountered wherever they lived and tried to make the most of their situation. And they are still doing the same. In *Bergantiños* they took advantage of its mineral and stockbreeding resources, as well as its abundant wheat harvests; in the *Sil Valleys* the narrow valleys favour the construction of dams; in *Barbanza* the piscicultural resources of its rias has given rise to a multitude of fishing ports...

It is easy to spot almost unrepeatable characteristics in one region after another. The numerous ancestral homes in *O Salnés* speak of a legendary past, aristocratic families and feudal fights. The Rey Cintolo caves in *Veiga de Mondoñedo* are an indication of a unique and different Galicia of limestone. The old streets of Allariz, situated between *Val de Arnoia* and *A Limia,* remind us of its importance in the High Middle Ages and Alfonso X's literary court.

Regional Map of Galicia.

Until now we have considered the geographical-descriptive aspects of the natural regions, i.e. a regional vision corresponding to an agricultural and pre-capitalist Galicia. Galicia now has a regional map approved by the Xunta de Galicia (20/2/97).

GALICIA'S REGIONAL DEVELOPMENT PLAN.

Galicia's regional development plan complements its territorial development. It began with the lessons learnt from previous development policies and has introduced a new strategic methodology based on administrative coordination and on taking local initiatives into account.

This plan combines the methodology of strategic planning and takes into account objectives of territorial and environmental regulation (considering the environment as a resource) and not only economic ones. It is capable of combining the philosophy of local development but with regional scope, and also enables the combination of a mixed system of bottom-to-top development, i.e. on a grass roots level, and top-to-bottom development, i.e. using a regional level. It can integrate the following elements:

a) The economy, territory and environment, as a unified medium of endogenous development.
b) The public and private sectors, with a mixed management formula.
c) The different socioeconomic parties and public administrations, by promoting coordination techniques.
d) Planning techniques, intervention and stimulation strategies, and promotion and marketing techniques applied to the territory.

The integrating of the above four components takes place in the region since it is the most suitable intervention level, due to its scale and dimensions. The region also favours the search for social cohesion and the participation of local initiatives as development driving forces.

The PDC is a development programme progressively encompassing all of Galicia and which adapts the principles of strategic planning to the new situations derived from spatial and sectorial processes taking place in Galicia, with the aim of improving the standard of living of the areas affected by the plan. This model was backed by the Council of Europe's Permanent Council of Local and Regional Authorities, according to Resolution 257 adopted on March 18, 1994.

Objectives of the Regional Development Plan.

The PDC has the following global objectives:

a) Standardizing the public installations of the different administrations.

b) Promoting the social development of the regions in their training, cultural and social fields.
c) Including the region in the general systems of communication, production, commercialization, promotion and others related to the economic and functional development of the region.
d) Determining the different aptitudes and land uses in function of their production capacities and environmental value.
e) Creating and improving infrastructures and local services favouring productive decentralization, innovation capacity and the use of new technologies in order to compete in an open market.
f) Organizing the system of settlements, promoting the intermediate level, i.e. small towns as regional development centres and sub-centres, as growth centres.
g) Favouring a local strategy aimed at creating employment in the secondary and tertiary sectors and seeking alternatives in the primary sector.
h) Promoting the creation of voluntary joint communities in order to provide services in all or some of the municipal districts making up the region.
i) Encouraging the creation and promotion of intermediate organizations of internal development.
j) Establishing a decentralized territorial structure, adapted to the habitat dispersion, in order to provide the population with the services required by a modern society.
k) Rationalizing a flexible decentralization of administrative services in order to attain a better relationship between them and local needs.

The region as a strategic unit for comprehensive territorial planning. While municipal districts are too small and lack the necessary resources in order to implement coherent and realistic policies, the Autonomous Community is frequently too extensive in order to generate development on a grass roots level. The region, as a stable territorial group of municipal disricts and parishes, is therefore, in Galicia, the basic functional and traditional space for territorial organization, and represents one of the traditional frameworks of coexistence and settlement.

The region acts as a strategic unit for coordinating the administrations' territorial policies and whose associative nature is based on voluntary unions, being able to attain its objectives without having to introduce new local entities into an already extraordinarily complex hierarchic structure. Due to its dimensions, the region is seen to be the most suitable territorial reality in order to implement the integrated planning models included in the PDC. Furthermore, in the case of Galicia, there exist geographical characteristics that show the region to be the ideal level for implementing a decentralized development process.

The PDC envisions the existence of 4 kinds of regions, functionally classified as:

- Metropolitan.
- Urban.
- Rural-urban.
- Rural.

It deals similarly with each kind as regards organizing, functioning and objectives, although with some particularities.

The regional development centres are the region's economic and functional centres.

The regional development sub-centres are the sub-regional functional Units (group of municipal districts within a region among which there are secondary economic, social, functional,...links) in which specialized sub-regional services may be located.

ORGANIZING THE REGIONAL DEVELOPMENT PLAN.

Galicia's Regional Development Plan involves the drawing up of a development plan for each region. In this way, each PDC becomes a comprehensive strategic plan for coordinating the territorial development. The development plans that are drawn up for each region are structured in three sections:

-Socioeconomic study.
-Physical environment study.
-Programme of objectives and strategic actions.

The socioeconomic study includes a profound analysis of aspects such as the structure of the productive fabric, demographic evolution, quality of life and housing, population's degree of training, urban network, and existing and planned infrastructures and installations.

The physical environment study aims at obtaining a synthesis of the territory's potential in function of the region's natural resources. This leads to a classification of the regional space according to productive aptitudes, in order to combine the socioeconomic development with the environment and quality of life. This section includes, among other matters, the drawing up of an environmental map and a natural resources map, and a profound study of the region's environmental situation, paying special attention to the state of its rivers, risks of forest fires, soil erosion and landscape impacts.

These two parts are used to draw up a functional synthesis, which forms the basis of a programme of actions and development strategies. The programme determines the region's distinguishing factors, strategic objectives and development actions to be carried out. Once the aforementioned studies are finished, and based on the diagnosis obtained, the necessary actions are established during the plan's validity so that the objectives are transformed into a development strategy. Such actions can be divided into two kinds:

a) The investments of the public administrations required to provide each region with the minimum level of necessary infrastructures and installations.

b) The promotion of endogenous resources and local initiatives.

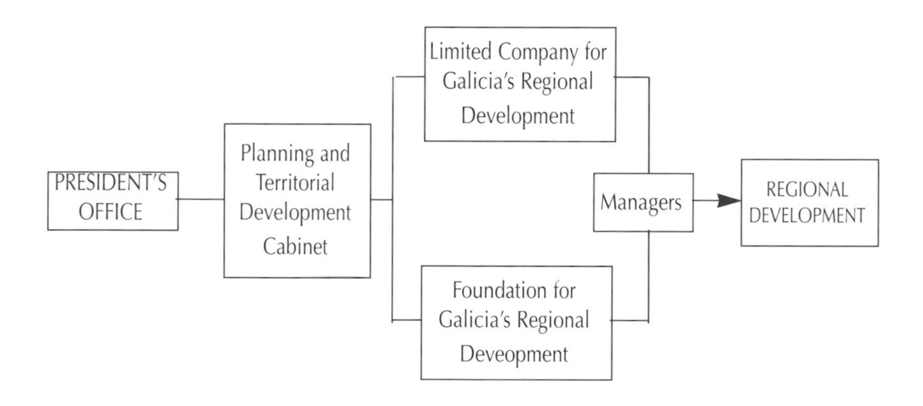

PLANNING, COORDINATION, PROMOTION AND TECHNICAL MANAGEMENT ORGANS.

Coordination, planning, promotion and technical management organs, whose specific powers are established in the Regional Development Law, were created in order to draw up, approve and monitor each of the regional plans produced for each region.

Planning and coordination organs:
Planning and Territorial Development Cabinet. Regional Council. Regionalization Commission.

Technical management and promotion organs:
Limited Company for Galicia's Regional Development.
Technical regional units of the provincial governments, and of services, in support of territorial development, established by the Xunta de Galicia. The role of promoting the Plan is the responsibility of the Foundations for Galicia's Regional Development.

In each region a development foundation was created due to the need for a specific entity integrating the public and private sectors, representing a group of regional action aimed at promoting endogenous resources and development initiatives.

Application of Galicia's Regional Development Plan.

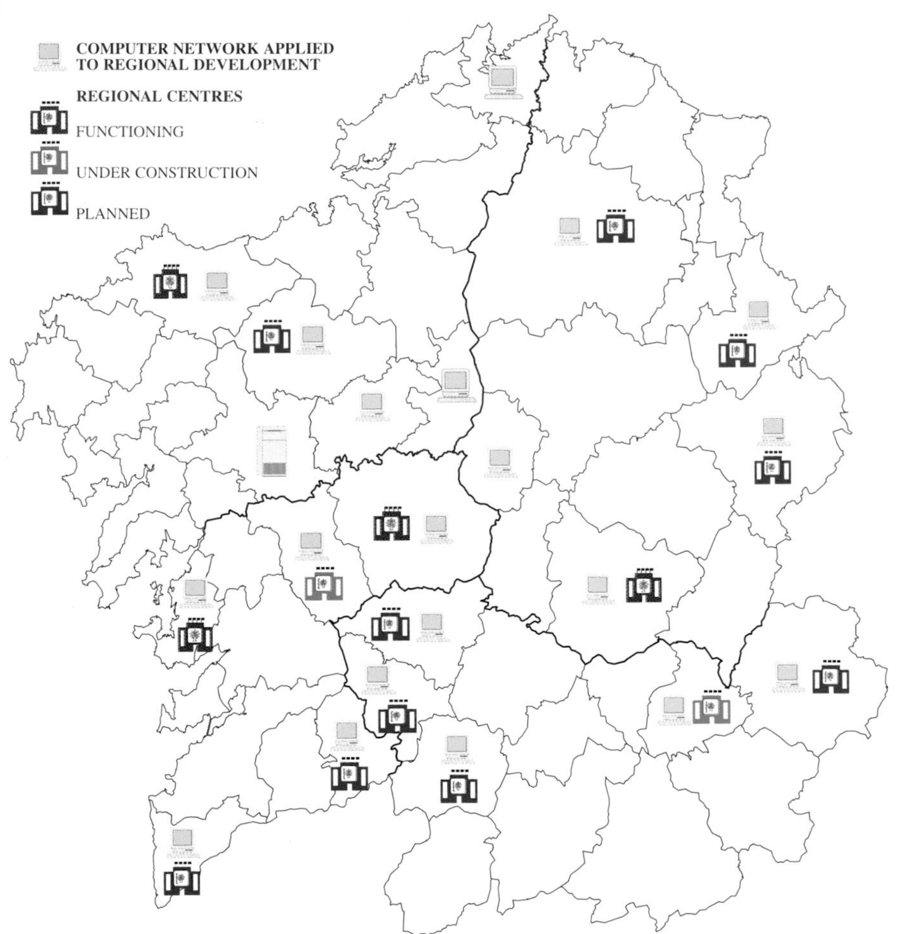

Structure of the Regional Development Plan.

Work is being done in each region in order to promote its endogenous development by means of six stimulation instruments:

1. A Strategic Plan and local planning organ called the *Regional Council,* for designing, monitoring and evaluating.
2. An organization for public-private cooperation: *Foundation for Regional Development.*
3. A regional development agency (managing regional development).

4. A Development and Innovation Centre, called the *Regional Exhibition and Promotion Centre*.

   Objectives:
   - Supporting small and medium-sized businesses, and micro-businesses.
   - Diffusion of new technologies.
   - Rural tourism and cultural information and reception.
   - Retailing of traditional products.
   - Exhibition of locally manufactured products.
5. A public company (Limited Company for Regional Development) providing technical support, with 4 fields:
   - Territorial Information System.
   - Planning of studies.
   - Local and Regional Development.
   - Marketing and communications.
6. *Planning and Territorial Development Cabinet,* an organ belonging to the Xunta de Galicia in charge of:
   - Horizontal coordination.
   - Vertical coordination.

Deza Regional Centre.

XI

EUROPEAN DEVELOPMENT POLICY IN GALICIA

- European policy.
- Community support framework. Programmes.
  - Galicia's Operational Programme 1994-1999 FEDER.
  - Galicia's Operational Programme 1994-1999 FSE.
  - Galicia's Operational Programme of Rural Development 1994-1999 FEOGA-O
  - Galicia's Operational Programme 1994-1999 IFOP.
- Community support framework. Community initiatives in Galicia.
  - INTERREG II initiative.
  - LEADER II.
  - URBAN initiative.
  - FISHING initiative.
  - PYME initiative.
  - ADAPT initiative.
  - EMPLOYMENT AND DEVELOPMENT OF HUMAN RESOURCES initiative.
  - RESIDER II initiative.
  - RECHAR II initiative.
  - RETEX initiative.

EUROPEAN DEVELOPMENT POLICY IN GALICIA.

EUROPEAN POLICY.

The European Union Treaty of 1993 establishes the policies and kinds of cooperation that will enable the European Communities to attain the said Union.

These set new objectives such as:
- -Implementing economic and monetary union.
- -Reinforcing economic and social cohesion.

Galicia benefits from the resources available for the structural Funds approved by the European Union.

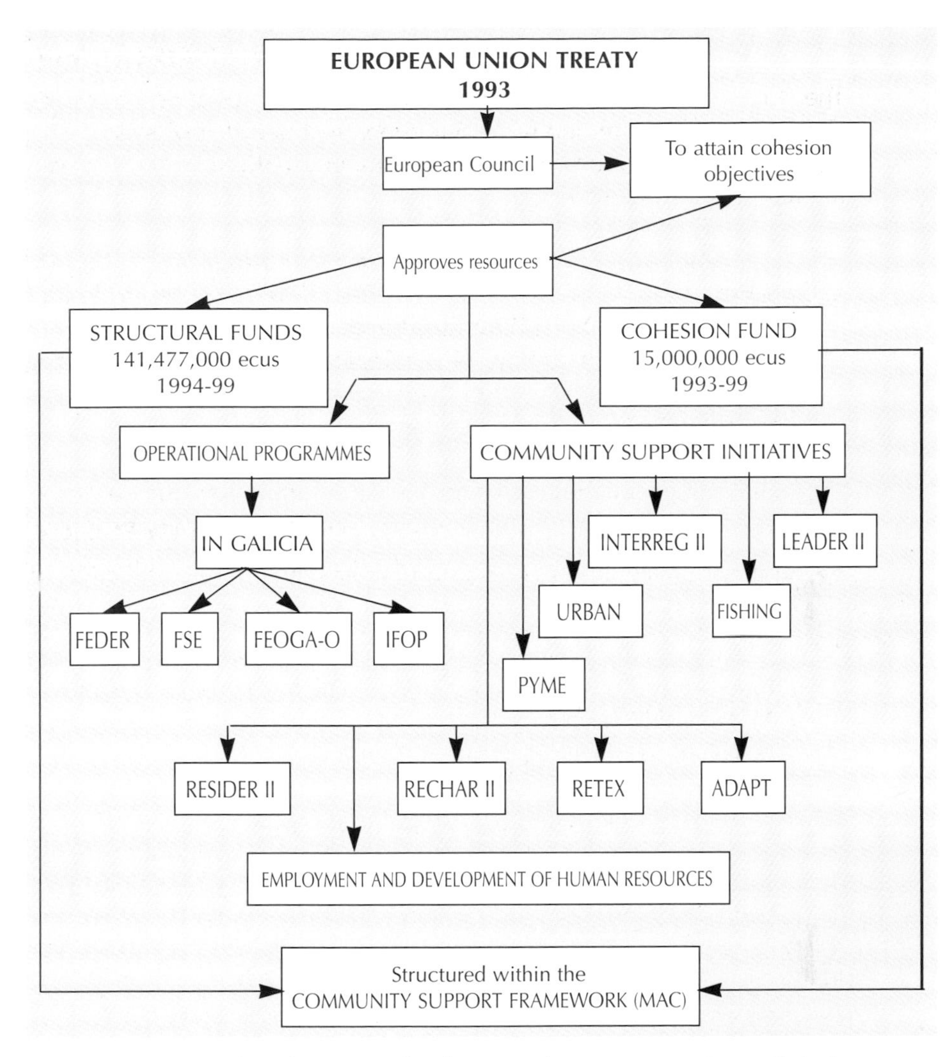

In order to attain the objective of cohesion, the European Council, in its Edinburgh meeting at the end of 1992, approved the resources available for the Structural Funds until 1999, establishing the sum of 141,471 million ecus for the FEDER, FSE, FEOGA-O and IFOP during the period 1994-1999 and 15,000 million ecus for the Cohesion Fund during the period 1993-1999. With regard to such resources, 70% will be used for objective No. 1 regions (less developed regions) and will benefit approximately 27% of the Union's population.

In order to reinforce economic and social cohesion, the European Union Treaty created the *Committee of Regions,* which has a consultative role.

The community interventions are structured within the Community Support Framework, which is developed by means of the *Operational Programmes,* non-Framework operations, established by *Community Initiatives,* and the *Cohesion Fund.*

COMMUNITY SUPPORT FRAMEWORK. PROGRAMMES.

The *Community Support Framework-1* (MAC-1), established by the Commission for community interventions in Spanish objective No. 1 regions, was approved with a total amount of 26,300 million ecus, with the following structure:

- *1 Community Sub-framework of Multi-regional Support,* corresponding to investment operations of the Central Administration, the Local Administration and public companies.
- *12 Community Sub-frameworks of Regional Support,* corresponding to operations under the jurisdiction of the Autonomous Administration of each affected region.

The total amount of structural fund resources approved for operations under the jurisdiction of the Autonomous Community of Galicia, for the period 1994-1999, is 1,225 million ecus (i.e. 191,677 million pesetas), excluding IFOP funds.

The Autonomous Community of Galicia drew up three Operational Programmes. In order to co-finance them, Galicia requested the totality of FEDER and FSE resources, and most of the FEOGA-O resources, assigned to Galicia in its Regional Sub-framework.

Galicia's 1994-1999 Operational Programme-FEDER.

The Operational Programme consists of operations corresponding to the Autonomous Administration and included in Galicia's Community Sub-framework of Regional Support, and operations corresponding to the Central Administration and public companies, included in the Community Sub-framework of Multi-regional support, in which the interventions are not regionalized.

The Autonomous Administration presents measures in all fields: integration and territorial organization, economic fabric development, tourism, agriculture and rural development, infrastructures in support of economic activities, assessment of human resources and technical assistance.

The interventions of the Central Administration and public companies are concentrated in the fields of integration and territorial organization, economic fabric development, infrastructures in support of economic activities, fishing and assessment of human resources.

The Operational Programme consists of two kinds of measures:

1. Infrastructures, of the following kinds: roads, ports, airports, telecommunications, industrial land, local development, rural development, water resources, natural environment, energy,

research, development and innovation, health facilities and training installations.
2. Economic promotion, in the following sectors: industry, crafts, tourism and fishing.

Galicia's 1994-1999 Operational Programme-FSE.

This Operational Programme-FSE only involves operations under the jurisdiction of the Autonomous Administration of Galicia.

The programmed operations are included in the different priority fields established in MAC-1 (1994-1999) for FSE interventions:

-Reinforcing technical-professional education.
-Supporting research and technological development activities.
-Continuous training of workers.
-Occupational insertion and reinsertion of the unemployed.

Galicia's 1994-1999 Operational Programme of Rural Development-FEOGA-O

The FEOGA-O resources assigned to Galicia are used to co-finance Autonomous Community operations in which the Central Administration also collaborates financially.

The Operational Programmes develop operations included in the totality of development fields.

The Operational Programme aims at improving the income of farmers and environmental quality.

It is divided into these Sub-programmes:

1. Improving the conditions of agricultural production.
2. Production and conservation of natural resources.
3. Reconversion, reorientation and improvement of agricultural productions.

Galicia's 1994-1999 Operational Programme-IFOP

The IFOP's Operational Programme, included in the 1994-1999 Community Support Framework for interventions in fishing, aquiculture, transformation and commercialization of fish products in Spanish objective No. 1 regions, was approved in Brussels in 1994 by the Decision of the European Communities' Commission.

Intervention fields:

1. Adjustment of fishing effort.
2. Renewal and modernization of fishing fleet.
3. Aquiculture.
4. Coastal areas.
5. Fishing port installations.
6. Product transformation and commercialization.
7. Product promotion.

Vilaxoán fishing port. Ria of Arousa.

COMMUNITY SUPPORT FRAMEWORK. COMMUNITY INITIATIVES IN GALICIA.

Community initiatives correspond to specific problems of the Union's citizens as a whole and not merely from a national point of view.

The most important differences between Framework and "Non-framework" are highlighted below:

1. The initiatives may be applied beyond national borders, which makes them an ideal resource for promotional transnational cooperation.
2. They are an essential element of Structural policies, in their community dimension, for the specific attention of supranational problems.
3. They enable the solution of temporary problems arising after the initial planning.
4. They support innovation experimentation.

The new Regulation of Structural Funds establishes that 9% of the pledged credits of the 1994-1999 Structural Funds will be assigned to community initiatives.

Having heard the opinion of the other interested parties (the other community institutions, member states, regions, local authorities, and economic and social representatives) about the said proposal, the European Commission decided to create the following Community Initiatives:

- **INTERREG II** initiative.

  Objectives:
  - Developing of trans-border cooperation.
  - Helping the European Union's interior and exterior border regions to overcome specific problems derived from their relative isolation with regard to national economies and the European Union as a whole.
  - Completing energy networks in order to connect them to more extensive European networks.

In recent years there has been a growing tendency, between the regions of Galicia and the North of Portugal, towards the development and execution of common projects and objectives.

Since the Galicia-North of Portugal area is the Spanish-Portuguese border's most integrated space and offers the best conditions and most important promoters of economic and social development, the Spanish State assigned, regarding the percentage of resources to be administered by the Autonomous Communities bordering Portugal, the largest portion to Galicia.

The subsidized measures were divided into 13 operational sub-programmes:

- *Business cooperation,* which aims at attaining joint industrial development. Joint development of the tourist sector is also included.
- *University cooperation,* based on cooperation in the field of R+D (Research and Development) between the technological centres of both regions and collaboration by means of the exchange of experiences, teachers and students between vocational training centres.
- *Natural heritage*: in order to reclaim, conserve and develop natural spaces with protected status.
- *Historical-artistic heritage*: in order to restore and conserve the border area's historical-artistic heritage.
- *Water resources*: in order to complete the supply and treatment network of border towns.
- *Ports*: involves modernizing and extending infrastructures in border area ports.
- *Roads*: projects to improve and modernize the communication infrastructures between both regions.
- *Phyto-sanitary measures*: the control of pests and diseases affecting vines and the development of a cattle treatment campaign in the border area.
- *European Social Fund Operations*: these aim at resolving the problems of the area's deprived population and developing joint actions regarding the youth of both regions.
- *Telecommunications*: in order to establish and promote the use of telecommunications between the two regions.
- *Regional and local development*: it endeavours to promote border cooperation actions by means of the Galicia-North of Portugal Working Community.
- Undertaking a pilot cooperation programme in the field of medical care and social insertion in the border area.
- *Fishing*: personnel and information exchanges will be carried out in the fields of fishing, aquiculture, and safety and rescue.

• The **LEADER II** initiative will support projects backed by local representatives. Emphasis will be given to the projects' innovative and demonstrational character, the exchange of experiences and transnational cooperation.

The following will benefit from this initiative:

- Groups of public and private representatives defining together a strategy and innovative measures for the development of a local-scale rural territory.
- Other public and private collective representatives from rural environments (local organisms, chambers of commerce and

agriculture, associations, cooperatives), as long as their project, of a predominantly thematic nature, involves the logical development of a local territory.

These operations will be financed by:
- Acquirement of capacities.
-Demonstrational and transferable rural innovation programmes.
- Transnational cooperation.
- Organization of a European network.

Themes related to agriculture and stockbreeding are extremely important for Galicia due to the socioeconomic consequences involved. The restrictions imposed by the Common Agricultural Policy have forced Galicia to seek new economic development alternatives. This is the objective of the Leader initiative.

• The **URBAN** initiative aims at seeking solutions for the serious social problems arising from the crisis of numerous urban neighbourhoods, by financially supporting activities of economic and social reactivation, the renewal of infrastructures and installations, and improvement of environmental quality.

The projects, generally planned for four years, should be of a demonstrational nature with regard to other urban areas. Preference is given to innovative projects included in long-term urban integration strategies.

The subsidized measures will be the following:
- Organizing new economic activities.
- Local-scale employment measures.
- Improving social, health and security services
- Establishing infrastructures and improving the surroundings.

Pontevedra, a city that has benefitted from the URBAN initiative.

• The **FISHING** initiative is designed to help the fishing sector overcome the social and economic consequences of the present crisis, contributing to production diversification in the affected regions by developing employment-creating activities.

The following will benefit from the FISHING initiative:

- Collective, public and private entities (town councils, chambers of commerce).
- Individual parties contributing to the diversification (small and medium-sized businesses).
- Public and private representatives affected by the transformations of the fishing sector (fishing cooperatives, charity associations).
- Fishermen and other sector workers.

The following measures will be subsidized:

- Diversification of activities in the subsidized areas.
- Business services.
- Maintenance and creation of jobs.
- Financial engineering.

General or transnational projects.

- Production investments in the sector.

Fishermen are the ones who receive most of the FISHING initiative's subsidies and benefits.

• The **PYME** initiative's objective is the adaption of small and medium-sized businesses in the face of the effects of the single market and the internationalization of economies.

The initiative will benefit small and medium-sized businesses (PYME) and producer cooperatives.

The subsidized measures will be as follows:
- Improvement of production system and organization.
- Consideration of environmental problems and rational energy usage.
- Consolidation of cooperation for R+D projects between research centres.
- Access to new markets.
- Increase in cooperation and the creation of networks among small and medium-sized businesses.
- Improvement of the small and medium-sized businesses' access to financing and credit.
- Improvement of the small and medium-sized businesses' economic context.

The small and medium-sized businesses' role in Galicia's industrial structure is of utmost importance.

Small and medium-sized businesses benefit from the PYME initiative.

The small and medium-sized businesses' participation, as a percentage of employment in 1990, in each of the industrial sectors reveals the existence of sectors that are mainly made up of small and medium-sized

businesses, such as the jewellery trade, the timber and furniture industry, the textile sector, the chemical sector, graphic arts, and the metallurgical and capital goods sectors.

• The **ADAPT** initiative is a key factor of economic growth since it produces first-class workers, capable of adapting to technological and economic changes.

ADAPT's objectives:
- The adaption of workers to changes.
- Increasing businesses' competitiveness by means of training.
- Preventing unemployment by increasing the workers' qualifications.
- Creating new jobs and activities.

The subsidized measures are divided as follows:
- Training, advice and orientation.
- Promoting the creation of networks and new employment possibilities.
- Adapting aid structures and activities.
- Training, diffusion and sensitization.

In order to be co-financed by ADAPT, such measures should:
- Be innovative.
- Have a transnational dimension.
- Be primarily aimed at improving the efficiency of training systems and services, as well as their openness.
- Promote active methods with the participation of all the interested parties.

• The **EMPLOYMENT AND DEVELOPMENT OF HUMAN RESOURCES** initiative is divided into three different sections with interrelated objectives:
- NOW (equal employment opportunities for women).
- HORIZON (integration of the handicapped and underprivileged into the job market).
- YOUTHSTART (integration of unqualified youths into the job market).

Objectives:
- Promoting the creation of employment.
- Promoting social solidarity in all of the Union.
- Promoting equal opportunities for women in the job market by developing human resources, improving the functioning of the job market and establishing transnational operations.

• The **RESIDER II** initiative was created by the Commission because many iron and steel regions are among the areas most affected by industrial restructuring and find it especially difficult to adjust quickly to changing economic circumstances.

Objective:

- Accelerating economic reconversion, concentrating on the iron and steel regions affected the most.

Priority will be given to improving the environment, promoting new economic activities and the advanced training of human resources.

• The **RECHAR II** initiative was created by the Commission for the same reasons and to pursue the same objectives as RESIDER II in coal-mining regions.

• The **RETEX** initiative was established to accelerate the diversification of economic activities in regions that are highly dependent on the textile and clothing sector, in order to reduce such dependency and facilitate the adaption of viable businesses.

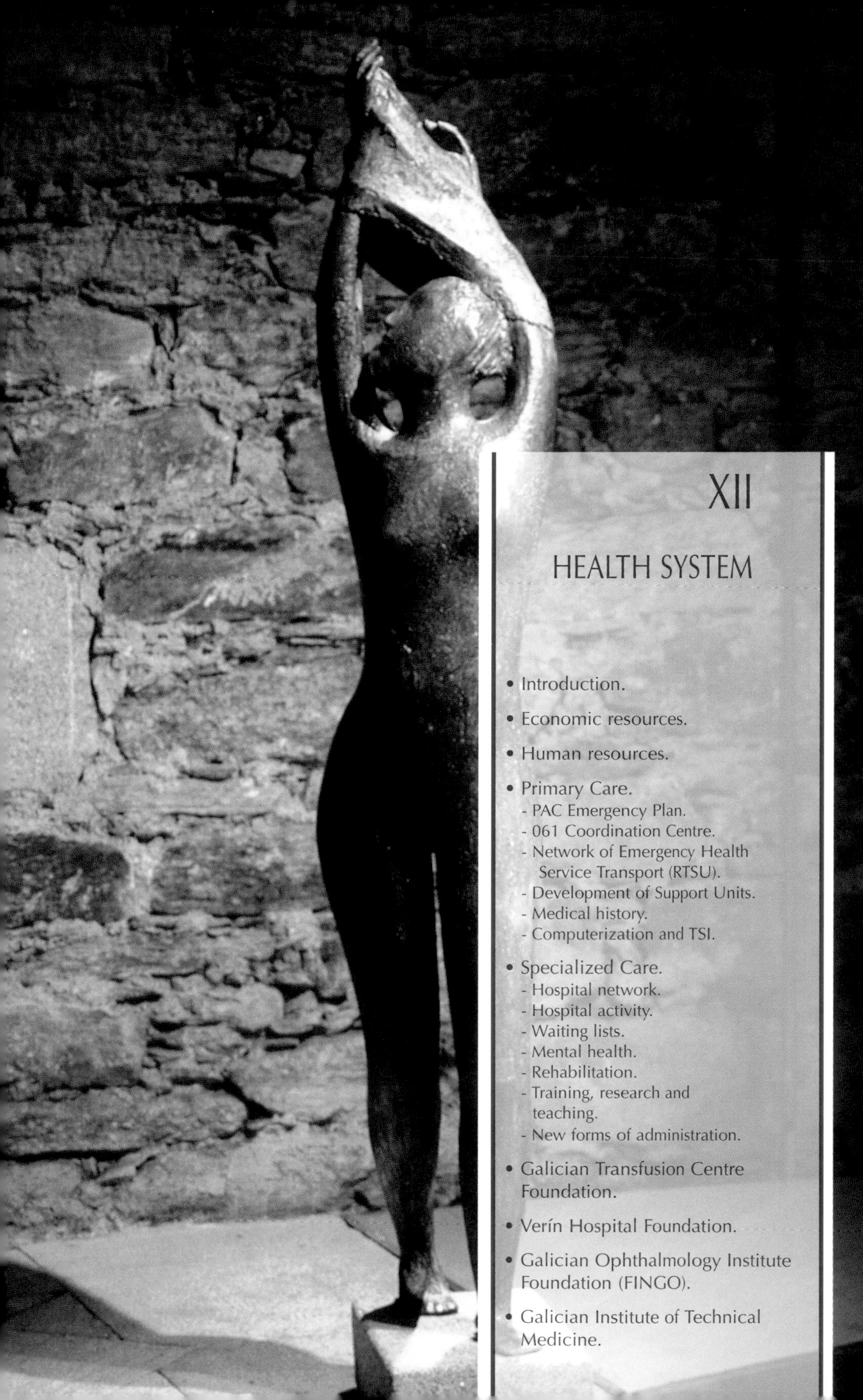

XII

HEALTH SYSTEM

- Introduction.
- Economic resources.
- Human resources.
- Primary Care.
  - PAC Emergency Plan.
  - 061 Coordination Centre.
  - Network of Emergency Health Service Transport (RTSU).
  - Development of Support Units.
  - Medical history.
  - Computerization and TSI.
- Specialized Care.
  - Hospital network.
  - Hospital activity.
  - Waiting lists.
  - Mental health.
  - Rehabilitation.
  - Training, research and teaching.
  - New forms of administration.
- Galician Transfusion Centre Foundation.
- Verín Hospital Foundation.
- Galician Ophthalmology Institute Foundation (FINGO).
- Galician Institute of Technical Medicine.

HEALTH SYSTEM.

INTRODUCTION.

Since 1991 the Galician health system has been run by the *Galician Health Service* (SERGAS), which aims at developing its own health policy, adapted to Galicia's territorial and demographic characteristics.

The health system proposed in Galicia is designed to maintain and administer efficiently the benefits of:

- Basic insurance.
- Public financing.
- The guarantee that each person will receive what he needs.
- The equality of access to all health care.

The future *Galician Health Law* will regulate the planned reform in Galicia as regards administration and health care. The reform aims at:

- Improving health care for patients.
- Increasing the capacity for choosing services, to be provided by the public sector and, in a complementary way, part of the private sector (concerted action).

Social services have been regulated by law since April 1993. Such services are now included in a comprehensive system of public responsibility, in order to promote, coordinate and regulate social initiatives.

BUDGET DISTRIBUTION

FIELD OF ACTIVITY	PESETAS
Administrative services	2,529 million
Primary care	16,809 million
Specialized care	44,463 million

Distribution of the SERGAS budget.
Period: 1991-1997.

HUMAN RESOURCES.

Presently, more than 90% of Spain's public health services is financed by means of general taxes. The rest comes from Social Security contributions by businessmen and workers.

January 1991, when the health functions and services were transferred to Galicia, saw the establishment of a financing system based on the costs of the previous year, and a fair amount below what it should have been in view of the protected population. In 1996 the Galician health system was put on a level financially with the other Autonomous Communities, although Galicia would like the financing criteria to take into account demographic differences and population aging, circumstances which are highly marked in Galicia and affect health expenses.

In order to meet the needs of primary health care and emergency services in the numerous health centres, new ones were built and others were adapted.

As regards hospitals, investments amounted to 44,500 million pesetas, a budget that includes the construction of a new university hospital in Santiago de Compostela and three hospitals located in the O Barbanza, Fisterra-Soneira and O Salnés regions, as well as the re-opening of the former military hospital of A Coruña.

From 1991 to December 31, 1996, the SERGAS' public hospital network was notably extended when it assumed the transfer of hospitals run by the provincial governments and the Vigo town council; it went from 12 to 21 hospitals to be precise.

Health centres built and/or fitted out:	
Up to May 1997	144
Planned by the end of 1997	23

HUMAN RESOURCES.

The lack of flexibility in the administration of human resources makes it difficult to obtain good results, despite having scientifically and technically well-qualified personnel. Overcoming this lack of flexibility is one of the priority objectives of Galicia's health system.

A. *In primary care,* continuous training is seen as an investment and has been oriented towards:

- Training internal and resident doctors in family and community medicine, in the medical care network's different teaching centres.
- Decentralized training in the seven primary care administration centres, integrating subjects dealing with clinical-medical matters, administration, and research and development.
- Training programme of the Ministry and Institute of Public Administrations, with decentralized application in the different primary care administration centres.
- Continuous centralized training, by establishing primary care schools.
- Completion of an advanced training course in order to obtain the title of specialist in Family and Community Medicine.
- Courses for administrators and department and primary care unit heads.

This sector has seen the creation of 800 new jobs, apart from the incorporation of 428 professionals involved in the transfer of the Navy's Social Institute in Galicia.

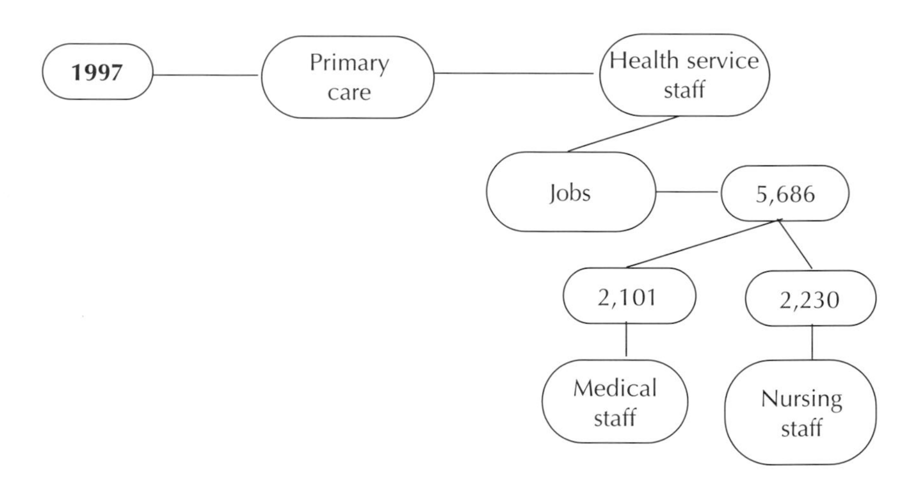

B. *In specialized care,* likewise the promoting of postgraduate training of the SERGAS' health service professionals, doctors (by means of the MIR examination), pharmacists, chemists, psychologists...in order to obtain the title of specialist.

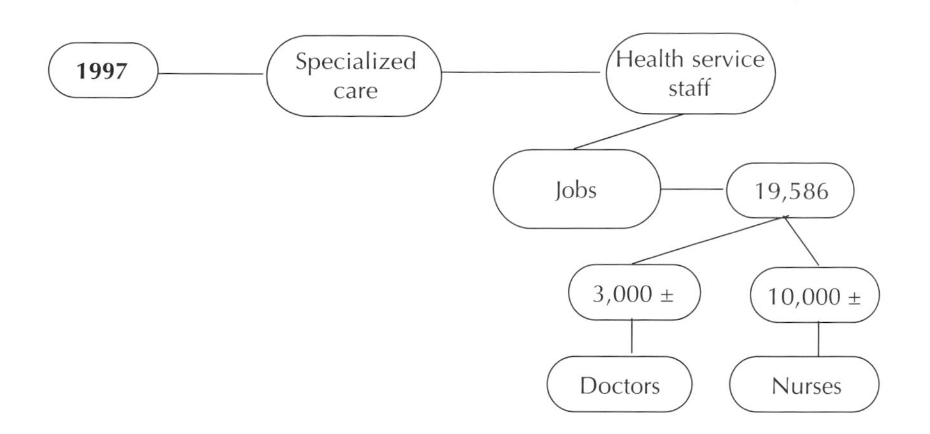
1997
Specialized care
Health service staff
Jobs
19,586
3,000 ±
10,000 ±
Doctors
Nurses

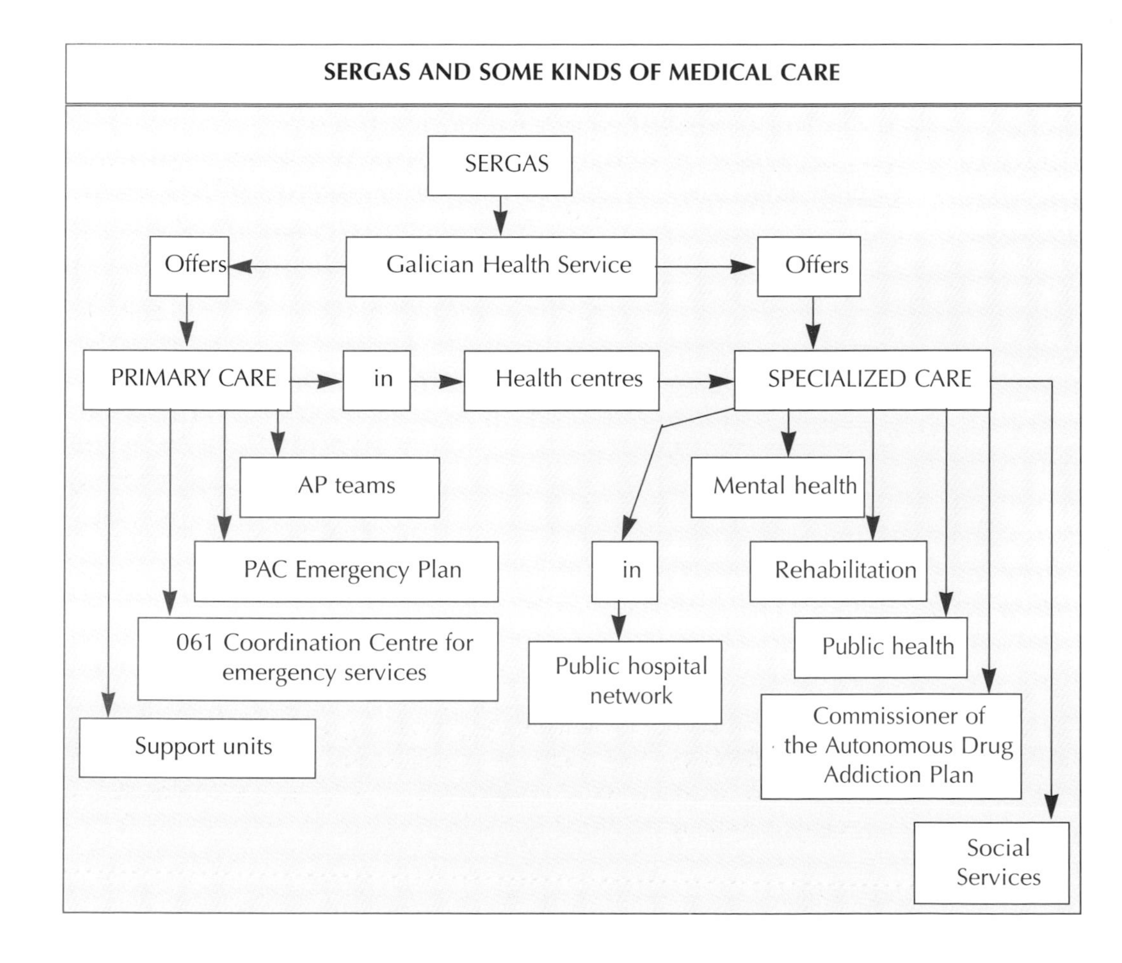
SERGAS AND SOME KINDS OF MEDICAL CARE
SERGAS
Galician Health Service
Offers
Offers
PRIMARY CARE
in
Health centres
SPECIALIZED CARE
AP teams
PAC Emergency Plan
061 Coordination Centre for emergency services
Support units
Mental health
Rehabilitation
in
Public hospital network
Public health
Commissioner of the Autonomous Drug Addiction Plan
Social Services

PRIMARY CARE (AP).

Primary care is the gateway to the health system.
Galicia's health service reform laid the foundation of the new primary care model, according to Decree 200/93, which is where patients first come into contact with the health services and where most problems arise.

Basic principles that should characterize primary care:

- High quality and safety guarantees for citizens.
- Easy access: a unit in each municipal district.
- Respect for the patients' autonomy and personal safety.
- Promotion of interdisciplinary cooperation among professionals and between them and citizens.
- A relationship of mutual trust between doctor and patient.
- A balance between individual care, the basic pillar of primary care, and community operations.
- The availability of a common range of minimum services in all Galicia.
- A workday adapted to medical care requirements while also providing professionals with sufficient rest.
- Rational distribution of resources and workloads.
- Emphasis on continuous training.

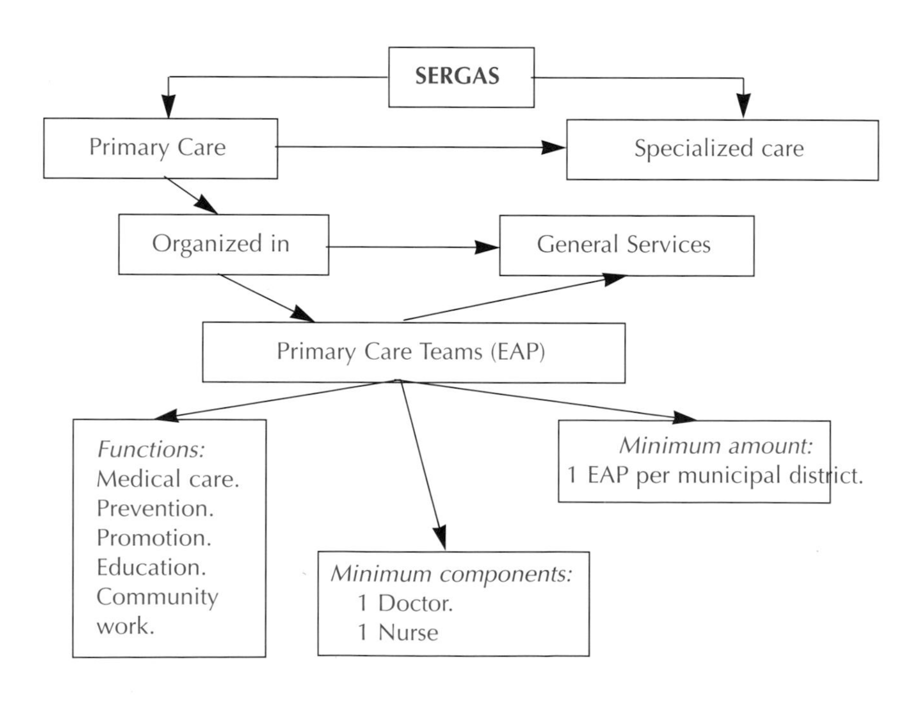

PRIMARY CARE HUMAN RESOURCES	
Population	2,700,000
Timetable	24 hours
Municipal districts	315
Health Centres and/or surgeries	525
General practitioners	1,624
Pediatricians	276
Nurses	1,767
Midwives	115
Administrative employees	283
Odontologists	80
Physiotherapists	46
Social workers	38

In Primary Care 23 million medical actions were carried out in 1996.

PAC emergency plan and physical presence.
The primary care reform includes a Galician Plan of Non-hospital Emergencies.

Emergency care has been an important source of dissatisfaction, both for patients and professionals, due to an excessive workload and the particular geographical dispersion. An Emergency Plan was therefore required that would:

- Provide continuous care 24 hours a day.
- -Be implemented by ordinary professionals or family doctors, who would be on call.
- Offer the population at hand more human and quality care.

Health centre.

The Emergency Plan is organized in Continuous Medical Care Points (PAC), which provide medical care 24 hours a day. The PAC are teams of doctors who provide emergency medical care, with a permanent presence, from a centralized point for several municipal districts, being situated in the district with the largest population and most central location.

The PAC are equipped with a telephone, support personnel, transport and all the necessary means for providing medical care to the entire population included in the corresponding municipal districts. They operate from 15:00 to 8:00 the next day, i.e. they begin when the primary care units close.

The PAC guarantee the localization of a doctor for patients, may avoid having to take patients to hospital and provide doctors with a suitable place for working and waiting while on call.

By 1996 25 PAC had been installed in Galicia, caring for 97 municipal districts and covering 73% of emergency calls with their physical presence. A population coverage of 90% is aimed for in the near future.

061 coordination centre for emergency services.
A single 061 Coordination Centre for emergency services has been set up, covering all of Galicia and with a continuous operation 24 hours a day and 365 days a year. It is a health centre that coordinates all of Galicia's existing resources, both public and private.

Services provided by the 061 health centre.
- Provides all users, both from rural and urban environments, with telephone access to a health centre.
- Offers consultation and medical advice by telephone.
- Coordinates and provides emergency transport to all citizens and professionals who so request.
- Sends health personnel out on house calls when required by the situation.
- Coordinates non-hospital emergency medical care.

Resources.
The 061 health centre has the following resources:
- 13 doctors who coordinate the demand and direct all the centre's activities.
- 19 operators in charge of classifying and transferring the different requests.
- 9 radio operators, who activate the resources and monitor the services.

The 061 centre was opened on December 4, 1995.

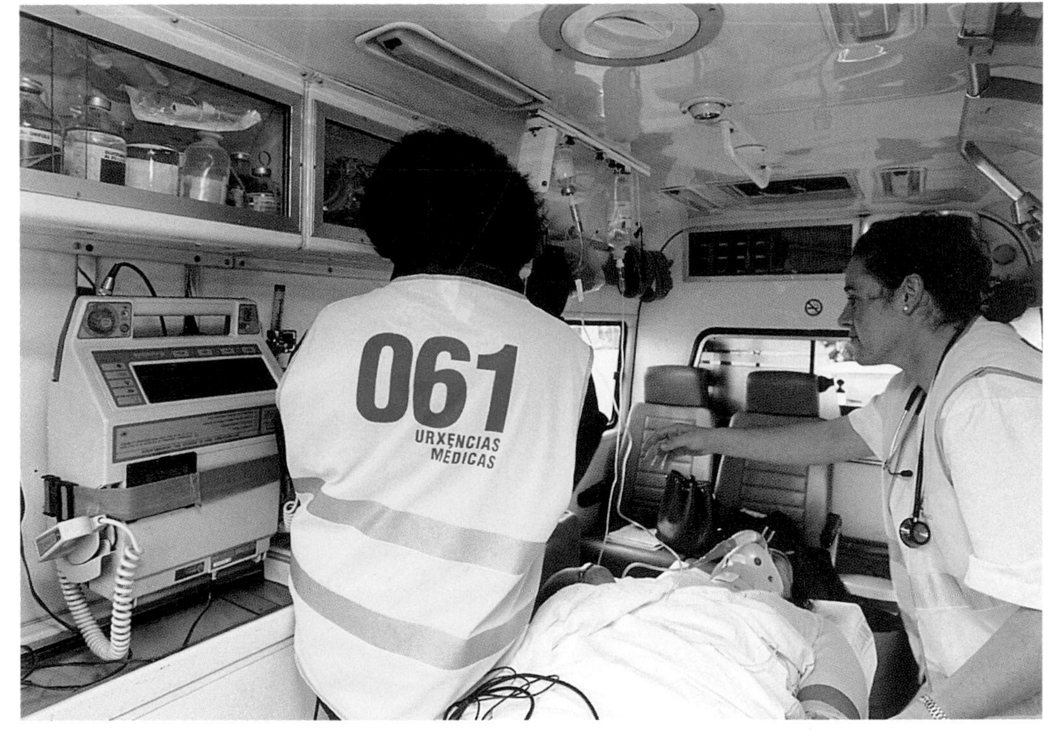

The 061 emergency service.

Network of Emergency Health Service Transport.

The *Network of Emergency Health Service Transport* (RTSU) created for the 061 emergency service consists of 100 ambulances that are especially designed for transporting critically ill patients. The emergency service has two bases, in Santiago de Compostela and Ourense, in which a medical team operates supported by a helicopter (belonging to SOS Galicia), covering all of Galicia.

Development of Support Units.

During the period 1992-96 SERGAS developed primary care support units by incorporating new personnel or integrating existing personnel. The following has been achieved in this field:

- Odontology. 100% coverage. By 1996 50 odontological units had been set up, which provide traditional dental care as well as a preventative programme of oral hygiene for children from 6 to 14 years old.
- Pediatrics. By 1996 30 new support units had been established and, along with the existing ones, a coverage of 96% for the population from 0 to 7 years old, with the prospect of reaching 100% during 1997.
- Physiotherapy. 30 support units were set up with a coverage of 100%. Such non-hospital physiotherapy units, in addition to those located in hospitals, are available to 81% of the population and, as more

services become available in administrative centres, this percentage is expected to increase to 90% by the end of 1997.

Medical history.
A model of primary care medical history, designed by the professionals themselves to help them with their work and improve the service, has been implemented.

Computerization and TSI.
In 1996 a primary care computerization plan was put into effect and during 1997 it was extended to all the primary care services. This plan, along with the issuing of a health card (TSI), which had been sent to almost the entire population by the end of 1997, and the development of the pharmaceutical services application, complete the nucleus of the computerization system for managing primary care in Galicia.

The health card programme, which began in 1993, provides the SERGAS' primary care centres with a *singular and individualized vehicle* between the health system and patients. The programme is presently on the point of completion and will therefore enable everyone to choose their own doctor.

SPECIALIZED CARE.

Hospital network.
SERGAS' public hospital network is presently made up of the following hospital complexes:

- Santiago de Compostela: *University clinic, Conxo, Gil Casares, Xeral.*
- A Coruña: *Juan Canalejo, Teresa Herrera, Marítimo de Oza, Abenti Lago.*
- Lugo: *Xeral, Calde.*
- Ourense: *Xeral, Rebullón.*
- Ferrol: *Arquitecto Marcide, Novoa Santos.*
- Vigo: *Xeral, Cíes.*
- Two general hospitals: *Meixoeiro* in Vigo and *Montecelo* in Pontevedra.
- Three regional hospitals: O Barco de Valdeorras, Burela, Monforte.
- A hospital for medium- and long-term stays in Vigo: *Nicolás Peña.*
- The regional hospital of Verín, administered as a public foundation.
- Povisa, a private centre, linked to SERGAS by a unique agreement. It provides specialized medical care to 125,000 people in the Vigo area.

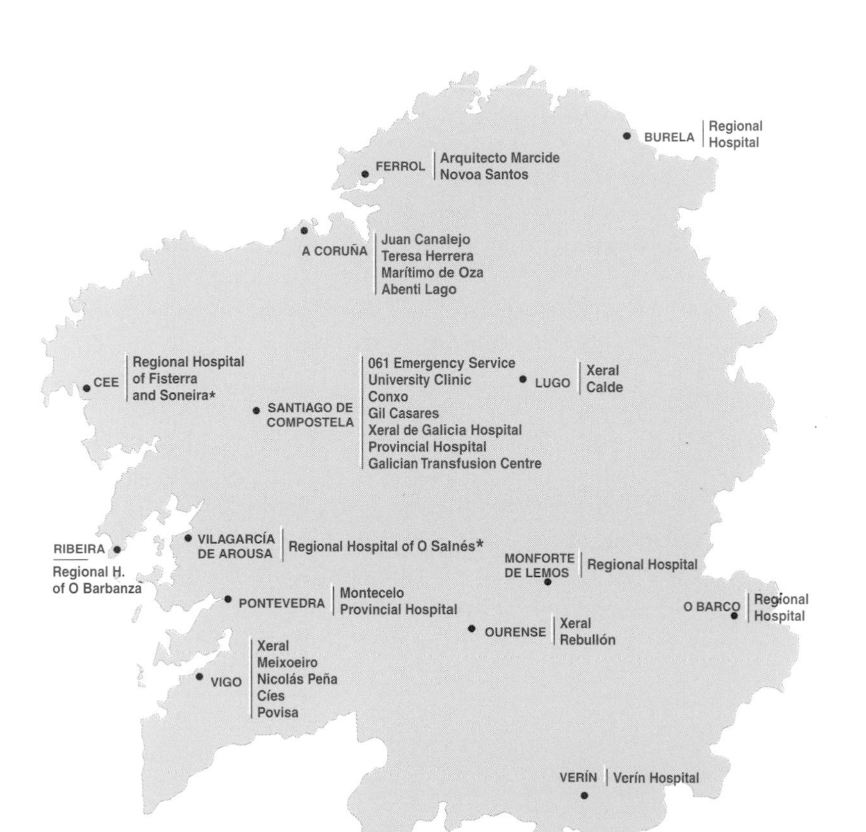

SERGAS' public hospital network.

New hospital under construction in Santiago. Galicia's public health system aims at providing patients with better medical care.

Hospital activities.

The hospitals presently included in the Galician Health Service's network provide all kinds of specialized treatment and, as a whole, cover all the demands of the Galician population, except in very special cases.

Galicia's hospitals boast a high technological level. The evolution in the matter of transplants is a good example; during the period 1989-96 the number of kidney transplants doubled. SERGAS has also extended this activity to the heart, liver, bone marrow and cornea.

The number of organ donors increased 162.7% during the period 1989-96, as opposed to 81.8% in the rest of Spain.

In order to combat cardiovascular disease two new haemo-dynamic wards were installed during 1984 in A Coruña's Juan Canalejo Hospital and Santiago's University Clinic. Two other wards and a cardiac surgery theatre were set up in Vigo's Meixoeiro Hospital.

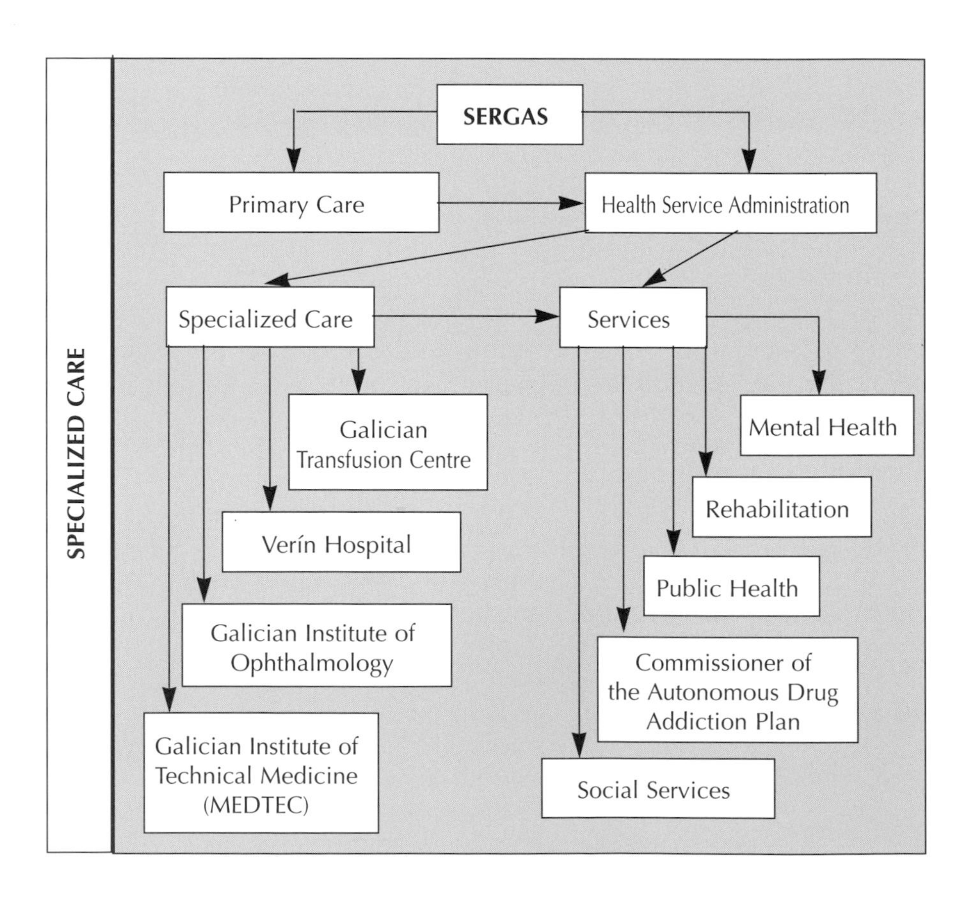

Waiting lists.
At present nobody has to wait for more than a year and most people do not have to wait more than six months. The average waiting time has been quartered, although the number of hospital admissions has doubled.

Such delays do not affect patients with urgent pathologies nor do priority 1 patients, requiring neoplasms, transplants..., have to wait more than is strictly structurally necessary (theatre programming, appearance of donors...).

Mental Health.
Starting in 1994 the general guidelines for providing psychiatric care were established in order to promote and protect mental health, prevent psychic illnesses and aid, rehabilitate and integrate the mentally ill.

Special emphasis was placed on providing care in Galicia and for Galicia. *Mental Health Units,* formed by an interdisciplinary team in support of primary care, were therefore established.

The psychiatric hospitalization units are located in the general hospitals. Halfway between the mental health units and hospitalization, there is the day hospital, which provides intensive and continuous treatment without separating patients completely from their social and family environment, as well as establishing the possibility of applying specific programmes for situations that require singular treatments, either temporarily or permanently.

The Mental Health Plan has been undergoing development in each health service area since 1995; integration of the psychiatric hospitalization units has been completed in the hospitals of Ferrol, A Coruña, Lugo, Ourense and Pontevedra, while the number of beds included in the three latter cities and Vigo has also increased.

Between 1990 and 1996 the Autonomous Administration has also signed agreements with other charity institutions and entities in order to implement and consolidate programmes regarding *alcoholism, smoking, childhood/juvenile mental health* and *psychosocial rehabilitation-reinsertion.*

Rehabilitation.
In the matter of rehabilitation there are presently insufficient resources and a certain lack of coordination between the different levels of medical care. In order to resolve this problem there is a plan to provide rehabilitation-physiotherapy services in all new hospitals, with the aim of changing the present system of payment per session to one of payment per process.

Training, research and teaching.
In specialized care there has been an increase in the training provided, not only for medical specialists but there are also training programmes being carried out in obstetrical-gynaecological matters for non-medical personnel. During 1997 946 residents (727 in hospitals and 219 in primary care centres) have been trained in SERGAS health institutions.

New forms of administration.
In Galicia three foundations in charge of administering health services (the *Galician Transfusion Centre, Verín Hospital* and the *Galician Institute of Ophthalmology*) and a public company, MEDTEC (*Galician Institute of Technical Medicine*), whose capital belongs entirely to the Autonomous Government, were created.

Galician Transfusion Centre.

Galician Transfusion Centre Foundation.
This centre was established in 1991 in order to confront the precarious situation of blood donations and blood therapy in Galicia, where a shortage of blood had traditionally been an endemic problem. The measures adopted by the Galician Transfusion Centre Foundation have led to a significant increase in unpaid donations, which has clearly improved the blood therapy situation.

Galicia has gone from 19.3 donated extractions per 1,000 inhabitants in 1989 to 34 donations/1,000 inhabitants. It is now on a par with the national average.

Galicia is presently self-sufficient in cell compounds and is working towards the same goal in plasma, used for preparing medical products (blood products).

Evolution of donation indexes per thousand inhabitants

	1989	1992	1993	1994	1995
GALICIA	19.3	24.5	27.4	30.1	32.30
SPAIN	26.4	31.4	32.4	32.0	33.26

Verín Hospital Foundation.
This foundation is run by a regional hospital located in an area of difficult access. The centre provides specialized care to the population and supports primary care.

Verín Hospital is linked to SERGAS by means of an agreement establishing its range of services and activities, quality criteria, admission conditions and financing.

The Galician Institute of Ophthalmology Foundation. (FINGO)
Its objective, which is of special interest to specialized care professionals, is oriented towards medical care, teaching and research activities in the field of ophthalmology and, more recently, it has extended its scope to include molecular biology.

Galician Institute of Technical Medicine. (MEDTEC)
The Galician Institute of Technical Medicine is a public company specialized in planning, assessing, acquiring and exploiting high-technology health service resources. Its priority activity since 1995 has been setting up and administering new high-technology health service units in SERGAS hospitals.

The Galician Institute of Technical Medicine's operations cover the following areas:

1. Administration of health services.
2. Medical physics.
3. Organization administration and consultancy.

1. Administration of health services.
MEDTEC's organization model applies business instruments to health service administration. The Institute's functioning includes mechanisms of financing, purchasing, invoicing, labour relations, incentives and production, which are normally associated with business practices but have been applied to the objectives of the public health service.

MEDTEC's administration is based on expert knowledge of the high-technology health service market. Medical equipment is complex and soon becomes obsolete, which is why a global and rigorous knowledge of available products is necessary before acquiring them.

MEDTEC is the only public consultancy company in Spain that is specialized in high-technology health services.

The Council of Nuclear Safety has recently approved the installation of a Radiotherapeutic Oncological Unit, which will equip Vigo with the Galician public health system's first two linear accelerators and the national health system's first virtual simulator.

On April 9, 1996, the *Cardiac Surgery Unit* began to function. From then on this service has carried out 387 operations, of which 306 were done using extracorporeal circulation, and in nine operations the surgical team employed a new laser system in order to recover heart tissue that was without any blood supply.

This Cardiac Surgery Unit has one of Spain's lowest average post-operational stays (6.4 days per patient) and an intra-hospital mortality index of 5.5%, far below the national average in this speciality.

The Galician Institute's second unit, in chronological order, is that of *Nuclear Medicine*, which began to function in July 1996 in Vigo's Meixoeiro Hospital. Since then it has carried out an average of 24 studies/day, which represents a planned operation of 7,000 explorations annually.

The *Interventionist Cardiology Unit* began its activity in September 1996 and has two examination wards at its disposal. The results are obtained and processed using digital technology and, for the first time in Spain, a CD-Rom system, which has important advantages over the usual video film.

The *Image Diagnosis Unit*, which the Institute has run in Vigo's Xeral Hospital since September 1996, is the first publicly-owned magnetic resonance unit, established in the south of Galicia.

2. Medical physics.
The Medical Physics Division (formed by physicists and engineers, this MEDTEC team of specialized professionals is the only existing one in the national health system as regards image diagnosis consultancy) has two main fields of activity:

- *Consultancy* in high-technology equipment and electro-medicine. The most important customer of this Institute division is SERGAS, for whom it has just finished a study on the situation of its hospitals' radio-diagnostic services, as well as giving advice regarding the acquisition of equipment. It also does consultancy work for outside Galicia, for international institutes (International Agency of Atomic Energy), state institutions (INSALUD), other autonomous communities and numerous public and private hospital centres.

The Medical Physics Division has signed agreements with SERGAS for covering *radiological protection* controls, with quality controls and protection barrier studies, in all of its radioactive installations providing specialized and primary care. Outside Galicia it also does similar work for Philips, General Electric, Siemens, Toshiba...

3. Organization Administration and Consultancy.

This MEDTEC field carries out its activities in health service organizations. Specifically, it has dealt with the administration of Galician health service organisms such as the 061 Coordination Centre for Emergency Services, the Socio-Health Care programme, as well as providing other advisory services.

XIII

SOCIAL PROTECTION

- Public Health.
  - Identification of health problems and their causes.
  - Modification of health factors.
  - Internal improvement of the organization.
- Commissioner of the Autonomous Drug Addiction Plan.
- Benefits and social promotion.
  - Social Services
  - Comprehensive family support plan.

SOCIAL PROTECTION.

PUBLIC HEALTH.

Galicia's public health has the following objectives:

- Improving the population's health, decreasing the incidence of illness by identifying health factors.
- Influencing social representatives so that they will act in favour of protective factors and decrease risk factors.
- Guaranteeing prevention services in the population and activities protecting and promoting health.

These objectives are organized in programmes divided into three strategic plans:

1. Identification of health problems and their causes.
2. Modification of factors.
3. Internal improvement of the organization.

1. Strategic plan to identify health problems and their causes.

By means of this strategic plan, systems of morbid-mortality information are carried out in the following fields:

- Diseases of compulsory declaration (EDO).
- Microbiological information. The data provided by the microbiology departments of Galicia's hospitals enables, among other things, the identification of the main etiological agents of different diseases, the detection of epidemic outbreaks or new agents and emerging pathologies, as well as the identification of possible microorganism resistance to different treatments.
- Morbidity (Recording tumours), with the aim of obtaining data about the incidence of breast cancer in Galician women. It will be subsequently extended to the recording of other kinds of tumours.
- Mortality, which encompasses the recording of general and prenatal mortality.

Likewise, this monitoring system includes data from other records, such as those dealing with tuberculosis, AIDS, metabolic pathologies and vaccines, so that its overall analysis offers a complete vision of the health situation.

- Operational programme to be implemented in situations of epidemics and outbreaks: In order to fulfill its objectives the *Galician System of Epidemiological Alert* (SAEG) has been set up, enabling the detection of problems which could, in a short time, pose a serious threat to Galicia's population. The SAEG involves compulsory and immediate notification with regard to declarers, guaranteeing, in addition, medical care from an epidemiologist on call 24 hours a day, whom may be contacted by telephone or by means of the 061 Centre.
- Programme of health assessment: Data about this matter is exchanged by means of agreements established with the Pan-American Health Organization (OPS) and the University of Santiago de Compostela. This has led to the creation of a computer statistical analysis programme and another estimating the delay in notification of AIDS cases, which is widely used in Spain and Latin America, as well as the development of joint activities, such as technical consultation and training courses in epidemiology, statistics, study design, mortality, etc.

2. Strategic plan for modifying health factors.

This Plan encompasses all the activities that are being carried out in Galicia in the field of hygiene-health prevention, by means of the following programmes:

- *Plan for preventing and controlling HIV/AIDS infection.*

The University of Santiago's Medicine Faculty.

Since this syndrome appeared in 1984, there has been a constant increase in the number of cases in Galicia. Nevertheless, this Autonomous Community has experienced a clear deceleration in the syndrome's incidence since 1991, with a tendency towards stabilization.

The Galician Plan for combating AIDS is scheduled to be updated in order to define an operational programme up to the year 2000.

Important steps in preventing the syndrome are continually informing the population, and the implementation of a school-oriented programme and another directed at parenterally administered drug users. The Health Department finances projects carried out by non-government organizations working in this field, so that terminal patients do not feel uprooted or rejected and to combat discrimination against those involved in order to ensure their full social integration.

• *Programme for preventing and controlling tuberculosis.*
There has been a considerable increase in this disease in Galicia in recent years, due to its association with AIDS, resistance to traditional drugs, delay in diagnosis and scarce monitoring of contacts. This has led to the creation, by means of SERGAS, of the Galician Tuberculosis Programme, with treatment units in the following hospitals: Gil Casares (Santiago), Juan Canalejo (A Coruña), Arquitecto Marcide (Ferrol), San José (Lugo), Montecelo (Pontevedra), Nicolás Peña (Vigo) and the centre of specialities in Ourense.

• *Programme of child vaccination.*
A continuous programme of vaccinations has been carried out in Galicia since the early sixties, with the objective of improving childhood health.

Thus, there have been no cases of poliomyelitis since 1982 and the cases of German measles, parotitis, tetanus and whooping cough have decreased considerably, while measles has experienced an oscillatory trend. In November 1993 the hepatitis B vaccination was included in the systematic vaccination programme, in addition to the following three sub-programmes for children: the systematic vaccination of all newborn babies, the systematic vaccination of pre-adolescents at the age of 12 and the control of high-risk newborn babies whose mothers are carriers of HBsAG (surface antigen of the hepatitis B virus), so that they may be vaccinated immediately and administered with specific immunoglobulin.

Hospital.

• *Programme of adult prophylaxis immunization.*
The first massive adult vaccination campaign, to combat tetanus, began in 1984. Ten years later, coinciding with the follow-up dose, a second campaign was held, especially targeting people at greater risk, such as workers in contact with the sea, farmers, stockbreeders, people over sixty-five and pregnant women.

As a preventative measure to avoid flu-related complications, anti-flu vaccination campaigns are usually held in the months of October-November, especially targeting people over sixty-five or suffering from cardiorespiratory pathologies, chronic and immune system illnesses, diabetes, hospital workers and those working in old people's homes, centres for the handicapped, prisons, etc.

• *Programme for preventing mental disability.*
It aims at avoiding mental disability arising from endocrine or metabolic illnesses that may be cured with early detection and treatment. In Galicia newborn babies undergo metabolic screening, with analyses and posterior controls being centralized in the University Hospital Complex of Santiago's metabolism pathology laboratory, and an approximate coverage of 97% has been attained in newborn babies.

• *Programme for preventing and controlling asthma.*
Its activities are centred on promoting self-care among asthma patients.

Every year subsidized summer camps for children with asthma are usually organized.

• *Programme for preventing and controlling diabetes mellitus.*
The prevalence of this chronic illness has increased in present-day society as a result of population aging. The activities carried out by this programme aim at postponing the appearance of diabetes-related complications, increasing survival rates and improving diabetics' quality of life, emphasizing the self-care of patients to that end.

• *Programme for the early detection of breast cancer.*
It began to function in November 1992.
Objective: Reducing, by 20 to 25%, the female mortality rate due to this cause in a period of 6 years, and attaining a coverage of 70% of women examined in this age group. The examination consists of a double mammogram examined by two different radiologists, and a new examination every two years is also being planned.

• *Programme for promoting a tobacco-free lifestyle.*
It began in 1993. Objectives:

- Reducing smoking-related mortality and morbidity.
- Reducing the number of smokers by 1% annually.
- Postponing the age of beginning to smoke by one year for every two years of programme application, by combining strategies of information, educational, legislative, participative (network of centres promoting a tobacco-free lifestyle) and clinical activities (campaigns to give up smoking).

There are presently 280 of such promotional centres.

During 1997 there are plans to increase the number of centres promoting a tobacco-free lifestyle, generalize anti-smoking medical advice in primary care and increase the number of smokers participating in campaigns to give up smoking.

• *Oral hygiene programme.*
It began with the 1986-87 academical year. Objective: reducing the incidence of oral disease in general and especially tooth decay.

In this programme priority is given to children, offering school children between the ages of 6 and 14 the possibility of fluoride mouthwashes at school.

Furthermore, the mouthwash campaign is complemented by an oral hygiene education programme at school.

• *Health education programme at school.*
In cooperation with the Department of Education and University Regulation that has been functioning since 1991. It aims at incorporating and take advantage of the potential of compulsory education in order to create habits and lifestyles promoting and protecting health, thereby contributing to the prevention of the frequent cases of illness overloading Galicia's health service. Health education has formed part of educational curriculums and objectives since the application of the LOGSE educational reform.

Operational strategies: continuous teacher training; designing, publishing and distributing, in schools, teaching material, contained in the guide *Health education experience at school*, as well as periodically assessing at school health-related knowledge, attitudes and behaviour.

HIV/AIDS infection, food and nutrition, oral hygiene, preventing drug addiction, sexual health, voice care for educators and accident prevention and first aid are priority themes in the design of teaching material and teacher training.

• *Programme of public health inspection in food industries.*
Various sub-programmes cover different food sectors. Objective: maintaining a suitable monitoring system of the equipment and production systems of establishments involved in making, storing, distributing and selling foodstuffs, in order to guarantee the public health quality of products produced for human consumption.

- *Sub-programme of cattle slaughter regulation and public health inspection of meat industries and outlets.*
- *Sub-programme of public health inspection of dairy industries.*
- *Sub-programme of public health inspection of establishments producing traditional dairy products.*
- *Sub-programme of public health inspection of egg-packing centres.*
- *Sub-programme of public health inspection of fish industries.*
- *Sub-programme of public health inspection of foodstuffs.*
- *Sub-programme of public health inspection of drinking-water bottling plants.*
- *Sub-programme of public health inspection of cake shops.*

• *Programme of public health inspection of foodstuffs.*
Objective: controlling the product itself and not the establishment producing it.
Various sub-programmes:

- *Sub-programmes of research into foodstuffs on the market and food alert network.*
- *Sub-programme to control residues in animals and fresh meat.*
- *Sub-programme of mollusk healthiness.*
- *Sub-programme of food handlers.*

• *Programme of public health inspection of drinking water for public consumption.*
Drinking water may be a vehicle for transmitting a large number of high-incidence diseases, which means that it is essential to guarantee its public health quality. This programme is especially important in Galicia due to the population's geographic dispersion and the large number of supply networks.
The programme is divided into five sub-programmes, defining the following actions:

- Census of supplies.
- Public health inspection of supplies.
- Coordination with the national information service regarding public drinking water.
- Public health inspection of chlorination.
- Analytical inspection of the public health quality of public drinking water.

• *Programme of public health inspection of collective swimming pools.* Bathing in a swimming pool is more dangerous than in sea water since recycled water is used, there is a greater density of bathers and a higher possibility of contamination. Such considerations and the increasing number of swimming pools functioning in Galicia make it necessary to inspect them regularly in order to guarantee their public health conditions.

An opening inspection is carried out in order to assess the water condition of the containers and complementary installations. During its functioning there are periodical controls, by both the operating company and public health personnel.

• *Programme of public health inspection in natural bathing areas (coastal and inland).*
Objective: the public health inspection of bathing areas in order to prevent morbidity that may arise as a result of bathing in contaminated water, as well as informing bathers and local authorities, so that they may take necessary action. It aims at monitoring the conditions of those coastal areas wishing to be awarded a "blue flag", in recognition of the European Union's best beaches.

• *Programme of public health inspection of chemical products.*
Objective: the public health inspection of the use and handling of chemical substances in order to avoid risks for people and the environment. Chemical products are divided into two main groups: pesticides and others.

a) Pesticides. During 1996 and as a continuation of the study carried out the previous year, the presence of pesticides in the drinking water of 100 Galician water supplies was monitored. An official register of pesticide establishments and services was created, regulations were drawn up for such registration and an official book regarding the movement of dangerous pesticides was regulated.

1997 saw the regulation of the standardizing of the training course for carrying out pesticide operations, as well as the issuing of licences for pesticide handlers. The control of Maximum Residue Levels (LMR) of pesticides in market products is also planned.

b) Other chemical products. In 1997 companies using such products were controlled, to make sure that they had the safety data cards regulated in the decree approving the regulations with regard to the classification, bottling and labelling of dangerous substances.

• *Programme of atmospheric air quality control (National Network Monitoring Atmospheric Contamination).*
Objective: enforcing the published legislation in order to protect people's health, especially those at greater risk: patients with respiratory problems, children and the aged.

The Public Health's head office receives data regarding the emission levels of controlled pollutants: sulphur dioxide, suspended particles, nitrogen oxides, lead, ozone, chlorine and fluorine compounds.

• *Programme of public health inspection of public tourist campsites.*
Objectives:
- Decreasing morbidity arising from poor public health conditions in campsites.
- Avoiding environmental degradation arising from the deficient installation of sewage treatment systems.

• *Programme of workplace public health.*
Objective: fulfilling the role assigned to the public health administration by the law of workplace risk prevention in the field of public health, such as setting up information and training systems regarding chemical substances used in production processes.

3. *Strategic plan for the internal improvement of the organization.*
• *Programme for the restructuring of veterinary surgeons and coordination of public health inspection.*
The requirement of adapting to the European Union's guidelines in the field of the official inspection of food products led to the restructuring of the body of official veterinary surgeons in 1994. There are presently 250 inspectors, divided into teams working in thirteen veterinary zones and 48 veterinary regions.

• *Programme for coordinating public health laboratories.*
Galicia has four public health laboratories, situated in the department's provincial centres. In addition to environmental matters, each laboratory is specialized in specific analytical techniques for controlling the public health conditions of different kinds of foodstuffs.

• *Programme of internal training.*
Objective: the continuous training of human resources. Since 1995 annual plans have been drawn up and extended regarding the training of the totality of technical and auxiliary personnel.

The annual plans' teaching-learning fields refer to strategic management and administration techniques, statistics and epidemiological information, computerized administration, administering and assessing health projects and programmes, administering inspection systems, quality administration and customer services.

COMMISSIONER OF THE AUTONOMOUS DRUG ADDICTION PLAN.

Created in 1993, it is responsible for coordinating, monitoring, carrying out and enforcing all activities in the field of combating drug addiction. It is in charge of presenting the Inter-department Coordination Commission in the matter of drug dependency with the Galician Administration's general policy in this field.

It also advises the minister, coordinates the relations of the Xunta de Galicia's departments with the social media regarding drug addiction, runs the programmes and budgets to that end, coordinates activities with other administrations and non-government organizations, as well as running the commissions and technical meetings that are organized.

The Autonomous Drug Dependency Plan was started in 1986, in reply to the intense social demand related to the excessive increase of drug consumption. The following basic principles were adopted: health service integration, zoning and territorialization, therapeutic continuity, comprehensive and interdisciplinary care and promoting community participation.

In 1996 the Galician Parliament approved a law providing the legal framework for all of the coordination activities dealing with this problem.

Operational fields: functions of prevention, care, integration, training, research and coordination.

The Commissioner has drawn up the 1997-2000 Galician Plan regarding drugs, a document that, for the three-year period that has now begun, will be the basis for planning, running and implementing the different programmes.

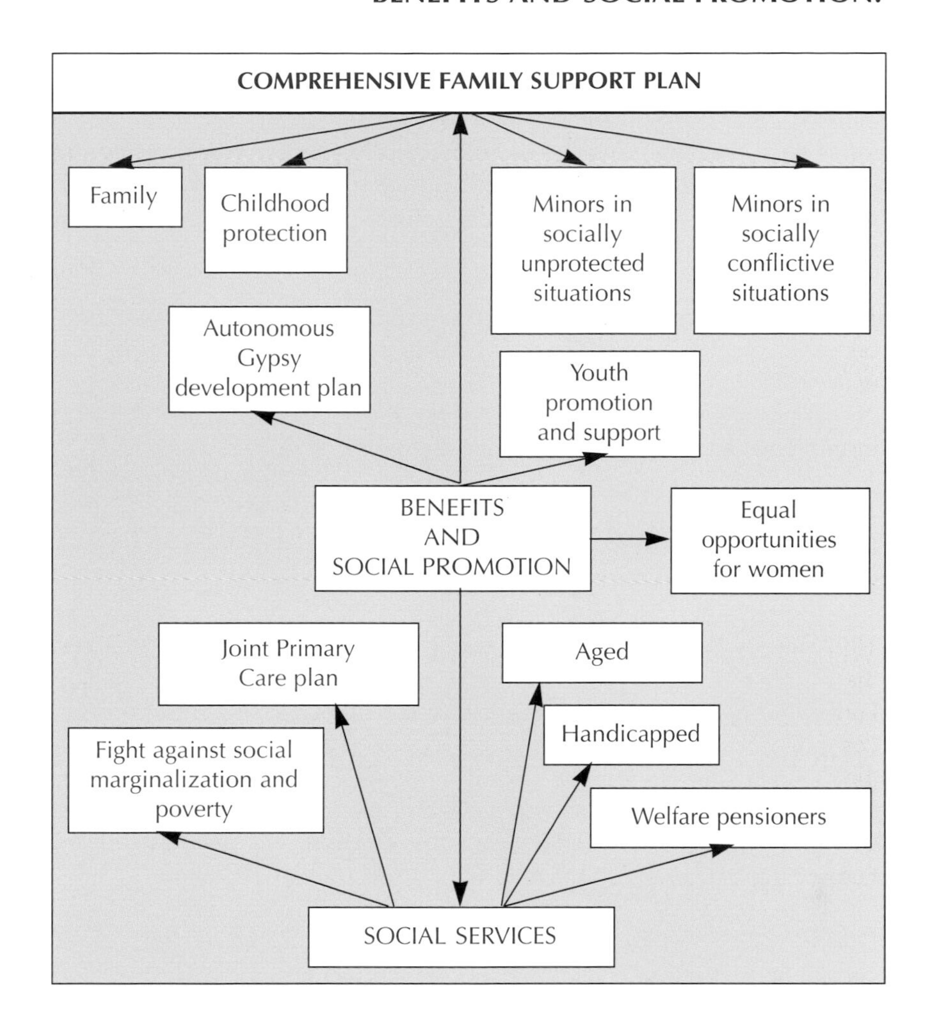

Social Services.
Galicia is working towards the consolidation of social rights, developing regulations and establishing a public system of social services in order to promote social welfare.

The Administration has to extend the present limits of public responsibility, going from the establishment of aid guidelines and economic benefit programmes to the stimulation and promotion of civil society's initiatives.

The Administration has the obligation to satisfy its citizens' basic needs and guarantee minimum levels of social welfare, but it would also like to enable civil society to fulfill its responsibility in matters of social interest.

• *Joint Primary Care plan.*
Primary care social services are one of the system's basic elements and the gateway to all social services. In addition to establishing a basic Primary Care network covering the entire Galician population, the plan aims at completing the municipal network of social installations and infrastructures, by means of co-financing agreements and the introduction of stable participation and administration mechanisms, to reinforce the joint Primary Care plan's philosophy of inter-administrative coordination.

The plan is designed to consolidate social services as rights not charity benefits, establishing a network of centres throughout Galicia, equipped with professionals undergoing continuous training and with the capacity of caring for the whole population. The Galician plan of social installations and services is presently being developed.

• *Fight against social marginalization and poverty.*
In 1996 3,705 people benefited from Galician Social Integration Income (RISGA).

1997 saw an increase in the number of people benefiting from RISGA and the number of those receiving social emergency aid was maintained. Furthermore, it is planned to optimize its usage, alleviating the consequences of the different situations of need and having an impact on their causes. This will be done from the perspective of the most deprived families, with the supportive implication of the main social, political and economic representatives and using the experimental methodology of European programmes designed to fight against social exclusion.

During 1995-96, for the first time in Galicia, an experimental comprehensive community development project was established and implemented, in the O Ribeiro region.

17 agents from the Foundation of the Regional Development of Galicia, who carried out operational projects in 17 regions, were also trained.

The 1996-97 biennium saw the application of the Itínere project for the social-workplace integration of deprived persons (preferably those receiving RISGA benefits), presented to the European Union's employment and human resources initiative.

• *Aged.*
Galicia has one of Spain's highest aging indexes (16.1% over 65 compared to 13.7% in all Spain). Objective: enabling this sector of the population to lead an independent life in their natural environment, fulfilling an active role in their community.

The different operations underway include fostering programmes, day centres, temporary stays in old people's homes and setting up custodial apartments.

Another objective is the social integration of the aged, by promoting their participation and cooperation in community activities; different activities are organized in the fields of sociocultural entertainment, and leisure and free-time promotion, as well as social tourism.

The family break programme "Health Holidays" was put into effect to provide temporary care in spas for old people with functional limitations. Other programmes deal with spa tourism, and sight and hearing improvement for the aged.

Old people's home.

For those who cannot be cared for in their own environment, there is a network of old people's homes that is designed to progressively meet the admission demand of disabled old people.

• *Handicapped.*

Handicapped persons are taken care of.

Objective: helping the handicapped to attain full citizen status, with the same rights and duties as the rest, by means of regulations and integration.

Priority is given to actions designed to facilitate the social-workplace integration of the handicapped and eliminate architectural barriers. There is an obvious need for joint action between the public sector and the associationism movement, consolidating the system of agreements with social entities.

Different programmes are underway as regards fostering, leisure and free time, sign language interpreters, the integration of persons with medullar injuries and early care.

During 1995 a census of handicapped persons was drawn up, as well as a services guide for their information.

Workplace insertion is being promoted by means of the HORIZON programme.

Specialized activities: NODUS, FORUM, CASTRO-NAVAS, PROMIGA and REDES projects for the physically handicapped, deaf, psychotic-autistic and psychic patients, presented to the European Social Fund by social initiative entities and co-financed by the Social Services head office.

• *Welfare pensions.*
Galicia is one of the autonomous communities with the highest level of population dependent on subsidies provided for handicapped and retired persons who have never paid Social Security contributions.

At present there are 70,000 old-age or disabled residents of the Autonomous Community receiving social and welfare pensions, administered by the Social Services Department, thereby benefiting from medical and pharmaceutical care and the social services network.

Those benefiting from non-contributive pensions receive a maximum amount of 35,080 pesetas per month, which is increased by 50% in the case of disabled persons requiring a home help in their daily activities. For those benefiting from pensions controlled by the Law of Social Integration of the Handicapped, there is also a subsidy aid for the home help of 9,725 pesetas per month, and the mobility subsidy and transport expenses were set, in 1996, at 5,690 pesetas per month.

In 1995 the social register (an information system for social services users, SIUSS) began to function in fifteen municipal districts, and it is planned to be established in 144 more by the end of 1997.

The Social Services Law set the guidelines for Galicia's social policies. There is a need to continue financing the development of regulations in order to specify the levels of social care and rights to be attained.

In December 1993 the health system's social services were unified in order to satisfy needs situated in the grey area bordering social services and the health system.

In Galicia, for example, there are about 100,000 persons over 80 who need permanent medical or psychiatric care.

In recent decades the welfare systems of developed countries have faced new challenges (derived from the changes in epidemiological disease patterns and the evolution of demographic and social profiles), such as greater population aging, the increase in life expectancy with invalidity, the survival of patients with serious handicaps and the tendency of an increasing number of people, who used to be admitted to hospitals or social centres, being cared for in the community.

All of these factors imply a reorientation as regards providing services and administering permanently scarce resources.
The Autonomous Community of Galicia has set up a short- and long-term plan to reorient present services towards the needs derived from this new situation.

The designed model is based on the following principles:

- Orientation towards the user, defining the resources and services to be developed, in function of each need's profiles.
- Flexibility in the combination of the different kinds of services, regardless of whether they belong to the social services or health system field or the financing methods.
- Orientation towards the improvement of a person's quality of life.
- Multi-disciplinarity.
- Diversification of services (variety of professionals and technical aids) and organization methods (home care, health centre care, day and night care, technical aids, support for family in charge of care...), in order to adjust their offer to each person's different degrees of need.
- Orientation towards the promotion of community participation, helping informal support services for those providing care and favouring social initiatives with regard to providing non-productive services (voluntary) and care (promoting social charity initiatives and associationism).

The main points to be implemented, from a political-administrative point of view, are the following:

- Development of an administrative framework enabling social-health problems to be dealt with in a joint and comprehensive way, harmonized and coordinated with the different social representatives.
- A selective policy of public coverage of priority needs, combined with forms of private coverage and co-financing.
- Attaining equality in the distribution of resources, promoting the development of simpler forms of organization in rural environments (home care, fostering...), as a mechanism compensating for the lack of more specialized resources.
- Providing the ideal medium for informal community care, by means of specific services for providing family relief.
- Financial cooperation with social and private initiatives.

Comprehensive family support plan.

Operational programmes

1. Family policy

- *FAMILY:*
  - Housing.
  - Cultural-educational.
  - Social-workplace.
  - Social-health.
  - Family Orientation Councils.
- *CHILDHOOD PROTECTION:*
  - Childhood centres run by:
    Autonomous Administration.
    Social Initiatives.
    Local administrations.
- *MINORS IN UNPROTECTED SITUATIONS.*
  - Family support to integrate the minor.
  - Nurseries.
  - Children's hot line.
  - Fostering.
  - Detections of situations of:
    - risk
    - child battering.
- *MINORS IN SITUATIONS OF SOCIAL CONFLICT:*
  - Repairing the damage.
  - Health centre treatment.
  - Admission to therapeutical centre.
  - Temporary week-end internment.
  - Controlled freedom.
  - Admission to an open, semi-open or closed centre.

2. Autonomous Gypsy Development Plan:

- Insertion of the Gypsy community into society.
- Housing.
- Education.
- Employment.
- Health.
- Culture.

3. Youth promotion and support:

- Youth participation in and integration into community life.
- Youth installations, especially for youth tourism in rural environments.
- Youth associationism.
- Leisure activities.
- Galician Network of Information and Youth Documentation.

4. Equal opportunities for women:

- Associationism, participation and cooperation.
- Education and culture.
- Training and employment.
- Social services and health.

Improving public health, a priority objective of Social Protection programmes.

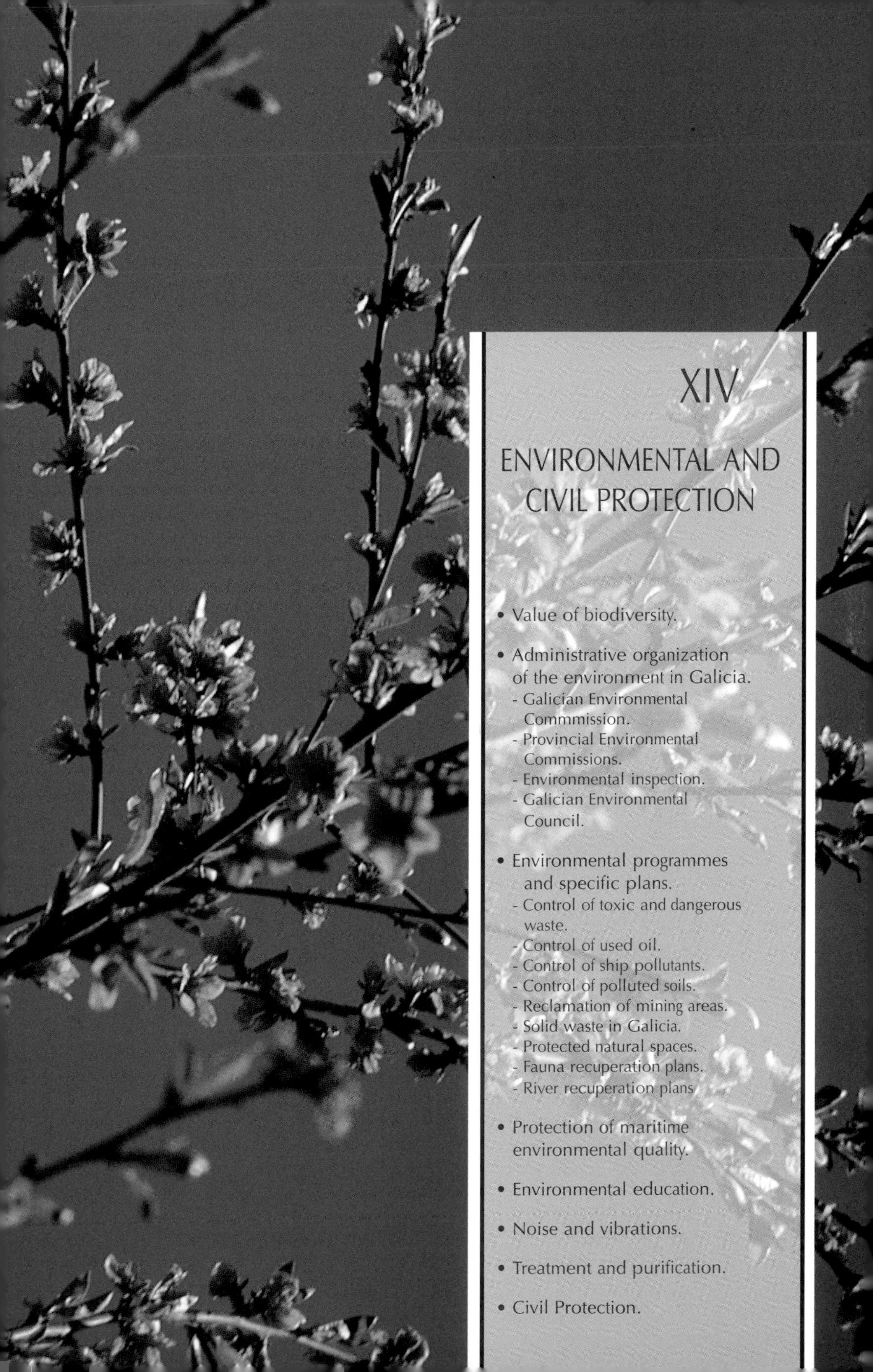

XIV

ENVIRONMENTAL AND CIVIL PROTECTION

- Value of biodiversity.
- Administrative organization of the environment in Galicia.
  - Galician Environmental Commmission.
  - Provincial Environmental Commissions.
  - Environmental inspection.
  - Galician Environmental Council.
- Environmental programmes and specific plans.
  - Control of toxic and dangerous waste.
  - Control of used oil.
  - Control of ship pollutants.
  - Control of polluted soils.
  - Reclamation of mining areas.
  - Solid waste in Galicia.
  - Protected natural spaces.
  - Fauna recuperation plans.
  - River recuperation plans
- Protection of maritime environmental quality.
- Environmental education.
- Noise and vibrations.
- Treatment and purification.
- Civil Protection.

ENVIRONMENTAL AND CIVIL PROTECTION.

"Everyone has the right to enjoy a suitable environment for personal development, as well as the duty to conserve it."
Spanish Constitution. Article 45.1.

VALUE OF BIODIVERSITY.

Present-day civilization, which is enormously consumerist, is degrading the environment: land, water and air. The environment contains a prodigious biological variety or *biodiversity*. Such bio-diversity should be taken care of because of its:

- *Economic value*: Natural ecosystems provide us with food and diverse materials.
- *Ecological value*: We depend on green plants, which transform light energy into chemical energy and, in addition, produce oxygen.
- *Aesthetic value*: The variety of shapes, colours, lifestyles and behaviour is so beautiful that it must be protected.
- *Ethical value*: All kinds of life are valuable per se.

Biodiversity is a guarantee of economic prosperity.

Biodiversity equals beauty.

According to the Spanish Constitution, "public authorities will ensure rational usage of all natural resources, in order to protect and improve the quality of life, and defend and restore the environment, based on indispensable collective solidarity." In order to implement this message, Galicia has the following administrative organization at its disposal:

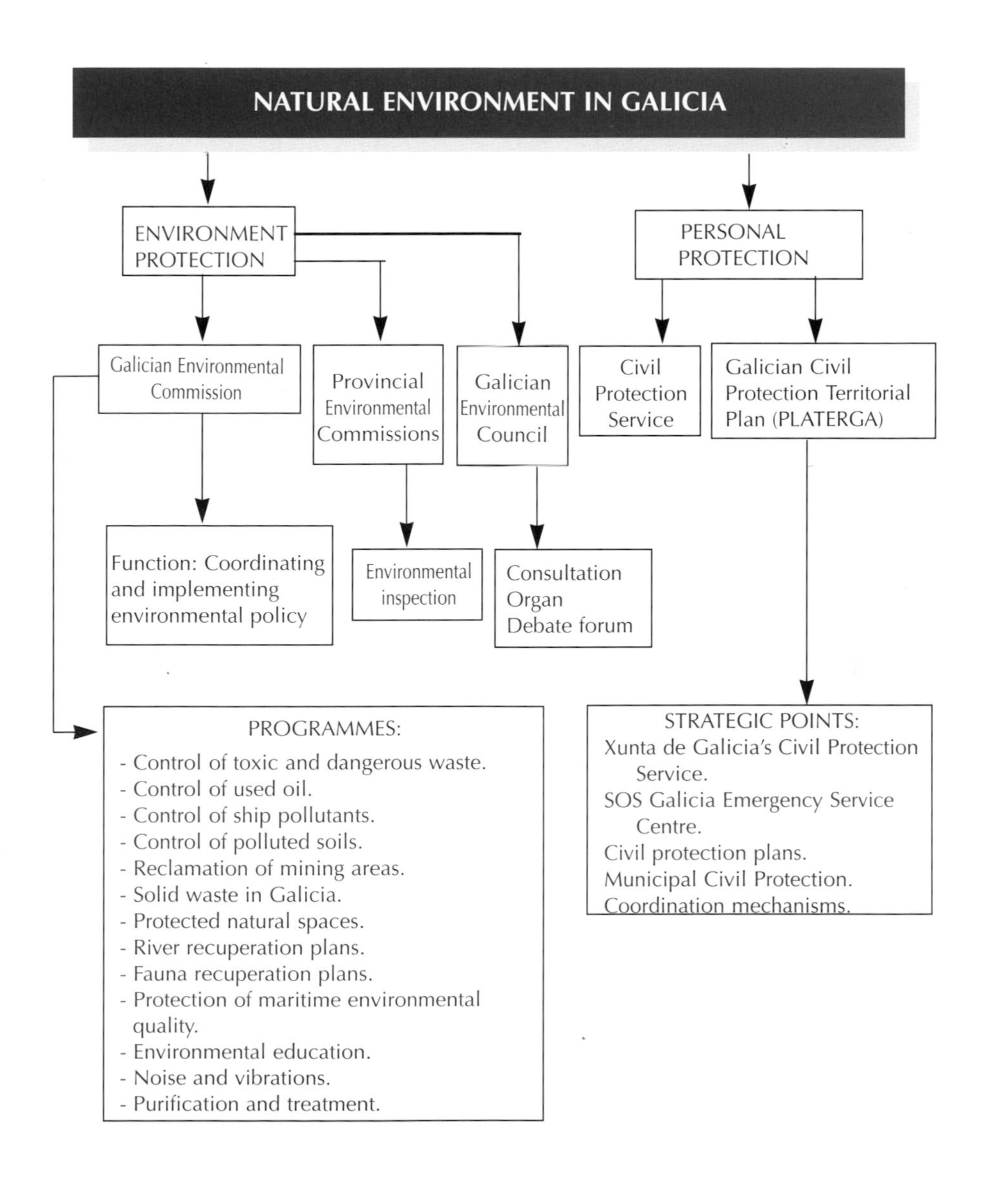

ADMINISTRATIVE ORGANIZATION OF THE ENVIRONMENT IN GALICIA.

Galician Environmental Commission.

The Galician Environmental Commission is the administrative organ in charge of the Autonomous Community's environmental policy. Functions:

- Drawing up and approving environmental impact declarations.
- Coordinating and ensuring the programming unity of all activities and projects in environmental matters.
- Knowing and informing about planned regulations related to protected natural spaces, or geological, flora, fauna or landscape protection.
- Compulsory notification of the final approval of applications that include, in environmental matters, the granting of financial benefits.

Provincial Environmental Commissions.

The Provincial Environmental Commissions coordinate the functions of monitoring and environmental inspection, informing about activities classified in the regulations of bothersome, unhealthy, poisonous and dangerous activities, and enforcing the corrective measures to be adopted by such activities.

Environmental Inspection.

Environmental inspection, coordinated by the Provincial Environmental Commissions, has the function of prior control and monitoring of the correct compliance of prevention instruments and regulations in the field of environmental preservation.

Galician Environmental Council.

This is the environmental administration's consultation organ.

Objective: Enforcing the principle of public participation and establishing a channel of collaboration between Galician society and the scientific community.

The following are represented: Autonomous Administration, environmental associations, trade unions, consumer organizations, businessmen, universities and town councils.

Function:

- Knowing and informing about general environmental projects and plans of unique importance.
- Drawing up proposals and issuing reports about environmental matters.
- Proposing measures to promote sustained development and the creation of employment in activities related to environmental administration and protection.
- Promoting initiatives for developing environmental education, scientific research and citizen participation in resolving environmental problems.

ENVIRONMENTAL PROGRAMMES AND SPECIFIC PLANS.

The different departments with environmental jurisdiction develop sectorial plans for administering the specific environmental aspects included under their own jurisdiction.

Control of toxic and dangerous waste.

Since 1995 Galicia's Industrial Waste Treatment Centre, situated in Somozas (A Coruña), has been functioning, with a waste treatment capacity of 85,000 t/year for all the Autonomous Community.

Control of used oil.

Since 1991 used oil has been collected by means of authorized vehicles and taken to treatment centres in Laracha (A Coruña) and Vilalonga (Pontevedra). Such oil is treated with a view to its energetic recuperation. The process is controlled by the Regional Industrial Environmental Laboratory.

Control of ship pollutants.

The control of waste from ships is defined in the MARPOL agreement. In Galicia it is carried out by private companies in charge of unloading waste and then transporting it to authorized centres, which extract its energetic value before eliminating it.

Control of polluted soil.

The control of polluted soil is implemented by means of an agreement with the Spanish Environment Ministry, which defines the operations to be carried out.

Reclamation of mining areas.

The Reclamation of areas impoverished by mining activities is divided into two aspects:

- *Deposits*: A 1997 environmental deposit decree sets the amounts to be deposited in order to restore and compensate for environmental damages caused by such activities.

- *Pacts*: Environmental pacts enable old mining operations, which had not made provision for reclamation measures, to meet present-day requirements.

Solid waste in Galicia.

Galicia's Solid Urban Waste (RSU) Control Plan, of 1992, defines a system of collection, selection and energetic recuperation.

Main points:

- Minimizing the production of solid urban waste.
- Installing transfer stations to centralize the collection of solid urban waste for its posterior transfer.
- Recuperation of recyclable materials.
- Production of waste-derived fuel.
- Production of electricity in power stations.

Protected natural spaces.

Operations carried out:

- Establishment of the Baixa Limia-Sierra del Xurés Natural Park and Governing Council.
- Creation and improvement of infrastructures in the Monte Aloia Natural Park.
- Setting up of the Interpretation Centre in the Natural Park of the Corrubedo sand dune system and Carregal and Vixán lagoons.
- Approval of the Natural Resource Regulation Plan of the Fragas del Eume Natural Park.

Plan of large herbivore reintroduction.

Common deer in Xistral and Invernadeiro.
Mountain goat in Baixa-Serra do Xurés.
Roe deer in Monte Aloia Natural Park.

Fauna recuperation plans.

The Autonomous Community is developing the following fauna recuperation plans:

- Application of the Cantabrian Brown Bear Recuperation Plan by means of the LIFE programme.
- Partridge recuperation plan, which included a 1996 count.
- Large herbivore and wild rabbit reintroduction plan.
- Control of the chamois' natural expansion in Os Ancares, from existing populations in Castile and León.

River recuperation plans.

Advances made by the River Recuperation Plan:

- Urgent measures for recuperating salmon populations.
- Creation of a network of wild trout capturers.
- Establishment of suitable ecological water levels for Galicia's rivers in harmony with the requirements of river species.

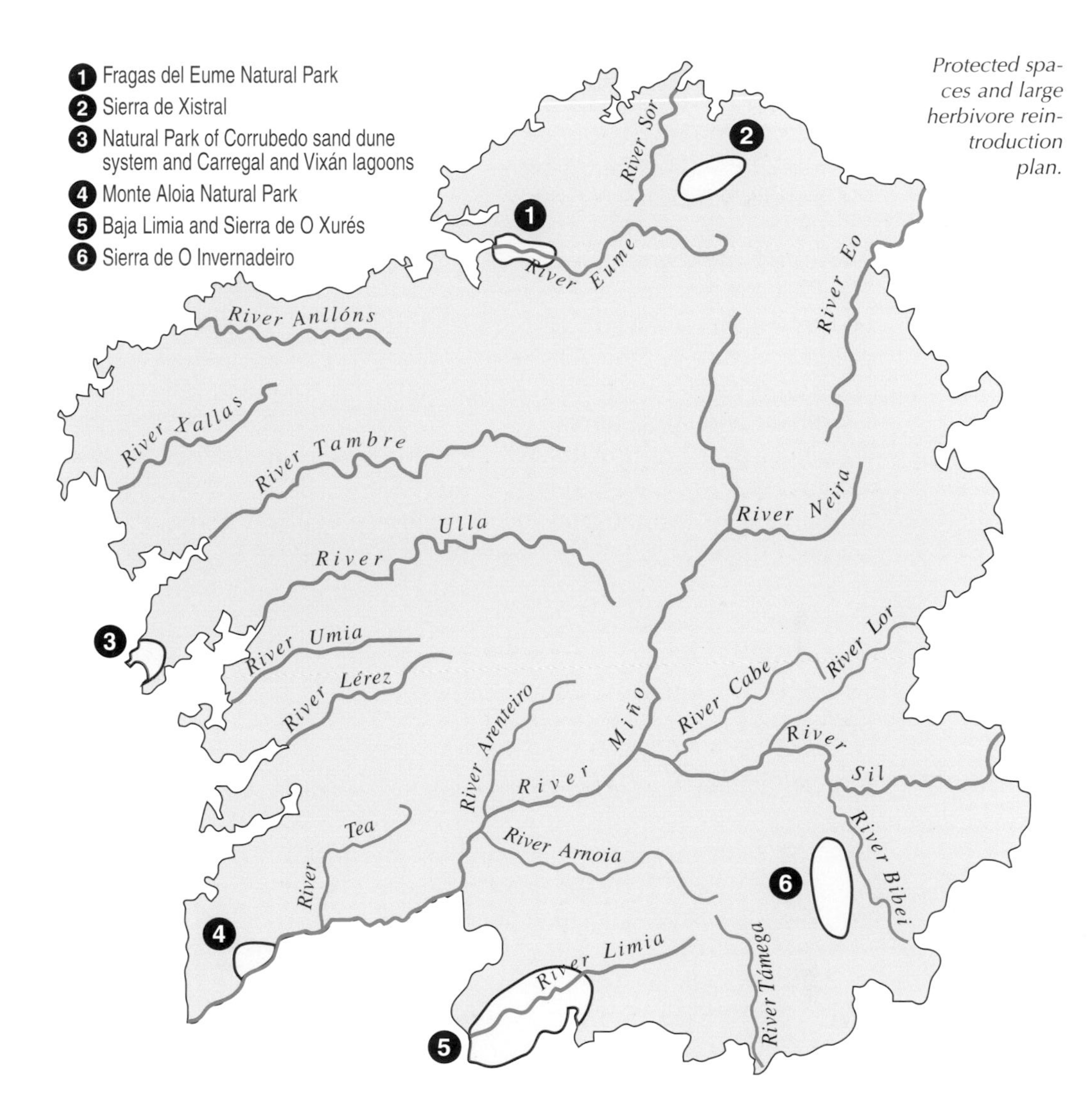

Protected spaces and large herbivore reintroduction plan.

Protection of maritime environment quality.

Galicia's Fish and Shellfish Resource Regulation Plan protects the quality of the maritime environment. A comprehensive analysis of urban and industrial sewage, which enters the rias, has been carried out.

This has led to the drawing up of a comprehensive purification strategy for the rias, defining the needs of constructing sewage treatment plants in order to minimize the effects of such sewage.

Since 1995 the *Vilaxoán Maritime Environment Control Centre,* which centralizes and unifies the different control networks (phytoplankton, water quality and bio-toxins), has been fully operational.

Environmental education.
Environmental education activities in Galicia are organized by means of different interpretation centres, nature classes and camps. The Administration has also signed agreements with associations that carry out specific environmental education activities.

Noise and vibrations.
The Galician Parliament, by means of an Acoustic Contamination Law, guarantees the protection of its citizens from problems and annoyance produced by noise and vibrations.

Treatment and purification.
Treatment and purification activities are based on the *Autonomous Community of Galicia's Purification Plan,* which established the programme to be implemented until the year 2005. Since 1989 40 sewage treatment plants have been put into operation.

CIVIL PROTECTION.

In 1990 the Autonomous Community of Galicia's Civil Protection Service was created.

Civil Protection is a public service with the participation of the different Administrations and citizens on a voluntary basis. Plans are drawn up with the participation of town councils by means of agreements and citizen collaboration is channelled by means of volunteer groups that are duly organized and situated in the municipal districts.

Since 1994, with the publication of Galicia's Civil Protection Territorial Plan (PLATERGA), the Autonomous Community of Galicia's civil protection service has been under the jurisdiction of the Autonomous Administration, which is responsible for its management.

PLATERGA determines the hierarchical and functional structure of the organisms that intervene in an emergency, as well as the system defining how to coordinate the equipment and resources used during situations of risk. This enables the implementation of a quick response and helps to resolve emergency situations.

In order to coordinate all the intervening services and establish planning regulations, different levels were created: local level or level 0, provincial level or level 1, autonomous level or level 2, national level or level 3.

At the end of 1997 more than 60 professionals were working in Galicia's Civil Protection.

Environmental education enables the recuperation and conservation of landscapes, rivers, seas, species...

Civil Protection's main strategies:

Xunta de Galicia's Civil Protection Service.
This service is divided into the following fields: Planning, Infrastructures and Installations, Information, Training, Radiological Safety and Intervention.
Due to the complexity of emergency situations, the Civil Protection and Environment's technical personnel are selected from different professional fields.

Creation and development of the SOS-Galicia Emergency Centre.
This service, created in 1990, is one of the most advanced in Spain.
Objective: responding to any request made during an emergency situation, coordinating equipment and resources belonging to the Autonomous Community or from other Public Administrations and entities.

The Emergency Centre enjoys the collaboration and participation of the Galician Health Service's 061 Service, the Sea Lifesaving and Rescue Service, the Forest Fire Prevention Service and other organisms.
SOS-Galicia has communication (telephone and radio) and advanced computer systems at its disposal. With regard to the day-to-day management of emergencies, the SOS-Galicia Centre employs a comprehensive management computer system called XESPRO, interconnected with a geographical data system.

The SOS-Galicia Emergency Centre is highly valued by Galicia's citizens, who made 159,535 calls in 1996.

Helicopter used in fire fighting.

Drawing up, approval and standardizing of Civil Protection plans.
In order to respond to possible risks, standard operational and coordination plans have been drawn up by the Galician Civil Protection Commission:

- Chemical Industry Emergency Plan.
- Autonomous Community of Galicia's Civil Protection Plan for Forest Fire Emergencies.

Plans have also been drawn up for specific activities, such as risks on the beach (SAPRAGA Plan), in snowfalls (NEGA Plan) and storms.

Promotion and Development of Municipal Civil Protection.
Municipal Civil Protection, since it is in close contact with citizens, is the first to act in an emergency situation, but not all municipal districts have the necessary means for responding efficiently to possible risks.
The following has therefore been promoted:

- Collaboration and cooperation with town councils in order to encourage citizen participation in Civil Protection, promoting the creation of the Civil Protection Service and first-intervention municipal groups.
- Training of Civil Protection volunteers in collaboration with the Galician Safety Academy.
- Creation of Local Civil Protection Councils as the promotional instruments of the following:
  - Establishing programmes for local emergencies.
  - Encouraging the drawing up of Municipal Emergency Plans (PEMUS).

Establishment of an effective and dynamic coordination mechanism.
Civil Protection in Galicia is coordinated by means of different organisms:

- Galician Civil Protection Commission.
- Xunta de Galicia's Autonomous Committee of Civil Protection Operational Coordination.
- Operational coordination centres.
- Galician Fire Risk Commission.
- Galician Chemical Risk Commission.
- Galician Commission for Risks of Flooding and Droughts.

XV

AGRICULTURE

- Climate.
- Agricultural regions.
- Crops.
- Stockbreeding.
- Forestry.
- Socioeconomic and agricultural indicators of the geographical regions.

AGRICULTURE.

CLIMATE.

Galicia's climate, due to its temperature range and precipitation, is suited to agriculture and stockbreeding, although there are important differences between regions, mainly due to geographical relief.

The main factors determining Galicia's varied climate are the following:

- The Atlantic-continental gradient of average temperatures from the coast to the interior.
- The shortage of water in the dry season.
- The precipitation range, conditioned by humid winds from the south-west and the position of mountain ranges and depressions.

Land usage in Galicia. 1997

Land classification	Surface area (ha)
Cultivated land	537,311
Meadows and pasture land	372,787
Forests	962,767
Sparse forests	82,60
Scrubland	799,143
Rivers and lakes	28,622
Unproductive lands	174,267
TOTAL	**2,957,506**

Agriculture only makes use of 18.17% of the territory.

Average annual precipitation ranges from 800 mm in southern inland valleys to 3,000 mm in western mountains.
Consequently, different climates exists: oceanic, oceanic-continental in the interior, oceanic-Mediterranean in the south and south-east, and mountain oceanic.

AGRICULTURAL REGIONS.

Galician agriculture is intensive and varied, with crops being produced in different stages throughout the year. Crops are adapted to Galicia's geographical relief and farmers take full advantage of available material resources.

The following agricultural regions may therefore be identified:
1. *North Coast.*
- Between the Central Plateau and the Bay of Biscay.
  - Rugged topography.
  - Wet climate all year round.
  - Mild temperatures, which rapidly decrease according to altitude.
  - Productivity depends on the land's altitude and topographical position.
  - Agriculture related to dairy cattle.
  - In mountain areas there is extensive cattle raising.
  - Eucalyptus forests on low-altitude slopes.
  - Oak forests in higher, more sheltered areas.
- In the depression situated between the Central Plateau and the Ares-Betanzos and A Coruña rias, the climate is hotter and drier.
  - Fruit and vegetable growing, maritime pine and eucalyptus forests.
  - Dairy cattle farms and advanced agriculture.

Intensive and multi-crop agriculture requires full-time work on the part of farmers but lessens the effects of droughts, pests and frosts, which are so frequent in mono-crop agriculture.

2. *Atlantic Coast.*

- Low-lying valleys of the Atlantic rias.
- Low-altitude coastlines, less than 500 m high.
- Atlantic climate.
- Shortage of precipitation decreases according to altitude.
- Multi-crop agriculture, frequently part-time.
- Small farms.
- In southern valleys, vine-growing and wine making ("Rías Baixas" appellation d'origine).
- Galician pine, eucalyptus and oak.

3. *Central Plateau.*

- The most extensive area.
- Continental climate, except the Bergantiños and Soneira regions, which have a more Atlantic climate.
- Shortage of precipitation towards the south.
- Multi-crop and cattle agriculture.
- Fodder production.
- Dairy cattle.
- Monterey pine forests, especially in the "Terra Chá" region or Central Galician Peneplain.
- Galician pine in the Bergantiños and Soneira regions.
- Mixed forests of Galician pine and eucalyptus in the central Melide-Arzúa regions.

4. *North-East Mountains.*

- Situated between the Central Plateau, Asturias and León.
- Steep and rugged terrain that rises to a height of 1,880 m above sea level.
- Mountain-continental climate.
- Shortage of precipitation in the south, bordering the Sil valleys and Lemos depression.
- Subsistence farming.
- Extensive cattle and goat raising.
- Well-cultivated chestnut trees.

5. *South-West Mountains.*

• Between the Atlantic coast and interior depressions.

- Heights above 1,100 m.
- High precipitation and water shortage in summer.
- Extensive cattle raising.
- Forest threatened by frequent fires.

6. *Interior Depressions.*

• Mid-range Miño basin and lower Sil basin. Támega and Viana depressions.

- Vine-growing in well-defined regions with "appellations d'origine":
    - Ribeiro.
    - Valdeorras.
    - Monterrei.
    - Ribeira Sacra.
- Rough terrain, with terraced cultivations.
- Cork oak.
- Small-scale farms.
- Omnivore raising.
- Predominance of potato and cereal crops in A Limia.

7. *Mid-range Mountains and South-East Mountains.*

- Situated in Galicia's south-east region.
  - Heights of between 600 and 1,700 m.
  - Large temperature range between winter and summer.
  - Notable water shortage. Precipitation does not exceed 1,200 mm.
  - Multi-crop agriculture in low-lying land.
  - Goat raising in high-altitude areas.
  - Decreasing population and abandoning of agricultural land.
  - Rye cultivation.
  - Predominance of community property.

Sheep raising in interior regions.

There is forest land in all of Galicia's agricultural regions. It occupies the greatest extension of Galicia's territory, although it alternates with farm land and pasture land.

CROPS.

- Fodder crops: They occupy the greatest extension of cultivated land.
  - Corn fodder: for green consumption.
for making silage.
  - Turnip.

- Corn grain: There is a long tradition of cultivation in southern coastal areas. It is the second crop in extension.

- Potato: It is the third crop in extension.
  It is predominant in the A Limia, Bergantiños and Terra Chá regions.
  Irregular annual production.
  Variable market prices.

- Cereals: Wheat and rye cultivation is decreasing.
  It is predominant in the Central Plateau and mountainous regions.

- Horticultural products: They are grown in the southernmost Atlantic coastal regions and A Coruña basin.
  Large variety of products, low degree of commercialization.

- Vines: The greatest extensions are located in the Rías Baixas and the sun-facing slopes of the Miño and Sil valleys.
  Monterrei is an almost exclusively vine-growing region.

Agricultural farms.
52% of agricultural farms consist of subsistence farms, which are the least specialized and with the lowest degree of commercialization.

They are located in the North-East Mountains, South-West Mountains, Mid-range Mountains and South-East Mountains, regions with a very small proportion of agricultural land.

Horticultural production, vine-growing and fruit trees make up less than 2% of the total. They are concentrated in the southern valleys of the Atlantic coast and Miño-Sil valleys.

STOCKBREEDING.

- *Cattle.*
Dairy cattle is extremely important to Galicia economically and socially.

Dairy cows. 1995*		
Heads	t of milk	Value (million pts)
453,000	2,110,000	100,562

Estimated data.

The number of dairy cows and farms has been decreasing in the last ten years. However, the total milk production, the milk delivered to industry, industrialized milk in Galicia, average production per farm and average production per cow has been increasing in recent years.

Furthermore, there are 185,000 adult cows, of breeds such as *"rubia gallega" (Galician brown),* which are highly valued for their profitable carcasses and quality meat. Galician beef is meat with a "Protected Geographical Indication". It is licensed meat. The number of heads of cattle sacrificed in 1995 made up 13% of the Spanish total.

-Pigs.
- Pig rasing increased greatly in Galicia up to 1987. The total figure is now near a million, representing 5% of national livestock.

-Poultry.
- Chicken breeding for meat has been steadily increasing in Galicia, with a net production of 111,000 tonnes, representing 12% of the corresponding national figure.

- Egg production has been decreasing since 1983. The present production amounts to 50 million dozens, less than half of the previous maximum. Nevertheless, the relative proportion has remained at 10% of Spanish production.

-Sheep and goats.
Sheep and goat raising is not highly developed in Galicia; the number of heads represents only 1.4% of the Spanish census. It is of some importance in inland mountain municipal districts.

Cattle farms.
- Herbivore farms, especially dairy, meat-producing and mixed dairy/meat-producing farms, make up the second most numerous group (45%). This sub-sector is well integrated with the food industry and is subject to constant market adaptions.

This group has its greatest presence in Central Plateau regions, where there are from 40 to 80 cows per km^2.

Dairy farms. 1995	
Dairy cows	454,000
Dairy farms	61,000
No. of farms with less than 10 heads	25,000 (est.)
No. of farms with more than 10 heads	36,000 (est.)
Cows per farm	7.4
Milk produced per cow	4,647
Average price paid (pts/l)	47.66

- Omnivore and granivore (pig, rabbit and poultry) farms have developed unequally. Galicia was once the leading Spanish producer of pork, but has now been displaced by other communities.

- Market trends have greatly reduced the consumption of eggs, which has led to a reduction of egg-laying hens since the eighties.

- Poultry production is still on the increase in Galicia and is becoming more and more important on a national scale.

- These landless farms are unevenly distributed throughout Galicia, but chicken and egg production is concentrated in the Ourense region.

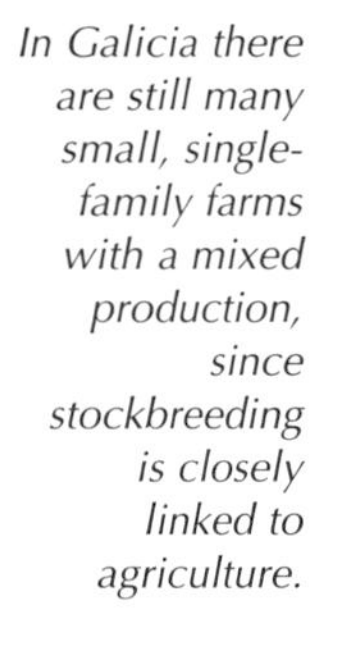

In Galicia there are still many small, single-family farms with a mixed production, since stockbreeding is closely linked to agriculture.

FORESTRY.

Galicia boasts magnificent conditions for forestry production, with high average increases. However, Galicia's forests are subject to very different climatic conditions according to the region.

The form of forestry ownership (individual and community) has influenced the present degree of capitalization and management system.

Forestry production. 1992	
Timber	78% of total production
Pasture for livestock	6%
Mushrooms and wild fruits	6%
Hunting and fishing	6%
Firewood	2%

Forestry, including lake and river fishing, and hunting, makes up 1% of the autonomous gross domestic product.

Timber produced in Galicia. 1995

Variety	Percentage (%)
Maritime or Galician pine	43%
Eucalyptus	41%
Radial pine	10%
Scotch pine, oak, chestnut, birch...	6%

Export/import ratio of 1/5.
Production/import ratio of 5/1.
Galician timber production represents 35% of Spanish total.

Forestry depends on the climate:

- Maritime pine grows in the Miño valley in Ourense and the river basins of the Atlantic coast.
- Radial pine is predominant in the Terra Chá region, below a height of 500 m. It is also present in mixed forests in Atlantic coast basins with minor water shortages.
- Scotch pine is found in the Lugo and Ourense mountains.
- The most abundant oak species are well suited to the Galician climate.
- Chestnut trees remain in inland mountainous areas.

XVI

FISHING, SHELLFISH AND AQUICULTURE

- Favourable conditions.
- Fishing legislation.
- Importance of fishing in Galicia.
- Shellfish.
- Aquiculture.
- Training and research centres.

FISHING, SHELLFISH AND AQUICULTURE.

Galician is Spain's leading fishing region due to:
- Volume of fish presently unloaded in its ports.
- Important fleet.
- Number of jobs generated.

FAVOURABLE CONDITIONS.

• The following geographical-biological conditions favour the development of fishing in Galicia:
- Galicia's situation in the rich North Atlantic fishing area.
- The great length of Galicia's broken coastline.
- The richness of its rias, ideal places for the growth of many species.
- The abundance of plankton.
- The beneficial influence of sea currents.
- Deep-water outcrops, with a high concentration of mineral salts, in the rias.

• Galicia's continental shelf is narrow, with a width ranging from 20 to 35 km. The total surface area, from Ribadeo to A Guarda, is 10,000 km^2. This negative factor is compensated by the favourable fish-habitat conditions.

Galicia's fishing policy is aimed at making full use of its abundant natural resources, without provoking their exhaustion or decline. It coincides with the European Union's Common Fishing Policy, which implements the following basic points:

a) Increasing the productivity of the primary section, by promoting technical progress and guaranteeing the rational development of the production, especially the work.
b) Guaranteeing a suitable standard of living for the fishing community by increasing the individual income of the people involved.

c) Establishing prices.
d) Guaranteeing the availability of supplies.
e) Guaranteeing that supplies reach consumers at reasonable prices.

In order to fulfill these objectives, the following measures will be implemented:

- Recuperating and conserving resources.
- Renewing and modernizing the fleet, fish product transformation industries and aquiculture installations.
- Professionalizing fishing for shellfish and transforming it into semi-farming.
- Stamping out poaching.
- Controlling water quality.
- Restructuring nautical-fishing education.
- Modernizing training and research centres and creating new ones.
- Enabling the modernization of the fishing sector to make it competitive.

FISHING LEGISLATION.

Galicia's Fishing Law is indispensable since Spain lacks a basic law in this field. The law is complemented by:

- The decree regulating fishing activities and authorized methods and equipment in Galicia.
- Decrees related to the commercialization of fish products.

These legal instruments led to a positive evolution of the sector. Other decrees renewed fishing structures, created the Ship Register and Register of Fish-Food Companies, approved the Floating Bed Regulations, and established quality Galician fish, shellfish and aquiculture products. The legal corpus also includes the law on infringements in the field of maritime-fishing resource protection and the law regulating fishing associations.

A large part of Galicia's fishing fleet is made up of coastal fishing boats. This kind of fishing is mainly family-based, using traditional methods and complemented by other activities.

Evolution of Galicia's fishing fleet.

Spain's fishing fleet has undergone a restructuring process oriented towards its modernization and viability. Galicia has followed a parallel path. Nevertheless, Galicia's relative importance with regard to Spain seems to be increasing total GRT, total power and the number of crew members. Galicia's industrial fleet has developed strongly in the last decade. Galicia's GRT now exceeds 40% of the national total. The number of crew members in Galician boats may be close to a third of the national total, while the number of Galicians enlisted in the national fishing fleet is close to 40%.

IMPORTANCE OF FISHING IN GALICIA.

Activity	No. of jobs generated
Fishing	41,600
Fish commercialization	6,730
Shellfish	9,200
Aquiculture	13,422
Directly-related services sector	13,000
TOTAL	**83,796**

The most numerous species in Galicia's rias and off its coast are: conger eel, whiting, grouper, pollack, red bream, monkfish, sole, ray, "faneca" cod. At certain times of the year: sardine, tuna, horse mackerel, mackerel. Cod, hake and bonito from distant fishing grounds are unloaded in Galician ports.

Population employed in fishing.

GALICIA TOTAL	**43,500 (4.6%)***	**41,600 (4.5%)**

**Percentage of working population employed in fishing.*

Galician fishing sector in terms of production.

	Million pesetas
Galicia's GDP	3,700,000
Value of fishing production	132,000
Fishing's proportion of Galicia's GDP	3.5%

Fishing fleet.

No. of boats	8,811
GRT	254,279
Power (hp)	895,748

SHELLFISH.

The habitat of Galicia's rias and coastline is ideal for producing shellfish, which is highly prized due to its quality and variety of species, including many that are highly valued commercially, such as oysters, scallops, goose barnacles, shrimps, lobsters, clams and different kinds of crabs.

Thousands of people fish for shellfish almost all year round. Fishing on foot is a residual activity. In order to take advantage of existing fishing resources, it is necessary to professionalize an activity that has been carried out almost in a hunting fashion.

The professionalization process started between 1990 and 1992, with the establishment of a new system of fishing, complemented by a programme for recuperating impoverished areas and the promotion of another incentive one dealing with the treatment and activities of shellfish beds, designed to make fishermen aware of their responsibility as regards substrate cleaning and removal, rinsing and sowing. Fishermen have to change from mere harvesters to cultivators.

A Department of Fishing, Shellfish and Aquiculture programme has multiplied production. Plan 10 or Plan Galicia aims at triplicating the income of around 9,200 people employed in bivalve mollusk fishing in Galicia.

Water quality centres.

Shellfish production requires controlling the environment in which species are bred, since the markets are becoming more and more demanding as regards the products entering them and community regulations set requirements regarding shellfish production.

The Department of Fishing, Shellfish and Aquiculture employs three maritime environment control networks:

- To detect and monitor toxic phytoplankton.
- To control bio-toxins in mollusks.
- To determine water quality.

AQUICULTURE.

Aquiculture or fish-farming refers to breeding fish and shellfish in enclosed sea or river installations.

Galicia already produces a large quantity of turbot, salmon, trout, mussels and oysters. Aquiculture is a technological innovation with a bright future.

TRAINING AND RESEARCH CENTRES.

Training is a key factor in order to deal successfully with the constant changes arising in the fishing sector. Research is indispensable for the associated industry. The Administration is concentrating on providing the 10 training and research centres with the best possible equipment.

Polytechnic Maritime-Fishing Institute of the Atlantic (Vigo).
This centres provides:

- First- and second-grade regulated education in the maritime-fishing branch with the following specialities: navigation and fishing, cabotage navigation and naval mechanics.
- Advanced course of regulated maritime-fishing vocational training.
- Permanent adult-training programmes, and refresher and specialized occupational training courses.

Official Nautical-Fishing School of Ferrol.
This centre teaches all the subjects included in the comprehensive training of future nautical professionals. It is equipped with the following: mechanical, oil-hydraulic and pneumatic technology teaching equipment; navigation, fishing and machine-room simulators; sea engines, library and a fully equipped administration unit. It also offers a safety, survival and fire-fighting course.

Crew members:

- First-class coastal fishing captain and deep-sea fishing captain, in the navigation and fishing speciality.
- First- and second-class naval mechanic; and cabotage captain, in the cabotage navigation speciality.

Official Nautical-Fishing School of Santa Uxía de Ribeira.
It offers the three regulated maritime-fishing training courses of the naval mechanics speciality's second-grade training course. It also offers a permanent adult-training course. The centre is equipped with installations for teaching about nets, electricity, refrigeration, safety and hygiene, a machine-room simulator, a navigation simulator, laboratories and 7 theory classrooms.

Galician Aquiculture Training Institute (IGAFA) in A Illa de Arousa.
The development of Galicia's traditional aquiculture, with the incorporation of new cultivated products, requires training plans for the sector's technicians and workers. This centre provides hands-on and experimental training in aquiculture.

Safety and Rescue Educational Centre of Ferrol.
It is the first of its kind in Spain. The centre, which forms part of the Official Nautical-Fishing School of Ferrol, is equipped with the necessary infrastructures, resources and materials to provide nautical-fishing students and fishing professionals with the knowledge and training they require regarding on-board safety and survival.

Maritime Research Centre of Corón.
It researches all the fields and matters related to aquiculture, estuary ecology and cultivation conditions of shellfish resources and others. It stands out as a result of its advanced technology and scientific apparatuses, which are on a level with the best of Spain, and even Europe.

Maritime Cultivation Centre of Ribadeo.
It consist of two buildings, one housing laboratories and administration facilities and another with tanks and cultivation installations. Outside there are two clam beds. Its buildings, laboratory material and equipment satisfy criteria of permanent updating as regards research and operational functionality.

Aquiculture Experimentation Centre of Couso.
It was created to satisfy the need of carrying out applied research on maritime cultivation technology. Its advanced installations and modern work methods enable the study and improvement of fish and mollusk farming, both in the experimental and industrial production phases.

Maritime Environment Quality Control Centre (Vilaxoán).
This centre directs the Department of Fishing's control networks regarding bio-toxins in mollusks, toxic phytoplankton and water quality.

Maritime Research Centre. Ria of Arousa.

XVII

MINING

- Mining tradition.
- Mining operations.
- Rocks.
- Energy products.
- Statistics.
- Mineral water.
- Exportation.

MINING.

"Among the Galicians in the north, the soil has veins of silver, tin and gold mixed with silver."
Estrabón

MINING TRADITION.

Galicia has always been sought after by the peoples of distant cultures, in order to obtain its mineral resources.

Helmet from Leiro. Archaeological Museum of A Coruña. Torques, bracelets, diadems, necklaces, rings, combs, helmets and vessels are the most frequent gold pieces from the Celtic period.

The Tartessians, the Phoenicians, the Romans... knew about the existence of tin, lead and gold in Galicia's soil and subsoil. Such resources are confirmed by the discovery of numerous pieces of jewellery, which are now housed in Galicia's museums.

The Greek historian Avienus spoke about the Casiterides Islands (perhaps the Cíes or Sisargas Islands) and their abundance of tin and lead.

The intense trade that was established between Mediterranean cultures and the North-West Iberian Peninsula influenced the inhabitants of those regions. The discovery of numerous utensils with diverse applications and pieces of jewellery confirms the development of metalworking.

Thus, Galicia became famous for its tin and presently produces 90% of the Spanish total.

From the Middle Ages to the end of the 19th century, iron ore was extracted to make tools and arms. More recently, tin, arsenic, antimony, wolfram, kaolin, lignite, quartz and titanium were extracted.

Galicia has large reserves of iron, lead, magnesite, titanium and garnet.

Wolfram production represents 40% of the Spanish total; since its importance has declined, a large part is now exported.

Iron ore reserves represent 30% of the Spanish total. The numerous deposits are spread throughout the north, centre and east of Galicia.

Minerals being mined.

MINING OPERATIONS.

Galicia's mining resources are not being fully exploited; with its present deposits, Galicia could become Spain's leading producer of coal, tin, copper, titanium, wolfram, kaolin, cyanite, quartz, dunite and industrial slate; its second producer of zinc and third of lead.

Most extracted minerals are exported to other parts of Spain or abroad in a raw state. Galicia thereby loses the opportunity of creating wealth and jobs. This is true in the case of wolfram, zinc, copper, quart and tin.

ROCKS.

Rock extraction deserves special mention. In Galicia granite, slate and clay are exploited.

Granite.

It is the dominant rock in western Galicia. It is extracted from open-cast mines: quarries. Although it is a very hard rock, it can be broken up into the following components: quartz, which can be used to provide find sand for white beaches; mica, which forms clay; feldspar, which also forms clay, especially kaolin.

The importance of granite is the result of a stonemasonry tradition and the fact that 90% of the granite produced in Spain is from Galician quarries, especially those in O Porriño, where the pink variety is extracted.

The numerous varieties of Galician granite are extracted from small mines, with a deficient employment of technology. Most granite is exported in a raw state, i.e. without being transformed.

Stone cross.

A large number of traditionally designed works have been sculptured in granite: crosses, granaries, Romanesque churches...

Slate.

Slate is predominant in eastern Galicia. Slate extraction has acquired great economic importance. Thousands of tonnes are extracted from open-cast mines for exportation. Slate is transformed in Galicia into manufactured products and exported to countries from different continents. Almost 50% of Spanish production is from Galicia.

Slate has traditionally been used for hearths, sarcophagus lids, public paving, boundary walls; it was also used in Lugo's Roman ramparts, but especially to roof houses. It is presently used in roofs, surfaces, facades, decorations and garden ornamentation.

85% of Spanish production is from the mines in the Sil, Ortigueira and A Fonsagrada valleys.

In construction it has the following advantages: inalterable colour, indefinite conservation of facades' initial aspect, eliminates the need for double walls due to its high heat insulation...

Open-cast slate mine. Valdeorras region.

Clay.

Galicia produces 50% of all Spanish clay. It is extracted from open-cast mines called "barreiras" and a fair amount is transformed here into roof tiles, fireproof bricks and floor tiles, crockery, kitchen pots, decorative objects...

Kaolin from Burela and Cervo, highly valued due to their exceptional purity, are used to make fine porcelain in factories such as Sargadelos-O Castro.

Clay has given rise to *baked clay* industries located near clay deposits.

ENERGY PRODUCTS.

Lignite is mined from the As Pontes de García Rodríguez and Meirama deposits, where it is used to produce electricity in the nearby power stations.

STATISTICS.

Galician mining represents 12% of the Spanish total.

GALICIAN MINING. 1995

	Mines	Production (million tonnes)
Energy products	2	10.67
Non-metallic products	29	0.60
Ornamental rock	184	1.55
Quarry products	137	19.50
TOTALS	**352**	**32.32**

	Production
Value of production before 1st transformation	63,211(1)
Proportion of Galician GDP	2.02%
Proportion of Spanish mining	14.40%
Value of production after 1st transformation	90,000(1)
Direct employment	6,550
Indirect employment	11,000

(1) Million pesetas

Most significant productions	Million tonnes
Lignite	10,675
Ornamental slate	305
Ornamental granite	1,186
Kaolin	118
Metallurgic quartz	315
Clays	585
Dunite	725
Feldspar	90
Magnesite	54
Aggregates	19,500

Mining resources according to latest estimates	Million tonnes
Lignite	374.5
Gold	0.86
Copper	20.13
Tin	57.23
Wolfram	24.00
Iron	93.50
Niobium/tantalum	0.04
Kaolin	24.00
Feldspar	8.00
Quartz	94.60
Magnesite	13.00
Peat	1.00
Ornamental granite	115.05
Ornamental slate	72.90 (m^3)
Serpentine	17.00

MINERAL WATER.

This sub-sector has 42 mines in Galicia, of which 22 produce mineral-medicinal water for therapeutic use in spas or bathhouses, one produces mineral-industrial water and 19 produce bottled natural mineral water.

Galicia's production of bottled water makes up 7% of the national total, i.e. around 160 million litres annually.

EXPORTATION.

Galicia's exports of raw mineral materials amount to 44,000 million pesetas, i.e. 14% of all Galician exports, with ornamental slate, ornamental granite, metallurgic quartz and kaolin exports being the most important.

XVIII

INDUSTRY

- Galician industry.
- Food and agriculture industry.
  - Dairy.
  - Meat.
  - Wine.
  - Other food industries.
- Canning industry.
- Animal feed industry.
- Wood industry.
- Granite and slate industry.
- Textile industry.
- Car industry.
- Ship industry.
- Crafts.
- European Projects.

INDUSTRY.

GALICIAN INDUSTRY.

Galicia has a low degree of industrialization. Galician industry is characterized by smallholding land division, an outdated structure, weak links between the different industrial sectors and an unbalanced localization. Neither is it integrated with the primary sector, since there are no transformation industries for its abundant horticultural products, nor does it have a complete production cycle, as is the case of wood, which is only used to produce wood pulp.

However, cooperation and competitiveness is being encouraged among the main sectors of Galicia's economy, such as the car, granite, maritime, slate and aluminium industries. Other important sectors, by virtue of their financial power, are electricity production, shipbuilding, the canning industry, the wood industry, meat and dairy production, and the clothing industry.

FOOD AND AGRICULTURE INDUSTRY.

The food industry derived from agricultural products is economically important, since it contributes more to the gross domestic product than agriculture and stockbreeding together. Galicia's food and agriculture industry represents 6.3% of the sector's national total.

-Dairy industry.

The dairy sector consists of a large number of companies, some of which are cooperatives. However, their number is decreasing while the transformation and turnover of some groups is increasing. Thus, 10 companies alone account for 70% of the turnover.

77% of the milk delivered to industry is transformed in Galicia.

- *Meat industry.*
The meat industry has not been highly developed; it has an export-import trade deficit.

The main meat industries are located in Ourense, O Porriño and A Coruña. There are many small transformation companies, although 5 large companies produce a high percentage of the sector's total. One Galician group is the leading Spanish company as regards the commercialization of chicken meat and one of the main national food companies in relation to turnover.

- *Wine industry.*
The climate of several Galician regions is well suited to the production of quality wine. Most producers are associated with wines with an "appellation d'origine": Rías Baixas, Ribeiro, Valdeorras, Ribeira Sacra and Monterrei.

- *Other food industries.*
In Galicia there is a lot of activity in this sector with many establishments that produce other foodstuffs. The most important are bakeries and cake shops as regards daily commercialization.

They employ traditional methods and are distributed throughout Galicia. These establishments represent the greatest percentage, within the food and agriculture industry, of the gross domestic product.

CANNING INDUSTRY.

The importance of fishing is Galicia is undeniable, as a generator of direct employment and a driving force of industrial activity.

Galicia's fishing complexes have a high level as regards the processing and handling of fish products. Galicia's refrigeration industry and the occupied population stand out.

Fish processing ranges from mere refrigeration for preservation purposes to the making of prepared dishes.

The fish-product transformation industry has a long tradition in Galicia, starting with sardine canning. The first canning industries were established along Galicia's coast at the end of the 18th century by Catalan businessmen. The industry has developed since then and continues to evolve.

ANIMAL FEED INDUSTRY.

The animal feed industry is well developed, due to the demand from landless stockbreeding and dairy farms.

The main factories are related to a large food group from Ourense and a multinational one from Holland. Both of them account for a third of the sector's total turnover. There are also various cooperative factories. The export-import ratio regarding goods and services is 1 to 15.

WOOD INDUSTRY.

Galicia's forestry industry has experienced a strong adaption process in relation to:

- The evolution of wood resources.
- The opening up of wood markets.
- Trade globalization.

The wood industry has great possibilities in Galicia, since forests occupy a third of Galicia's territory. The northwestern forests are made up of quality species such as oak, chestnut, walnut, ash and beech. Repopulation is presently dominated by pine and eucalyptus.

In order to analyze this sector, it is worth differentiating between first- and second-transformation industries.

The first-transformation industry is represented by a reduced number of large-sized companies that concentrate on production. These companies have an important presence in international markets, higher even than those in the rest of Spain. They base their competitiveness on technological initiatives oriented at automation and the possibility of creating new products.

On the other hand, the second-transformation industry is divided into a large number of small- and medium-sized companies, the majority of which are family businesses and highly dispersed geographically. They suffer the typical problems of small- and medium-sized companies:

- Difficult access to capital markets.
- Low negotiating strength with suppliers and customers.
- Lack of scale economies.
- High costs.
- Absence of research and development.

In Galicia's first-transformation industries, saw mills stand out from timber and wood pulp factories. The saw mills are the most traditional industries and the best suited to Galicia's forestry conditions.

Nevertheless, they are decreasing in number; they presently supply 36% of the sawn timber consumed by the national market.

The timber industry (boards, fibres, particles, medium density, panels, strips and plywood) has eighteen production lines. The wood pulp industry in Galicia has a factory that consumes a million cubic metres of eucalyptus wood.

GRANITE AND SLATE INDUSTRY.

Granite and slate are ornamental rocks that abound in Galicia, with a predominance of granite in the west and slate in the east.

This industry has a strong presence in international markets, on which it depends. Its technological initiatives of recent years have been oriented towards sawing and cutting techniques. There are excellent possibilities of creating a prosperous industry with these abundant but exhaustible resources.

TEXTILE INDUSTRY.

Galicia's textile industry is in a strong condition since:
- It has increased its market share.
- It has increased its investment per job.
- It has a well-qualified labour force.
- It offers a varied product for the different market sectors.

Galician fashion.

Until the beginning of the eighties, Spain was a mere fashion watcher - impassive, silent and surprised at the kind of sociocultural phenomenon that came from such highly esteemed neighbours as France and Italy. Some even interpreted the invasion that filled our screens and magazines as an evidence of our European partner's industrial and commercial power.

However, the Spanish authorities soon began to give consideration to this phenomenon arising from Europe's most established culture. They realized that our country should also participate in this grand show combining art and commerce. And at the same time, all the Autonomous Communities enthusiastically embarked upon the same pursuit of modernity.

Years later, looking back at the unequal effect of those initiatives, we may conclude that the general impression about fashion has changed, perhaps due to the existence of local brands and designs. Undoubtedly, it is precisely in Galician fashion where the change in ideas and structures is most noticeable.

The textile sector, which the majority of economists and technologists considered to be a field with scarce innovation possibilities, experienced a genuine creative revolution in barely a decade.

The essence of fashion, the basis of the finished product, is based on quality workmanship, on knowledge passed down from generation to generation and on creations that almost look as if they have been handcrafted. The figure of the *"costureiriña"* (seamstress) immediately comes to the mind of any Galician who hears something about Galician fashion -she appears as a relative, a friend or merely a childhood memory.

Galician fashion was founded on exquisite workmanship, careful and faultless creations, long before quality began to be considered. The first step consisted in giving this phenomenon, which had arisen naturally, a business-like structure. An important role in the transformation was played by family businesses, which, as in many other sectors of Galicia's economy, are the beginning of important industries.

Despite the experts' opinions, it was possible to innovate in the clothing industry, and as soon as this innovation came about, Galician fashion as we know it today was born.

The workmanship was enriched by design, something that regions with a longer textile production tradition have striven for but few have attained. The industry learned to sell, without establishing borders while doing so. Galician fashion is, above all, a phenomenon that knows no limits and does not feel small in international markets. A fashion show is the same anywhere, whether in Ourense, Barcelona or Paris. There is always the same challenge of creative professionalism.

A great brand-based image has been created, but perhaps the most positive aspect of this image is the fact that it arose from a common effort. The phenomenon of associationism in Galician fashion is undoubtedly an innovative experience within the Galician business world.

CAR INDUSTRY.

It is mainly located in Vigo and the surroundings, centred on the Citroën Hispania, S.A. company and the different auxiliary car-related industries, as well several companies that manufacture chassis and specialized vehicles, which are situated in different areas of Galicia.

The main auxiliary industry companies are presently grouped together in a cluster that has recently been formed under the name CEAGA.

At present it is the industry with the highest growth in Galicia's economy, as regards both its employment figures and its sales outside the Autonomous Community.

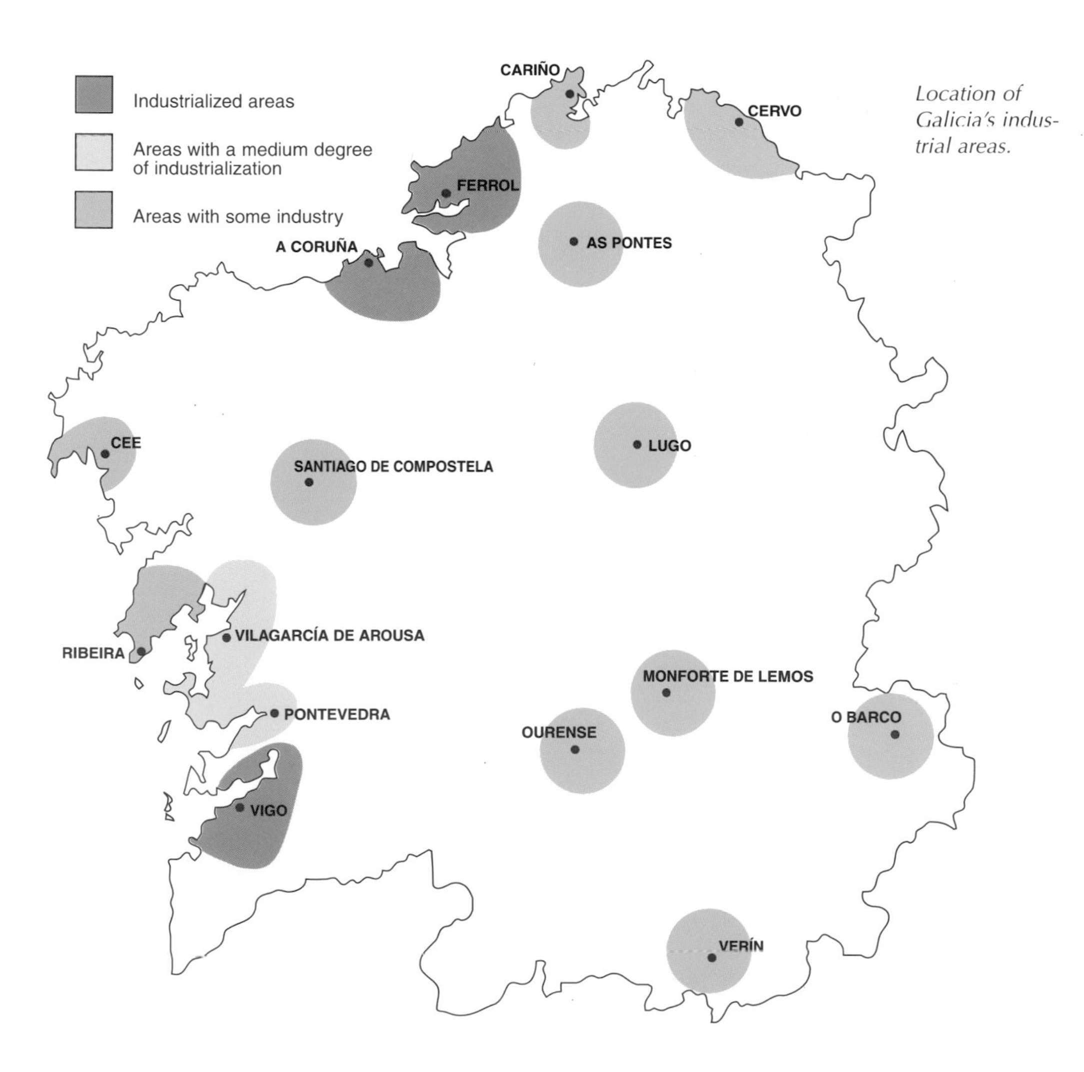

Location of Galicia's industrial areas.

SHIP INDUSTRY.

After experiencing the crisis of the early nineties, with unequally distributed effects, Galician shipyards in general now have their order books filled will enough work until the end of the decade.

In order to increase the guarantees offered by new work orders placed with Galicia's shipyards, the Galician Administration has signed agreements with PYMAR (Reconversion Society of Small- and Medium-sized Shipyards), thereby contributing to the Patrimonial Fund of Guarantees and making it possible to supplement the sureties obtained by the shipyards upon signing contracts for new projects.

In order to maintain the sector's competitiveness, the creation of a ship building cluster has been promoted, by taking advantage of the synergies produced by company cooperation, and should be established by mid-1998.

Since 1996 the Autonomous Administration has formed part of the Administration Councils of the three public shipyards with factories in Galicia. Due to a worsening in market conditions, ASTANO, which has a prestigious reputation in the off-shore sector, is undergoing a period of adaption and intense commercial activity. BARRERAS is the most profitable public shipyard and its order book is filled until 1999. The formalizing of the contracts of the F-100 frigates and second LPD ship have guaranteed BAZAN's work until the year 2005.

Alumina-aluminium factory on the Bay of Biscay coast.

CRAFTS.

Craftsmanship is important to Galicia, for economic reasons and as part of its cultural heritage. It employs more than 5,000. Galicia's Craftsmanship Law enabled:

- The creation of the Galician Craftsmanship Commission.
- The establishment of Galicia's General Register of Craftsmen.
- The regulation of the conditions and requirements in order to obtain a craftsman's licence and craft workshop certification.
- The establishment of the Craftsmanship Centre of Lugo.

The Craftsmanship Project, for the 1995-99 period, carried out a study of the craft sector, produced a Craftsmanship Guide of Galicia, a CD-ROM, a commercialization catalogue and a video about crafts.

The following craft sectors have a long tradition in Galicia: jewellery, lace, tapestry, dressmaking, leather goods, pottery, carpentry, brassware...

EUROPEAN PROJECTS.

The Galician Autonomous Administration is involved in important European projects:

ESTREIRA Project (Regional Innovation Strategy).
During its 18-month duration it aims at drawing up an innovation strategy to direct technological policies, under the consensus of the public authorities, private sector and universities.

QUALYMAN Project.
Within the framework of the ADAPT Community Initiative 1995-97, this project was created to administer human resources under quality criteria in order to optimize the competitiveness of Galician companies, paying special attention to the small- and medium-sized ones (PYMES).

Handcrafted objects are still being produced despite having to compete with industrial production.

XIX

INFRAESTRUCTURES, TOWN PLANNING AND HOUSING

- Roads.
- Railways.
- Ports.
- Airports.
- Water resourcess.
- Energy.
  - Electricity distribution.
  - Natural gas.
  - Renewable energy sources.
  - Wind power.
  - Small-scale hydroelectric projects.
  - Other renewable energy sources.
- Housing policy.
- Autonomous housing policy.
  - Public housing.
  - Rehabilitation and improvement.
  - Rural rehabilitation.
  - Other programmes.

INFRASTRUCTURES.

The creation of infrastructures is fundamental for industrial development.

Infrastructures	
Roads Ports Airports Railways	Industrial land Information and communication technology Energy: Electricity Natural gas Renewable energy sources

ROADS.

Spain's becoming a member of the European Union required the urgent modernization of communication networks in order to improve our economy's competitiveness.

GALICIA'S ROAD NETWORK.

GROUPS	CLASSIFICATION	ROUTE
Atlantic axis	A-9 motorway N-550 road	Ferrol-A Coruña-Santiago-Pontevedra - Vigo-Portugal
North-West dual carriageway	A-6	A Coruña - Lugo - Benavente
Rías Baixas dual carriageway	A-52	Vigo - Ourense - Benavente
Autonomous road network	Autonomous	Throughout Galicia
High-capacity roads	Expressway Salnés expressway Motorway Barbanza expressway Motorway Central expressway	Ferrol - As Pontes Curro - Sanxenxo A Coruña - Carballo Ribeira - Vacariza Puxeiros - Val Miñor* Monforte - Lalín

**Under construction*

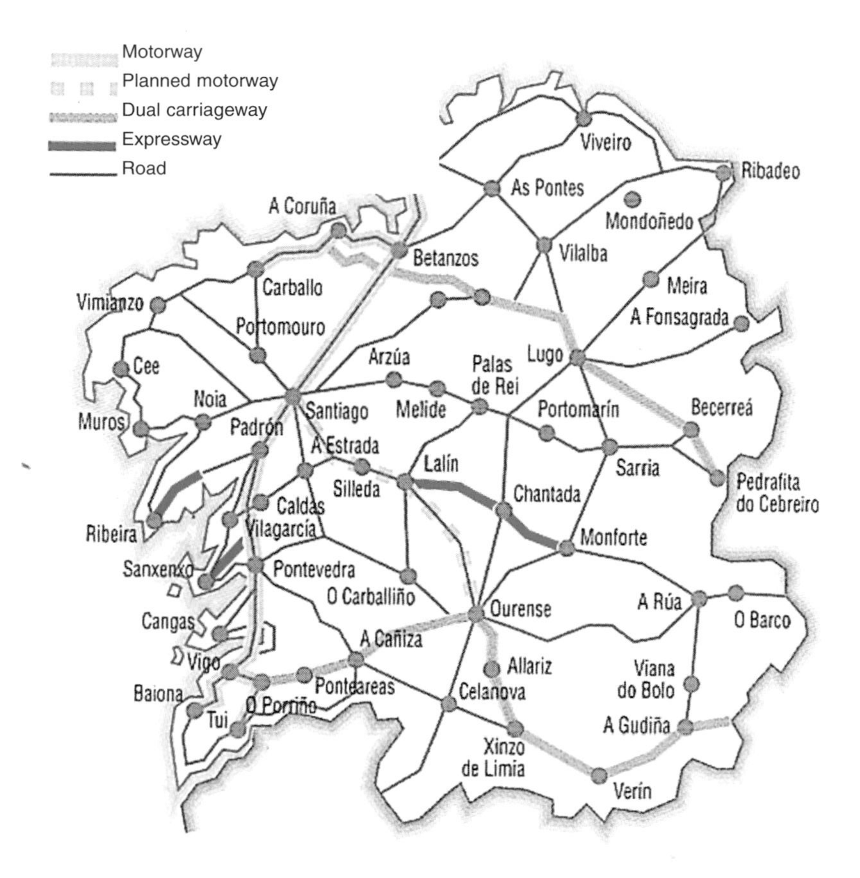

Galicia's Road Plan has improved inter-regional communications and stimulated commerce.

RAILWAYS.

The RENFE network in Galicia is 920 km long, representing 7.5% of the national railway network. It has three exterior connections:

- With Portugal via Tui.
- With Central Spain via Zamora.
- With North and North-East Spain via León.

• Railway network problems.

- Few kilometres of double-track sections.
- Radial conception.
- Very short electrified section: Ponferrada-Monforte and Monforte-Vigo.
- Complex and winding geographical relief:

• Too many sharp bends.
• Slopes steeper than 1.5%.
• High number of tunnels.
• High number of level crossings.

- Technical characteristics:
  - Modern tracks, never more than 30 years old.
  - Restructuring of Vigo-Ourense-Monforte section, with comprehensive track modernization.
  - Modernization of access to Portugal in the Guillarei-Tui-border section.
  - Relatively modern signalling and communication systems, with automatic blocking in single-track sections with centralized traffic control directed from Ourense, for the following sections:
    - Vigo-Ourense-Monforte.
    - Ourense-Puebla de Sanabria.
    - Redondela-Santiago-A Coruña.
    - Ourense-Santiago.
    - Monforte de Lemos-Ponferrada.
  - Along with the RENFE network, there is another network, run by FEVE, with a single coastal route, 153 km in length, between Ferrol and Ribadeo. It is a winding low-speed route, with steep slopes.

PORTS.

Galicia has a very broken coastline, with numerous sheltered areas that provide small natural ports.

Galicia's coastline is 1,309 km long. 52% of the population is situated along the coastal strip. These circumstances have promoted fishing, shellfish and maritime transport activities.

Shipping. Galicia	Total merchandise
Merchandise between Galician ports	35%
Foreign-bound shipping	40%

Note: Other kinds of shipping make up the other 25%.

The port system is important to Galicia's economy because:
- The added value produced by the percentage of the port-dependent industries' activity amounted to 15.6% of the gross added value.
- Fishing and shellfish activities alone directly employ 44,000 people.
- Complementary activities (preparation, transportation and commercialization) also create an important number of jobs.

Galicia's port network		
CLASSIFICATION	**RUN BY**	**NAMES**
5 large ports of general interest	Central State Administration	Ferrol - San Cibrao, A Coruña, Vilagarcía Marín, Vigo.
33 main ports	Autonomous Administration	Ribadeo, Foz, Burela,Celeiro, Cariño, Cedeira, Sada, Malpica, Laxe, Muxía, Camariñas, Cee, Fisterra, Portosín, Muros, Ribeira, A Pobra do Caramiñal, Tragove - Cambados, O Grove, Portonovo, Bueu, Baiona
49 complementary facilities.	Autonomous Administration	

There is an important network of general-interest ports, with suitable docks, shipping services and commercial storage facilities. These ports account for 95% of shipping of energy products, cars, granite, iron and steel, wood, grain, fruit, fertilizers, animal feed, minerals, building materials, chemical products and fish. The ports of Vigo and A Coruña occupy the leading positions in Europe as regards the unloading of fresh and frozen fish.

Their strategic geographical location in relation to the main traditional sea-routes between Europe, America and Asia, means that these ports are potential points of entry into the European market. Such good perspectives must be accompanied by improvements, since the ports need better connections with other means of transport, especially the railway, in order to access Spanish and European markets.

Port of Sta. Uxía de Ribeira, in the Ria of Arousa.

The ports run by the Autonomous Administration stimulate the economy of coastal towns. They generate employment in:

- Fishing and shellfish activities.
- Recreational sailing.
- Urban and tourism development.
- Commercial shipping.

Description of selected ports.

Vigo: It is Galicia's largest fishing port and one of the most important in Europe, especially in deep-sea fishing. The majority of fish-freezing ships, cod-fishing trawlers and factory ships, as well as an important number of trawlers, are based in Vigo. It is less important as a merchant port, although it ships great quantities of cars and granite. Along with A Coruña, and Vilagarcía sporadically, it is visited by large ocean liners during the summer season.

A Coruña: It is Galicia's second fishing port, with an important level of deep-sea and coastal fishing activities. On the other hand, it is Galicia's first as regards merchandise transportation, mainly due to the loading and unloading of oil products.

Ferrol: It is an important commercial port due to the transportation of regional industrial products and materials, mainly related to its shipyards and the As Pontes power station.

Marín: It is another important fishing port oriented towards deep-sea and coastal fishing.

Sta. Uxía de Ribeira: A fishing port in which trawlers, seiner boats and traditional fishing boats are based. It is Spain's leading coastal fishing port.

Vilagarcía de Arousa: A commercial port that stands out in the transportation of dry goods and grain.

Ribadeo: Commercial port, handling general merchandise, whose hinterland extends into the western part of Asturias.

Burela and Celeiro: Important fishing ports.

Cedeira: A tourist resort with a small fishing port and sheltered anchorage. It handles an important amount of recreational sailing.

Sada: A mixed port with commercial, fishing and sports activities.

Malpica, Laxe, Muxía, Camariñas and Fisterra: Typical fishing ports on the Costa da Morte.

Cee: A commercial port with a suitable area for recreational boats in Corcubión, 2 km away.

Portosín: A fishing port and marina with a Yacht Club. It has 150 berths for recreational boats, along with the corresponding services.

Muros: It has a fish market and docks for trawlers.

A Pobra do Caramiñal: An important port due to the amount of frozen fish unloaded there. It is also an important base for unloading mussels and has floating berths for recreational boats.

Tragove-Cambados: A fishing port that provides services for 160 floating mussel and oyster beds.

O Grove: A fishing and shellfish port with floating jetties for recreational boats.

Portonovo: A fishing port with suitable anchorage for recreational boats. Sanxenxo, a tourist resort where recreational boats anchor, is 2 km away.

Bueu: A fishing and shellfish port that provides services for floating mussel and oyster beds.

Baiona: A fishing port in a touristic region. Its Yacht Club, which is highly regarded throughout Spain, provides services for 320 boats.

AIRPORTS.

Galicia has three airports for commercial flights:

- Lavacolla, 10 km from the centre of Santiago.
- Peinador, 8 km from the centre of Vigo.
- Alvedro, 8 km from the centre of A Coruña.

Airports and selected ports of Galicia.

Airports. 1996			
	Lavacolla	**Peinador**	**Alvedro**
Passengers	**1,295,339**	**441,219**	**370,000**
Percentage of passengers leaving from and returning to Galicia.	60%	25%	15%

Among Spanish airports, Lavacolla is number 14 in merchandise and number 16 in aircraft and passengers.

The three airports have the main navigation systems at their disposal.

Galicia's airports are easily reached from the different regions of demand, which makes air travel very competitive for short and mid-range distances. The airports' operational capacities have been improved in the last decade, with runway extensions, the installation of navigation systems and the construction of better-equipped terminals.

WATER RESOURCES.

Water is a scarce natural resource and, as such, should be administered. Galicia's Water Administration Law of 1983 created the autonomous *Galician Waters* organism, with the following functions:

- Administering the sewage treatment tax.
- Water resource planning.
- Galician sewage plan.

• Water resource planning.

This aims at satisfying demands on water, balancing and harmonizing regional and sectorial development by increasing water availability, protecting water quality and rationalizing its usage in harmony with the environment and other natural resources.

As regards water administration, Galicia is involved in two different territorial groups:

- Inter-community hydrographic basins in Galicia and other neighbouring communities: Eo, Navia and Miño/Sil river basins.
- Intra-community hydrographic basins: all other river basins of the Bay of Biscay and Atlantic coasts.

• Galician sewage plan.
The Community Regulation 91/271 regarding urban sewage treatment established objectives that called for sectorial sewage planning. The Autonomous Community drew up Galicia's Sewage Plan, which should result in improved water quality.

ENERGY.

An energy policy is fundamental for economic and social development. Basic energy planning has already been carried out by means of Galicia's Energy Plan, aimed at rationalizing the sector as regards its different fields: exploitation, production, distribution and usage.

- Electricity distribution.
The Mega Plan, 1990, coordinates the electrical companies operating in Galicia: Unión Fenosa, Begasa and small distributors grouped together in APYDE.

Thanks to this plan, the lack of electricity will no longer hold back industrial development, since any company will be able to establish itself wherever it wishes.

The tertiary sector may now enjoy the advantages of efficient electrical installations and rural population centres may now have public lighting and water supplies.

- Natural gas.
Natural gas is presently being developed comprehensively throughout the Galician Community, so that it may be used by all sectors of the market: domestic, commercial, institutional, industrial, heat and electricity co-production, petrochemical applications.

The initial gas supply for North-West Spain is the Maghreb-Europe pipeline, via Portugal. Connection with the national network of gas pipelines is being completed via Asturias.

The infrastructure is presently under construction and will have the following characteristics:

Section	Length km
Main gas pipeline Tui-Vilalba-Ribadeo	**277**
Networks and branch pipelines to Tui, Vigo-Ourense, Pontevedra, Pontecesures-Catoira, Santiago, Lugo, A Coruña and Ferrol	342

The Repsol butane gas company is in charge of small distributions in towns and villages that are far from the natural gas network.
A propane-air mixture is presently being distributed in Lugo, Santiago, Ourense and Ferrol as a natural gas substitute until the construction work is completed. Propane gas is being distributed in Foz, Sarria and Cuntis. The number of users amounts to 10,000 inhabitants.

- Renewable energy sources.
The increase in energy consumption will worsen environmental problems, which makes it necessary to promote renewable energy sources.

The European Union's Commission has set the objective, for the year 2010, of producing 15% of primary energy from renewable energy sources. Galicia already produces 25% of Spain's renewable energy.

- Wind power.
Galicia enjoys excellent conditions for wind power production. The Strategic Wind Power Plan is the instrument created by the Xunta de Galicia in order to guarantee the full and harmonious exploitation of this natural resource.

The Wind Power Plan is presently being fully developed. Three wind farms (Malpica, A Capelada and A Barbanza) are already functioning, representing more than 50 MW of installed power. We should mention four other wind farms (Coriscada, As Paxareiras I, As Paxareiras II and Zas) whose construction is now nearing completion, which will produce more than 80 MW, as well as others whose construction is about to begin, with a total power output of around 100 MW.

- Small-scale hydroelectric projects.
Galicia is Spain's second community as regards small-scale hydroelectric production.

Wind farm in Malpica, on the Costa da Morte. Galicia has excellent wind-power possibilities.

-Other renewable energy sources.
Studying the possibility of developing the biomass is important to Galicia. The construction of a biomass power station in now being completed in Allariz.

Galicia is also experimenting with the exploitation of geothermal energy, wind or tidal power, and solar energy, but there is a lack of technological maturity in order to extend their usage.

TOWN PLANNING AND HOUSING.

"All Spaniards have the right to enjoy a decent and suitable home."
Spanish Constitution. Article 47.

HOUSING POLICY.

In 1985 the jurisdiction of housing matters was transferred to the Autonomous Community of Galicia and in 1988 the Galician Institute of Housing and Land Use was created, being an autonomous commercial and financial organism in charge of implementing land-use and housing policy.

The Xunta de Galicia wants each municipal district to have its own town planning regulations. Of the 315 town councils, 29 have a General Urban Regulation Plan, 164 have Subsidiary Regulations and 38 have Urban Land Demarcation.

AUTONOMOUS HOUSING PROGRAMME.

The Xunta de Galicia collaborates with the Central Government in the administration and financing of the Four-Year Housing and Land Use Plan, which aims at filling a large section of the population's need for a home, specifically those families whose calculated income does not exceed 5.5 times the interprofessional minimum wage.

Drawn up by the Ministry of Public Works in collaboration with the Autonomous Communities, the Galician Institute of Housing and Land Use played an important role in applying the 1992-95 Plan in our Community, by way of its administration capacity and the quantity of resources contributed to subsidize specific operations.

The Four-Year Plans, designed to fill Spain's global needs, proved to be deficient from the outset. The Xunta de Galicia immediately set about correcting the situation by means of its own plans with regard to public housing projects, the rehabilitation of rural homes, the eradication of shanty dwellings, benefits for large families (more than four children), rented homes for old people, etc.

The Autonomous Administration established subsidies for first-time home-buyers and buyers of public-sector (general category) homes whose calculated family income does not exceed 2.5 times the interprofessional minimum wage.

Public housing.
Public-sector housing fulfills the objective in Galician of providing low-income sectors of the population with the opportunity of owning a decent home.

It also provides an important number of high-quality homes at a reasonable market price and functions as a price-regulation mechanism.

With the creation, in the framework of four-year state plans, of the special category, many Autonomous Communities stopped investing their own resources in public housing. In Galicia public housing continued to be promoted and was complemented by private-sector housing under the special category. Consequently, the number of homes for families whose calculated income does not exceed 2.5 times the interprofessional minimum wage, has been increasing year after year.

A new set of technical regulations was also drawn up in order to establish the minimum quality requirements for public-sector housing. It is presently being applied to the construction of public housing.

Public-sector housing is one of the Administration's priority objectives.

Rehabilitation and improvement.
Since 1990 more than half of the transferred homes, many of which are fairly old and all of which are of poor quality, have been rehabilitated and improved.

Rural rehabilitation.
Rural housing initiatives are a priority in a community such as Galicia, with a widespread population. In these circumstances, it is only possible to carry out customized projects, financed by autonomous government money, since the benefits established in the Four-Year Plan do not satisfy rural needs.

Since 1987 a programme of rural home rehabilitation has been functioning in Galicia. It was further invigorated in 1990, which has led to a substantial increase in the number of projects and contributed funds.

From 1990 to 1996 the Xunta de Galicia contributed 10,000 million pesetas to 31,000 projects, with an average subsidy of 33%.

One of the challenges facing the Xunta de Galicia is the recuperation and rehabilitation of rural homes.

Other programmes.
Other initiatives financed by autonomous government funds are benefits for large families (more than four children), the eradication of shanty dwellings, substandard rural housing, DIY rural construction, rented homes for people over 60 and young people, etc.

All of these initiatives are designed to provide solutions for housing problems experienced by certain sectors of society, i.e. those with low incomes or all kinds of added difficulties.

XX

TRADE AND CONSUMPTION

- Past and present.
- Quality Galician.
- Domestic agricultural trade.
- Fishing trade.
- Foreign agricultural trade.
- Consumption.
  - Consumer protection.
  - Galician Institute of Consumption.

TRADE AND CONSUMPTION.

"Galicia has exclusive jurisdiction in the matter of domestic trade and consumer and user protection."
Autonomy Statute. Article 30.1.4.

PAST AND PRESENT.

Commerce has traditionally been carried out in Galicia by means of fairs and markets. Markets are usually held weekly or fortnightly, with a small area of influence and specialized in certain products. Fairs are generally less frequent, with a larger area of influence and a variety of products. With the improvement of rural communications, some commercial areas became less important, while others remained the same or were given a boost. Traditional and modern commerce presently coexist together.

Characteristics of Galician commerce.

- Abundance of small, non-specialized, single-family establishments.
- High prices due to the reduced turnover.
- Low level of professional training among many shopkeepers.
- Presence of large shopping centres in the main cities.

Galicia's jurisdiction in the matter of trade is to be exercised according to autonomy and general economic regulations, the State's monetary policy and the European Single Agreement, which established the single domestic market in 1993.

Promotion and Modernization Plan for Galicia's Commercial Sector.
This plan, which took effect in 1994, establishes measures for:

- Adapting traditional commerce to the demands of present-day economic circumstances.
- Adjusting structures to new commercial distribution formulae.
- Providing Galician society with supply services and a diversified supply.

These measures are implemented by initiatives such as the following:

- Renewal and improvement of commercial infrastructures and commercial town planning.
- Training, information, advice and technical assistance for the sector's businessmen and workers.
- Promoting the commercial sector.
- Encouraging associationism.

Small, specialized shops sell high-quality products.

QUALITY GALICIAN.

The 1991 institutional campaign slogan promoting Galician products, *Galicia Calidade (Quality Galician)*, was so successful that in 1994 it was chosen as the name for all Galician products of suitable quality.

Galicia calidade therefore represents global quality and refers to Galician companies, products and services that stand out from their competitors due to their optimum quality.

Up to August 1997 the following had been awarded the Appellation d'Origine "Producto Galego de Calidade" (Quality Galician Product):

"Galicia Calidade" Products

Mel de Galicia. (Galician honey)
Patata de Galicia. (Galician potatoes)
Ternera gallega. (Galician beef)
Orujo de Galicia (Galician eau-de-vie)
Cheeses:
- -Queixo de Arzúa
- -Queixo de San Simón.
- -Queixo de Tetilla..
- -Queixo do Cebreiro.

Wines:
- -Rías Baixas.
- -Ribeiro..
- -Valdeorras.
- -Viño da Terra Ribeira Sacra
- -Monterrei.
- -Viño de Terra Val do Miño.

"Galicia Calidade" Companies
Cooperativas Ourensanas. S.C.L. "COREN" • Poultry. Jesús Alonso, S.A. JEALSA • "Rianxeira" canned fish. Productos Koala, S.A. • Electrical material. Corkscrews. Ice-cube tongs. Champagne stopper. LEYMA, alimentos de Galicia, S.A. • Milk and dairy products. Hijos de Rivera, S.A. • Special "Estrella Galicia" beer.

Galicia Calidade satisfies the needs of small- and medium-sized companies as regards adapting to the demand of markets that are becoming more and more competitive and saturated.

In order to obtain a licence authorizing the use of the *Galicia Calidade* brand, interested companies must:

- Have their registered office and legal residence in Galicia.
- Complete their production cycle in Galicia.

The brand may be awarded to:

- *Companies,* when a product licence is not feasible because the product varies according to fashion, as in the case of textiles and furniture, or because it is a specific service.
- *Products,* when they have permanent characteristics.

Galicia Calidade promotes Galicia's products and image in Galicia, Spain and the rest of the world.

Objectives:

- Protecting typical Galician products.
- Standardizing and promoting their production and industrialization.
- Guaranteeing their quality by means of a Regulatory Organ.
- Product marketing.
- Protecting the name and Guarantee of Origin.

DOMESTIC AGRICULTURAL TRADE.

Spanish market

Galician trade surplus in:	
Dairy products.	Sawn timber.
Animal feed.	Boards.
Rough timber.	Pulp.

Spanish market	
Galician trade deficit in:	
Agricultural products. Meat products. Wine.	Furniture. Paper.

FISHING TRADE.

Treating and handling fish products at the point of origin, from the moment of capture until their delivery to destination markets or distribution centres, is of the utmost importance because:
-This determines how long fresh fish will keep and, therefore, its value.
-The product may be handled and treated so as to increase its added value.

In order to optimize these processes, the following are fundamental:
-*Fish markets,* where part of the fish is commercialized. Fish market deficiencies are being resolved by means of modernization investments and benefits. The *Fishing Information Service* interconnects all the fish markets and enables consultation about species, available quantities, prices...

Galicia's coastline and rias are privileged places for producing shellfish. Such richness is due to the quantity, quality and variety of species, many of which are very highly valued commercially.

-*Handling and preparation facilities.* The European Union has a shortage of fishing products but many species are undervalued and are not easily marketed. The transformation of such products may increase their consumption -Galicia has a long tradition of canning and freezing species such as sardine, tuna, hake, cephalopods...

-*Freezer facilities.* An important sector in Galicia, also because of the employment it generates.

FOREIGN TRADE.

The evolution of Galicia's trade balance in recent years has reflected its economy's progressive internationalization.

Foreign Galician trade. Period 1989-1996			
	Exports (million pts.)	Imports (million pts.)	Balance (million pts.)
1989	244,414	350,831	-106,417
1990	267,658	381,270	-113,992
1991	261,387	403,374	-141,731
1992	278,754	426,757	-148,003
1993	423,903	499,946	-76,043
1994	487,966	593,684	-105,718
1995	562,910	640,211	-77,300
1996	731,582	750,622	-19,039
Variation 96/89	199.32	113.95	

Galician exports increased 200% from 1989 to 1996. Imports increased 114% during the same period. The trade balance, 1989-1996, decreased 82.10%.

SECTORIAL DISTRIBUTION Main exported products		
Sector	**1996**	**% total exports**
Motor vehicles, tractors, mopeds and other land vehicles, their parts and accessories.	269,342	36.82
Shipping or river transportation.	79,962	10.93
Fish and crustaceans, mollusks and other aquatic invertebrates.	65,724	8.98
Manufacture of stone, plaster, cement, asbestos, mica and similar materials.	32,157	4.40
Products of meat, fish, crustaceans, mollusks or other aquatic invertebrates.	25,802	3.53
Mineral fuels, mineral oil and distillation products, bituminous materials, mineral wax.	24,518	3.35
Aluminium and aluminium manufacture.	22,953	3.14
Clothes and clothing accessories, except woollen ones.	21,677	2.96
Timber, charcoal and timber manufacture.	19,514	2.67
Wood pulp or other fibrous cellulose materials, waste paper and coal.	15,662	2.14
SUBTOTAL	**577,311**	**78.91**
TOTAL (million pesetas)	**731,582**	**100**

In 1996 the first ten sectors represented 78.91% of Galicia's total exports.

Growth in 1996.
In 1996 Galicia's exports experienced a 30% increase with regard to the previous year, and imports increased 17%. On a national level, Galicia is the Autonomous Community whose exports have increased the most.

Foreign agricultural trade. Galicia's exported products. 1993

ORDER	PRODUCTS	ORDER	PRODUCTS
1.	Boards.	5.	Drinks.
2.	Beef.	6.	Sawn timber.
3.	Milk and dairy products.	7.	Fruit.
4.	Pork.	8.	Poultry meat.

Main imported products

Sector	1996	%
Motor vehicles, tractors, mopeds and other land vehicles, their parts and accessories.	201,399	26.83
Fish, crustaceans, mollusks or other aquatic invertebrates.	114,919	15.31
Mineral fuels, mineral oil and distillation products, bituminous materials, mineral wax.	110,054	14.66
Nuclear reactors, boilers, machines, mechanical apparatuses and devices, parts for such machines.	66,592	8.87
Timber, charcoal and timber manufacture.	19,663	2.62
Animal feed, food industry waste.	15,947	2.12
Cast iron, iron and steel.	14,735	1.96
Machines, apparatuses and electrical material and their parts.	12,773	1.70
Seeds and oily fruits.	12,574	1.68
Clothes and clothing accessories, except woollen ones.	12,090	1.61
SUBTOTAL	**580,746**	**77.37**
TOTAL (million pesetas)	**750,622**	**100**

Citroën Hispania of Vigo's imports (mainly car parts and accessories) and the nine following sections represent 77.37% of all Galician imports.

In Galicia there is an important amount of intra-industrial trade in sectors such as cars, fishing and textiles, which is progressively bringing us up to the intra-industrial trade levels of other European Union countries.

Mineral fuels (crude oil) is imported by the Repsol company located in A Coruña.

Imported products

ORDER	PRODUCT
1.	Cereals and animal-feed products.
2.	Rough timber, sawn timber and boards.
3.	Pulp and paper.
4.	Plant agricultural products and foodstuffs.
5.	Meat.

Trade relations. 1996

EXPORTS	%
France	27.58
Portugal	17.49
United Kingdom	10.42
Other countries	44.51

IMPORTS	%
France	35.32
Portugal	8.10
United Kingdom	5.42
Other countries	51.16

76.36% of exports went to European Union countries.
64% of imports came from European Union countries.

Regulation of foreign trade.
Trade between countries is regulated by numerous international laws and treaties. Spain is a member of the main international economic and trade organizations, such as the World Trade Organization (WTO).

Foreign trade strategies implemented by the Xunta de Galicia, in collaboration with the Central State Administration, aim at internationalizing Galician trade with strategies and programmes such as the following:

- Plan for Promoting Galician Exports (FOEXGA), a joint plan between the Xunta de Galicia and Galician Chambers of Commerce.
- Collaboration with the Galician Chambers of Commerce by means of an agreement in order to contribute to the internationalization of small- and medium-sized companies (PYMES).
- Confederation of Galician Businessmen (CEG).
- Galician Chambers of Commerce and the Federation of Galician Businessmen Abroad (FEGAEX).
- Foundation for Investments of Galician Origin (FIOGA).

In 1996 2 FIOGA offices were opened in Buenos Aires, 2 in Sao Paulo and 1 in Montevideo.

CONSUMPTION.

Consumer protection.

In order to protect consumer and user rights and interests within the Autonomous Community of Galicia, the *Galician Consumer and User Statute* was published in 1985. This law established the following consumer and user rights:

- The protection of health and safety, and an appropriate environment.
- The protection of economic and social interests.
- Information and education as regards usage and consumption.
- The right to create consumer organizations in order to represent and defend consumer interests.
- Legal, administrative and technical aid and the awarding of damages.

Galician Institute of Consumption.

The *Galician Institute of Consumption was created* in 1994, with a wide range of responsibilities as regards information, training and promotion.

1. *Consumer protection.*

It takes care of complaints.

• Market control.

- It carries out European, national and autonomous government campaigns in relation to the inspection and control of the market's establishments, goods and services.
- It investigates complaints about alleged infringements.
- It exchanges information about risks derived from products in use or being consumed (Alert Network).

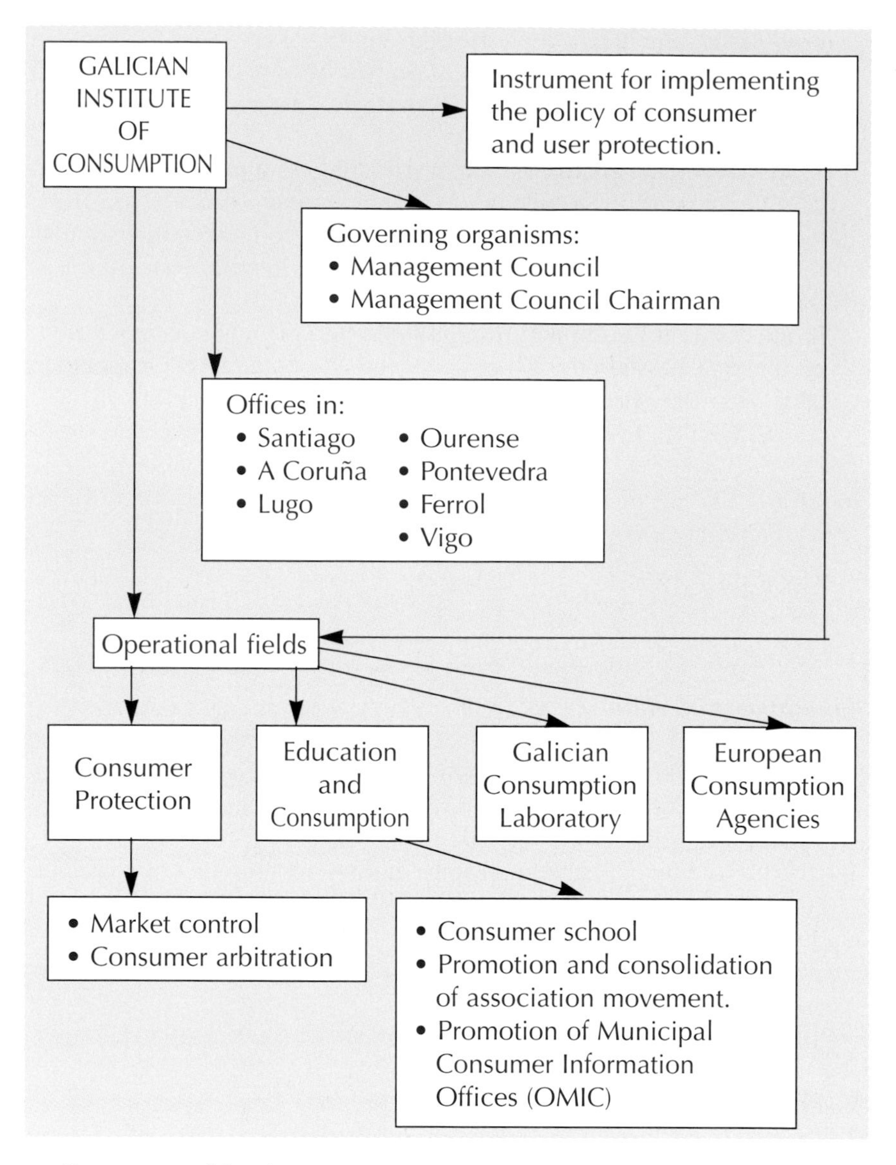

- Consumer arbitration.
  - Enables consumers' and users' disagreements to be resolved voluntarily, quickly and out of court.

2. *Education and consumption.*
- Consumer school.
  - Programmes and organizes courses, seminars, meetings... for consumers.
  - Cooperates with the authorities and educational centres as regards consumer-training programmes.
- Promotion and consolidation of association movement.
  - Subsidizes consumer associations.

- Promotion of Municipal Consumer Information Offices (OMIC).
  - Provides subsidies for OMIC creation, functioning and activities.

3. *Galician Consumption Laboratory.*
   - Carries out expert analytical tests, trials, studies, analyses and quality controls regarding bleaches, cleaning products and cosmetics, textiles, toys and small electrical devices.

4. *European consumption agencies.*
   - Provides public administration organisms, consumer associations, media entities and educational centres with consumer information on a European, state and autonomous government level.

XXI

TELECOMMUNICATIONS

- Telecommunications and development.
- Autonomous Television.
- Spanish Television and private television companies.
- Galician Radio.
- Press.
- Communications networks and new technology.
- Other Xunta de Galicia activities in the telecommunications field.

TELECOMMUNICATIONS.

TELECOMMUNICATIONS AND DEVELOPMENT.

The strategic value of telecommunications is higher in Galicia than in non-peripheral communities, since it shortens distances and brings decision-making centres, and information and documentation sources, closer.

Technological innovations and deregulation processes in the telecommunications sector, are presently promoting the presence of telecommunications services in all areas of society and creating magnificent possibilities, as regards the use of such technology in the socio-economical development of regions.

The deregulation of telecommunications is a process now underway that will be highly beneficial as regards developing services and support infrastructures, but which may imply important risks if market criteria are

Galician Television and Radio installations. San Marcos, Santiago de Compostela.

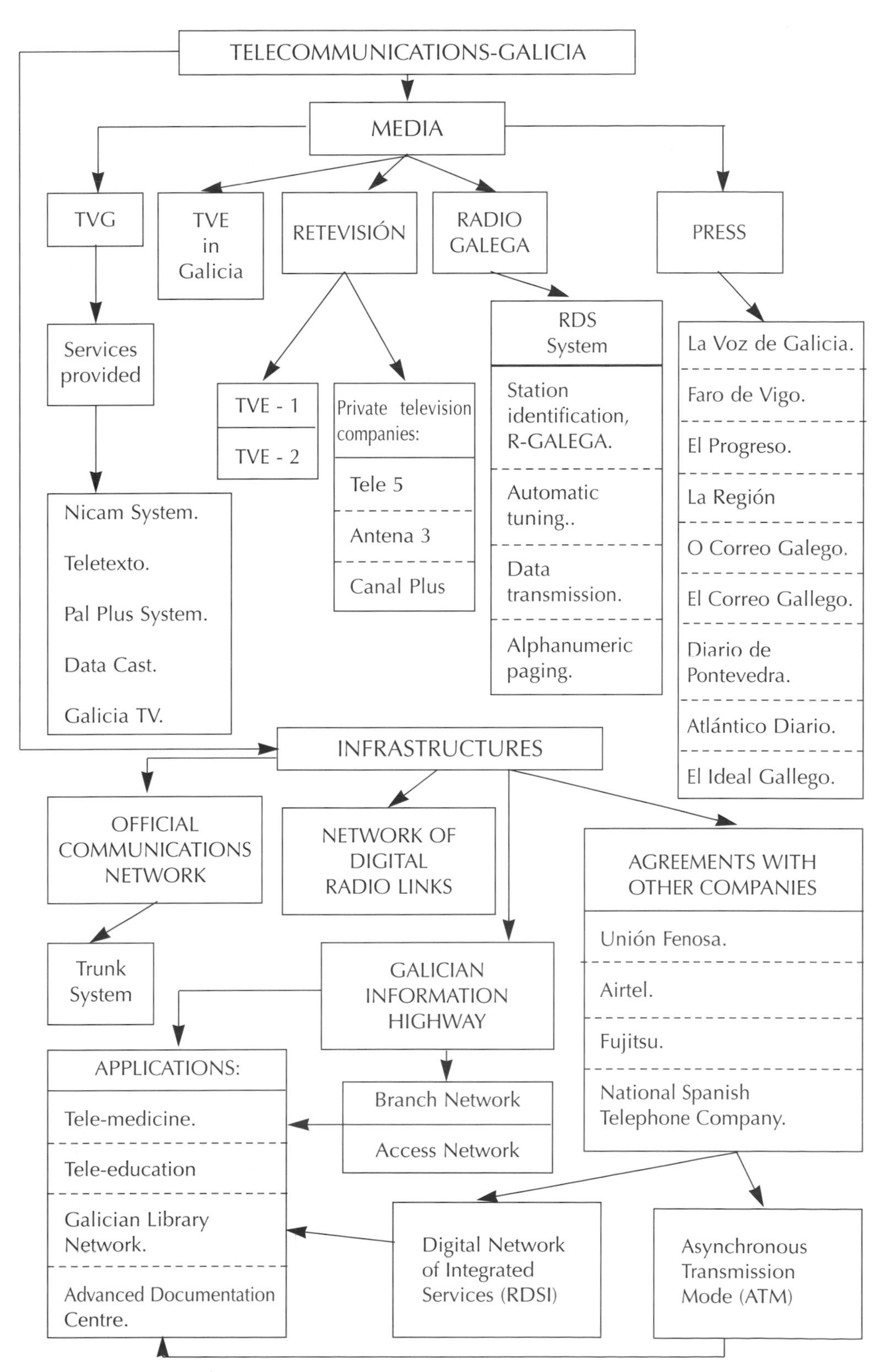
TELECOMMUNICATIONS-GALICIA
MEDIA
TVG
TVE in Galicia
RETEVISIÓN
RADIO GALEGA
PRESS
Services provided
Nicam System.
Teletexto.
Pal Plus System.
Data Cast.
Galicia TV.
TVE - 1
TVE - 2
Private television companies:
Tele 5
Antena 3
Canal Plus
RDS System
Station identification, R-GALEGA.
Automatic tuning..
Data transmission.
Alphanumeric paging.
La Voz de Galicia.
Faro de Vigo.
El Progreso.
La Región
O Correo Galego.
El Correo Gallego.
Diario de Pontevedra.
Atlántico Diario.
El Ideal Gallego.
INFRASTRUCTURES
OFFICIAL COMMUNICATIONS NETWORK
NETWORK OF DIGITAL RADIO LINKS
AGREEMENTS WITH OTHER COMPANIES
Unión Fenosa.
Airtel.
Fujitsu.
National Spanish Telephone Company.
Trunk System
GALICIAN INFORMATION HIGHWAY
APPLICATIONS:
Tele-medicine.
Tele-education
Galician Library Network.
Advanced Documentation Centre.
Branch Network
Access Network
Digital Network of Integrated Services (RDSI)
Asynchronous Transmission Mode (ATM)

allowed to exclusively direct and control the development of basic infrastructures for future societies. In this sense, the Xunta de Galicia is implementing specific proposals:

- Infrastructures: cable, Galician Television and Radio Galega links with Galician populations abroad and boosting existing infrastructures.
- Expansion of digital technology. High definition.
- Boosting resources to increase permanent mobile communications.
- Urban telephone systems and elimination of rural concept, and conception of Galicia as an urban area.
- Other technologies. Galician Information Highway.

AUTONOMOUS TELEVISION.

The Galician Radio and Television Company's main objective is to serve the Galician community, as an important means of standardizing Galicia's own language and disseminating its culture.

Galician Television (TVG)

Galician Television was created in 1986 in order to inform the Galician people about their land's message, its history, its inhabitants and promote its culture and language.

At present it has six transmitters, 133 re-transmitters and 700 micro-transmitters throughout Galicia, which provide the best coverage of all television channels available in Galicia, which means that all of the territory is covered.

Services provided by Galician Television.

Nicam. Teletext. Pal Plus.

In January 1995 TVG began regular broadcasting of the **Nicam** System. This system, of sound transmission in digital form, enables stereo and Dual (two different languages from which spectators may choose) broadcasting.

Likewise, TVG was one of the first television companies in Spain to provide regular broadcasting of **Teletext**, in January 1996.

In October 1995 TVG began regular broadcasting of the **Pal Plus** System, which, apart from improving colour reception, enables wide-screen (16/9) television-viewing similar to cinema format.

Data Cast.

Since the beginning of 1997 TVG broadcasting has been used for data multi-diffusion using the **Data Cast** System, by means of which access can be totally or partially conditioned by way of the broadcasted signal itself, thus enabling or disabling its reception by each receptor unit.

Galicia Abroad: Galicia TV Channel.
Galicia TV is a new television channel that is broadcast via satellite in order to maintain a permanent line of communication between Galicia and Galicians abroad. Its first phase employs the PANAMSAT satellite system, covering practically all of the American continent, from the United States to Tierra del Fuego. It began on April 1, 1997, with 24-hour, encoded-signal broadcasting oriented mainly towards cable networks. It should be available in Europe by the end of 1997.

Digitalizing of TVG.
TVG's own productions, as well as its archives and documentation service, are presently being digitalized. New equipment, including a mobile digital production unit, and the digital formatting of documentary archives are examples of TVG's technological evolution.

Better picture quality of programmes produced in digital format and better conservation of documentary archives are the two main advantages of the digital system, compared with the previous analogous one.

The resources of TVG's archives and documentation services are not only materials for internal use but rather a documentary collection, a cultural and historical heritage unequalled in Galicia, that is worth conserving.

Spanish Television's Regional Centre in Galicia.
TVE's Regional Centre in Galicia complements each day's general programming with locally produced programmes. Regional centres began as correspondent offices providing local coverage for the national news service.

Although the Regional Centre has been producing supplementary material for news broadcasts since it began operating, since 1972 its production has increased due to its news-coverage possibilities.

Spanish Television's Regional Centre in Galicia. Santiago de Compostela.

SPANISH RADIO AND TELEVISION AND PRIVATE TELEVISION COMPANIES.

Retevisión, the telecommunications company in charge of transporting and broadcasting television and radio signals in Spain, is aiming to achieve comprehensive television coverage.

Attaining this coverage and undertaking the technological adaption of the telecommunications network are the two main objectives of **Retevisión**'s investment programmes, which envision a global volume of 5,387.7 million pesetas for Galicia during the period 1994-99. Galicia has experienced an increase in the number of public television centres in the last five years, 54% for TVE-1 and 61% for TVE-2.

Retevisión now has the following broadcasting centres in Galicia: 105 for TVE-1, 98 for TVE-2 and 21 for private television channels (Tele 5, Antena 3 and Canal Plus, which is encoded via satellite).

In order to improve present coverage, which is strongly dependent on Galicia's geographical relief and dispersion, **Retevisión** has drawn up a Comprehensive Coverage Plan that is to be implemented in all Spain during the period 1994-99.

The plan's first phase, which envisions the extension of the private television channels' coverage to small population centres, will see the installation of 41 new centres in Galicia.

RADIO GALEGA.

Radio Galega is Galicia's most powerful and extended radio network, providing comprehensive coverage throughout the entire community. It is equipped with the latest technology and its broadcasts include the RDS System, which enables a station to be identified (R-GALEGA), automatically tuned in case of displacement and data transmission.

The RDS System is also used to provide an extensive alphanumeric paging service. Radio Galega is presently being digitalized and since mid-1996 has been broadcasting via Internet, which means that it may be listered to in any part of the world.

PRESS.

Galicia has a wide range of newspapers, which provide social, political and economic information about the Autonomous Community, supplemented by national and international news coverage. The region's main newspapers are *La Voz de Galicia*, which publishes several local editions, and, to a lesser degree, *Faro de Vigo*, which has a large distribution in the south of Galicia.

El Correo Gallego and the Galician-language *O Correo Galego* are also widely distributed in Santiago de Compostela and its area of influence, and in Ferrol to a lesser extent.

Lugo's *El Progreso* and Ourense's *La Región* are widely distributed and influential in their respective provinces, while *Diario de Pontevedra*, Vigo's *Atlántico Diario* and A Coruña's *El Ideal Gallego* are mainly distributed in their respective cities and, to a certain extent, in their areas of influence.

The daily press is supplemented by two weekly newspapers distributed among Galicians abroad (*La Región Internacional* and *Galicia en el Mundo*) and monthly publications such as *Galicia Autonómica y Municipal* and *Eco. Revista del Arco Atlántico*. There are also periodical publications dealing with specific Galician subjects.

The range of publications also includes national newspapers with sections of Galician news coverage. The main national newspapers are printed in Galicia.

COMMUNICATIONS NETWORKS AND NEW TECHNOLOGY.

The Xunta de Galicia has established, jointly or alone, the following services and infrastructures:

1. *Official Communications Network.*

The Xunta de Galicia presently operates a Mobile Communications Network (Trunk System), which covers all the different administrations. It has a control centre in San Marcos (Santiago de Compostela) and 24 radio-based stations distributed throughout Galicia, all of which are connected by means of high-capacity digital radio links.

This Network enables data transmission and fleet localization by way of the Trunk Network. The Network presently receives around 80,000 calls per month. Its main users are the Galician Health Service (O61 Service), Civil Protection, Autonomous Police, Forestry and Port Services, town councils and others.

2. *Network of Digital Radio Links.*
The Xunta de Galicia operates a powerful Network of Analogical and Digital Radio Links (PDH and SDH technology), which form a solid Transportation Network that is used by all the telecommunications services that are functioning at present, such as Radio Galega, TVG, Official Network of Mobile Communications, Paging or Galician Information Highway.

3. *Galician Information Highway.*
The Galician Information Highway consists of a Branch Network and an Access Network.

The Branch Network includes the following nodes: Pedroso, San Marcos, Bailadora, Domaio and Meda.

The Access Network is used by the following centres:
Galicia's Supercomputer Centre, the university campuses of Ferrol, A Coruña, Santiago, Vigo, Ourense, Lugo and Pontevedra, Vigo's Marine Research Centre, Vigo's Xeral Hospital, A Coruña's Juan Canalejo Hospital and Santiago's Xeral Hospital, Galicia's Technology Park and Ferrol's CIS.

It has a high communication capacity -sending peak traffic that was formerly sent via the Conventional Network only occupies 1% of its capacity.
Sending images from one hospital to another takes a second, compared to 3 hours in the past.

Applications in the near future: tele-medicine, tele-education, access to the Galician Library Network, access to Galicia's Advanced Documentation Centre, which will include Galicia's Virtual Library, a newspaper and periodicals library, a music library, a video library and a virtual museum.

Researchers, scientists and Galician companies will be able to implement broadband applications and services, which will be standard next century.

4. *Collaboration with other companies.*
In order to promote written and audiovisual communications as a means of transmitting the situation in Galicia to its citizens, to favour its comprehensive development, to boost Galician identity and improve the Xunta de Galicia's public services, collaboration agreements have been signed with important companies such as **Unión Fenosa, Airtel, Fujitsu** and the **National Spanish Telephone Company (Telefónica).**

The agreement with **Telefónica** has improved telecommunications, with beneficial results for the economy. The development of cellular-access **rural telephone systems** has enabled Galicia to be the first Autonomous

Community that has universalized its telephone service, something that has not yet been attained in many areas of the European Union.

Galicia's experience has attracted interest from abroad and requests are received for information about its achievements in the field of rural telephone systems.

This cellular-access system (TRAC) sends the telephone signal using mobile-telephone technology to an antenna in the customer's home. All of Galicia's inhabitants now have access to the telephone system within the same period of time, for the same price and with the same conditions.

By the end of 1994 all of the population centres had access to the telephone system, with users from more than 108,000 rural homes. These recently installed lines increased telephone traffic by more than 50 million calls in one year. Galicia is the first Autonomous Community in which the waiting time for having a telephone installed does not exceed 7 days. It has been one of the most important sociological changes experienced by Galicia in recent times, since all kinds of services may now be accessed from any population centre.

The primary element of development, according to European Union criteria, is the telephone service. This process began in Galicia on January 1, 1993, when the rural surcharge was eliminated and Galicia became, for telephone purposes, a single urban zone. Before then having a telephone installed in a rural area cost more then 300,000 pesetas. With the elimination of this surcharge, having a telephone installed in the remotest corner of Galicia costs the same as in any town.

An agreement has been reached with Telefónica to **extend the Digital Network of Integrated Services (RDSI) to Galicia's rural territory**. Objective: digitalizing Galicia's conventional rural networks, equipping them with the Network's services, especially in places where there are medical-health centres, educational centres, agricultural or stockbreeding organizations, etc, under the Autonomous Administration's jurisdiction, in order to enhance their social function.

Two Digital Network of Integrated Services projects, regarding specific social applications, are being planned: tele-medicine and tele-education.

Protocol of RDSI tele-medicine in the health field.
Tele-medicine offers numerous advantages, since it eliminates the unnecessary transferring of patients from primary health care centres to hospitals and optimizes human resources, by means of support units whose specialists are consulted from primary health care centres.

Santiago de Compostela' Xeral Hospital is equipped with the first Trans-Telephone Cardiological Centre, which enables cardiograms to be carried out and analyzed using the telephone system, either by cable or by means of the radio spectrum.

Protocol of RDSI tele-education in the school education field.
The Digital Network of Integrated Services provides various telecommunications services, such as voice, data, image and text transmission by means of a single and common interface. Such services enable the establishment of new teaching and educational systems, in addition to traditional ones, in which students do not have to leave home, e.g. Computer-Aided Teaching enables students living in isolated areas to teach themselves.

Protocol of the university sector's incorporation into the ATM (Asynchronous Transfer Mode) experimental project.
The technological nucleus of broadband communications consists of the Asynchronous Transfer Mode (ATM), a technology that transmits and switches data in the form of fixed-length packets (cells), thereby providing an extremely flexible method of data transmission. ATM is a telecommunications superhighway. Users may access the system and choose the band width they desire.

This protocol enables collaboration between the research and development centres of Galicia's universities and that of Telefónica.

The Xunta de Galicia's agreement with Unión Fenosa enables the sharing of fibre-optic and radio-link infrastructures in order to speed up the creation of the Galician Information Highway (AGI).

The Xunta de Galicia's agreement with Fujitsu will enable the development of data transmission projects such as tele-education, tele-medicine, tele-work and remote access to libraries, based on the Galician Information Highway.

OTHER XUNTA DE GALICIA ACTIVITIES IN THE TELECOMMUNICATIONS FIELD.

1. *Galicia's Telecommunications and Audiovisual Advice Council.*
The Xunta de Galicia created the Telecommunications and Audiovisual Advice Council with the following functions:

a) Presenting the Galician Government with any measure it considers beneficial regarding the telecommunications and audiovisual field.
b) Knowing and informing about strategic lines of action, established in the telecommunications white paper, as well as Galicia's future audiovisual white paper.

c) Knowing and issuing reports about legislative projects and regulations in telecommunications and audiovisual matters under the Xunta de Galicia's jurisdiction.
d) Issuing reports about telecommunications and audiovisual subjects presented by the Council chairman.

2. *Telecommunications Marathon.*
In 1996 the 1st Telecommunications Marathon was held in Santiago de Compostela, with conferences on the subject.

In 1997 the 2nd Marathon was organized as a travelling exhibition and visited Galicia's main towns and cities. It included conferences and displays regarding the latest technology: virtual reality, 3-D, Internet access, multimedia...

3. Retegal was created in response to the need for promoting, administering and undertaking telecommunications projects directed at public and private sectors that find it difficult to access new technologies and services.
Other specific agreements have also been signed: hostelry, mobile telephones for professionals working in rural areas, RDSI equipment for small- and medium-sized companies, and the elimination of RDSI installation fees.

Telecommunications Marathon.

XXII
AUTONOMY AND FINANCES
• Jurisdictional development in financial matters.
• Autonomous Government income and expenditure.

AUTONOMY AND FINANCES.

"The Autonomous Communities will enjoy financial autonomy in order to develop and implement their responsibilities in line with the principles of coordination with the State's Treasury and solidarity among all Spaniards."

Spanish Constitution. Article 156.1

"The Galician Autonomous Community will have its own Treasury and Patrimony in order to carry out its responsibilities."

Statute of Galician Autonomy. Article 42.

JURISDICTIONAL DEVELOPMENT IN FINANCIAL MATTERS.

Galicia's Treasury is basically financed by means of the following resources:

- State-transferred taxes.
- Autonomous taxes and fees.
- Share of State income.
- European Union transfers.
- International Compensation Fund transfers.
- Government stock and borrowing.

These resources are administered by the Treasury.

The Autonomous Community's General Budget, its content, approval and drawing up are controlled by Galicia's Financial and Budget Regulation Law.

Internal economic-financial control is carried out by the Autonomous Community's General Audit, while respecting the jurisdiction of the Galician Audit Council and, in turn, the National Audit Office.

The Galician Parliament is responsible for annually approving the Autonomous Government's General Audit, which includes all the budget operations carried out during the previous year.

AUTONOMOUS COMMUNITY INCOME AND EXPENDITURE.

The planned income according to Galicia's 1997 General Budget amounts to 870,051 million pesetas.

Consolidated income budget
Economic distribution

(million pesetas)

Chapters	1997	Relat. value
I. Direct taxation	14,956	1.7
II. Indirect taxation	30,201	3.5
III. Fees, prices and other income	25,500	2.9
IV. Current transfers	653,147	75.1
V. Patrimonial income	1,691	0.2
Total Current Operations	**725.495**	**83,4**
VI. Alienation of actual investments	7,983	0.9
VII. Capital transfers	88,556	10.2
Total Non-Financial Income	**822,034**	**94.6**
VIII. Financial assets	12	00
IX. Financial liabilities	48,005	5.5
Total Financial Income	**48,017**	**5.5**
Total Capital Operations	**144,556**	**16.6**
TOTAL INCOME	**870,051**	**100**

General budget. 1977
GALICIA

(million pesetas)

Income	870,051
Source	**%**
Central State Administration and European Union	85.3
Resources administered by Autonomous Community	9.2
Government stock operations	5.5

Consolidated income budget. 1997
Contribution per sector

SECTOR	%
Galician Autonomous Community's general administration	68.3
Administrative and commercial Autonomous Organisms	31.7

Consolidated expenditure budget Economic distribution (million pesetas)		
Chapters	**1997**	**Relat. value**
I. Personnel expenses	299,927	34.5
II. Current goods and service expenses	101,036	11.6
III. Financial expenses	36,093	4.1
IV. Current transfers	223,993	25.8
V. Current surplus and repayment fund	0	0.0
Total Current Operations	**661.049**	**76,0**
VI. Actual investments	104,229	12.0
VII. Capital transfers	79,836	9.1
Total non-financial capital operations	*184,065*	*21.1*
Total Non-Financial Expenditure	**845.114**	**97,1**
VIII. Financial assets	45,322	0.5
IX. Financial liabilities	20,405	2.4
Total financial capital operations	*24,937*	*2.9*
Total Financial Expenditure	**24,937**	**2.9**
Total Capital Operations	**209,002**	**24.0**
TOTAL INCOME	**870,051**	**100**

Personnel expenses (34.5%), linked to the provision of essential services, stand out in the consolidated expenditure budget.

Fishing modernization requires large investments.

Consolidated expenditure budget Organic distribution (million pesetas)		
SECTIONS	**1997**	**Relat. value**
01 Galician Parliament	1,799	0.2
02 Audit Council	627	0.1
03 Galician Culture Council	225	00
04 President's Office and Pub. Adm. Dpt.	14,180	1.6
05 Treasury	17,898	2.1
06 Dpt. Terr. Policy, Pub. Works and Housing	32,712	3.8
07 Dpt. Education and University Regulation	205,433	23.6
08 Dpt. Industry and Trade	14,457	1.7
09 Dpt. Agricul., Stockbreeding and Forestry	49,080	5.6
10 Dpt. Culture and Social Communication	20,989	2.4
11 Dpt. Health and Social Services	32,127	3.8
12 Dpt. Fishing, Shellfish and Aquiculture	17,559	2.0
13 Dpt. Law and Labour Relations/Home Office	7,133	0.8
14 Dpt. Family, Women and Youth	18,350	2.1
15 Galician Advice Council	229	0.0
16 L.C. transfers	74,061	8.5
17 National Debt	56,488	6.5
18 Expenditure various Departments	2,242	0.3
Total sections	**565,589**	**65.0**
AUTONOMOUS ORGANISMS		
01 Galician School of Public Administration	414	0.0
02 Galician Statistics Institute	583	0.0
03 Galician Inst. of Housing and Land Use	17,338	2.0
04 Galician Water Service	10,701	1.2
05 Galician Consumer Institute	662	0.1
06 Galician Dairy and Stockbreeding Institute	259	0.0
07 Galician Inst. of Stage Arts and Music	663	0.1
08 Galician Health Service	273,128	31.4
09 Galician Security Academy	152	0.0
10 Galician Service Prom. Sex Equality	562	0.1
Total autonomous organisms	**304,462**	**35.0**
Consolidated total	**870,051**	**100**

Education and health service expenditure stand out:
Education administers 23.6% and the Galician Health Service administers 31.4%.

XXIII

ECONOMIC POLICY

- Galician Institute of Economic Promotion (IGAPE).
- Strategic Galician Investments (INESGA).
- Industrial Development Corporation (SODIGA).
- Industrial land.
  - Business parks.
  - Galician Technology Park.
  - Business Reserve Parks (PRE).
  - Vigo Duty-Free Zone.
- Business-Galician University Foundation (FEUGA).
- Municipal companies.
- Local and provincial economic development institutes.
- Vocational training.
- Youth employment plan.
- Working Community: Galicia-North of Portugal.

ECONOMIC POLICY.

GALICIAN INSTITUTE OF ECONOMIC PROMOTION (IGAPE).

The Galician Institute of Economic Promotion (IGAPE) was created in 1992, as one of the Xunta de Galicia's basic operational instruments for competitively developing Galicia's production system.

The IGAPE has the structure of a public body, associated with the Treasury. The Institute has its own legal status and patrimony; its external relations, patrimonial administration and hiring are regulated by private law.

The law establishing its creation sets out the following functions and objectives:

- Promoting economic activities that favour the balanced and comprehensive development of the different regions.
- Promoting the creation of companies in the different economic sectors with the greatest impact and comparative advantages in relation to Galicia's economic development.
- Favouring the modernization, and technological and organizational innovation of Galician companies, especially small- and medium-sized ones.
- Promoting dissemination activities regarding the instruments and funds at the disposal of Spanish and European public administrations in support of economic activities.
- Providing market information and favouring the development of exports and agreements with foreign companies.
- Promoting the creation of companies that generate employment and use Galician resources, as well as economic activities that favour balanced and comprehensive development in terms of sectors and territory.

In order to attain its objectives, the IGAPE may carry out all kinds of economic and financial activities, may create trading companies or participate in existing companies or foundations, may obtain subsidies and guarantees from the Xunta de Galicia or other Spanish or European institutions and establish all kinds of agreements with companies, organisms, associations, institutions or experts.

The Galician Institute of Economic Promotion is therefore the Xunta de Galicia's most powerful, flexible and dynamic direct-action instrument as regards Galicia's economic activity.

The IGAPE's activities are regulated by the economic promotion guidelines established by the Xunta de Galicia's Delegate Commission for Economic Affairs, presided by the president of the Xunta de Galicia, thereby guaranteeing coherence between sector and general regulations, in line with economic principles of public expenditure, systematization of benefits and their coherence with European regulations.

IGAPE organization.

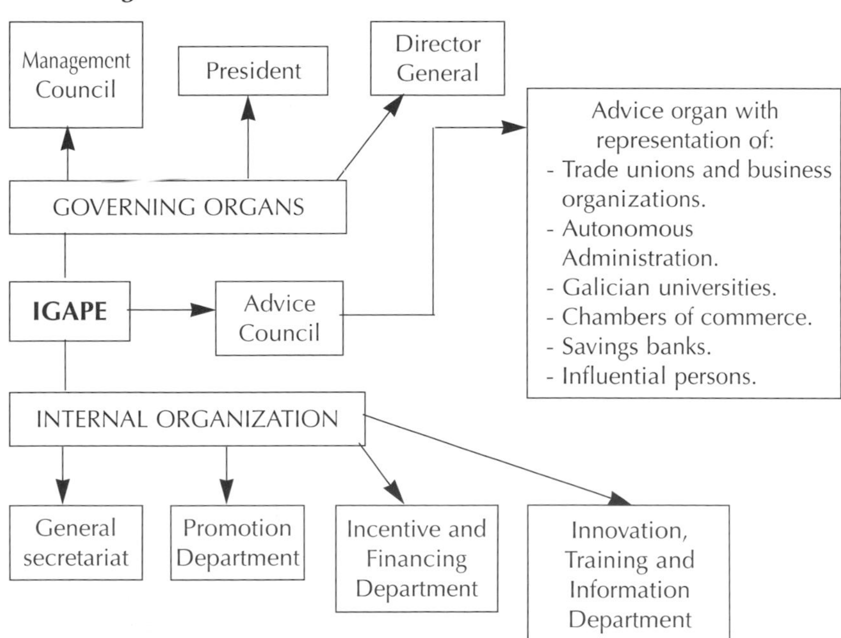

IGAPE'S internal organization.
The **General Secretariat** has the following functions:
providing the Institute with legal advice, hiring, payments, accounts and preparing each year's budget.

The **Promotion Department** has the following lines of action:
- Favouring and stimulating the creation and location of companies in Galicia.

- Supporting the penetration and consolidation of Galician products in foreign markets.

The IGAPE has a network of Business Promotion Centres and agents abroad, which provide Galician companies with information and support regarding their foreign expansion, apart from their own activities aimed at directly promoting Galicia.

The IGAPE annually awards a variable number of foreign promotion grants, which enable university graduates to gain experience in international trade by working in IGAPE's Business Promotion Centres and commercial offices. It organizes business meetings and gatherings, and market research trips.

The Promotion Department also coordinates financial support programmes for inter-company cooperation and the foreign expansion of Galicia's companies, described below:

Trade cooperation programme: Provides help aimed at partially financing company costs and expenses linked to the signing of cooperation agreements, and arising during the different stages of the cooperation process.

Incentives to promote the foreign expansion of Galician companies: They are divided into two categories:
1. Financial help to support the insuring of the risks involved in export operations: nonrefundable subsidies of the cost of the insurance policies taken out, in order to cover commercial, political or disaster risks linked to export operations. Help is only provided to cover export operations outside the European Union.

2. Financial help to support the establishing of companies abroad.

The **Incentive and Financing Department** administers the different IGAPE programmes aimed at financially supporting commercial investments within the Galician Autonomous Community and helping companies with financial restructuring.
Programmes:
Regional incentives. Galician Economic Promotion Zone: subsidies designed to finance commercial investment projects within the Galician Autonomous Community, co-financed by Spanish and European funds.

Investment programme: consists in subsidizing the interests of loans or long-term leasing contracts.

Company restructuring programmes: designed to reorganize activities included in a strategic plan to make companies experiencing difficulties viable by means of long-term subsidized loans.

Guarantee programme: the Institute provides businesses with subsidiary guarantees placed before credit institutions or finance companies, in order to set up, expand, reconvert and restructure businesses.

The **Innovation, Training and Education Department** is in charge of promoting technological research and development (R+D) in Galician companies, endeavouring to boost training, innovation and industrial design regarding processes and products in order to increase their competitiveness.

In order to attain theses objectives, the following programmes have been established:

1. *Programme of financial help to improve company competitiveness,* divided into the following sub-programmes:

- *Diagnosis projects:* subsidies to diagnose a company's present situation, analyze and define future lines of development, define organizational structures, design the system of quality, certify the company or develop administration improvements.
- *Projects for implementing improvement plans,* with nonrefundable subsidies.

2. *Programme of financial help to provide personnel with specialized training,* with subsidies for training activities.

3. *Programme of financial help to hire specialized personnel,* with nonrefundable subsidies for hiring highly-qualified management or technical staff considered indispensable for the implementation or viability of a business project or operation.

4. *Programme for promoting business initiative.*
Lanza programme: designed to favour the creation of innovative companies, especially those proposed by young people under 30.

5. *Igatel programme:* A computerized business database developed by IGAPE in order to promote the use of telecommunications technology and improve information access.

Furthermore, IGAPE's policy of actively promoting innovation and industrial design is boosted by the activity of its Innovation and Services

Centres (CIS): Design CIS and Technology CIS, based in Ferrol, and Wood Technology CIS, located in Ourense's Technology Park.

IGAPE budget.

The IGAPE budget for 1997 amounted to 9,865 million pts, distributed as follows:

IGAPE EXPENDITURE FOR 1997	Amount
I. Financial help for the establishment, modernization, consolidation and viability of companies	**6,686**
- Programme of interest subsidies	4,609
- Participation in companies	667
- Capital participation programme	100
- Programme of reciprocal guarantees	90
- Subsidization, creation and expansion of companies	**1,220**
II. Business services	**928.5**
- Innovation and Services Centre	440.5
- Training and business improvement activities	400
- Specialized information services	88
III. Obtaining investments and business promotion	**826.5**
IV. Other activities	**1,424.8**
Institute's actual investments	1,424.8
TOTAL	**9,865.8**

STRATEGIC GALICIAN INVESTMENTS (INESGA).

The existence of large-scale industrial projects requires an important volume of financial resources, easy access to such resources and suitable financial conditions as regards costs and terms.

The Xunta de Galicia promoted the creation of a company to administer a fund for financing large-scale industrial projects, with the participation of all of Galicia's financial institutions or those operating in Galicia. The fund presently has guaranteed resources amounting to 18,000 million pesetas.

The administration company, INESGA, is also backed by the Xunta de Galicia, which cooperates in the organization of business financing operations by assuming 30% of the financial risk involved in each operation.

The important volume of operations makes it advisable to syndicate them among the participating financial institutions, and to establish reduced interest rates in order to attract business investments.

GALICIAN INDUSTRIAL DEVELOPMENT CORPORATION (SODIGA).

The **Galician Industrial Development Corporation** (SODIGA) was established in 1972.

Corporation objective: industrial promotion by means of minority or temporary participation in companies, a formula known as risk capital or development capital. SODIGA is the oldest of Spain's capital-risk corporations, in both the public and private sectors.

The SODIGA's financial operations were strengthened by the participation of the Galician Administration on a majority basis, thereby enabling it to extend its activities to operations aimed at consolidating businesses and protecting the production fabric.

The SODIGA presently has financial resources in excess of 5,000 million pesetas and annual investments, in participation operations and loans required by the shared companies, of around 1,000 million pesetas.

The SODIGA actively participates in capital-risk associations and organisms in Spain and Europe. It has a special relationship with NORPEDIP, a capital-risk corporation in the North of Portugal, which is its partner in a joint project to administer a Galician-Portuguese development fund included in the INTERREG II European initiative.

INDUSTRIAL LAND.

Industrial land enables the localization of companies in specific zones, clearing urban areas and increasing their quality of life, by moving industries that alter or disturb the population's social life to specific industrial estates.

In order to fulfill the demand for this kind of land and facilitate the coordination of jurisdictions, the Xunta de Galicia created the Inter-

Departmental Commission for the Development of Industrial Land in Galicia (CIDESEGA), which approved Galicia's Industrial Land Plan, establishing the following categories:

- Business parks.
- Technology parks.
- Business reserve parks.

Business parks.

They consist of updated industrial estates. However, the new parks lay more emphasis on a quality environment and telecommunications infrastructures.

Each park has established areas to be developed in the short, medium and long term, characterized by different requirements.

The main promoter, as regards the number of operations, is the Galician Institute of Housing and Land Use (IGVS), either directly or by means of Urban Administration Corporations (XESTUR), with a participation level of 60%. In the case of surface area, the main promoter is the State Corporation for the Promotion and Equipping of Land Use (SEPES), with 40% of the total. Other promoters include Industrial Land of Galicia Ltd (SIGALSA), provincial councils, town councils, financial institutions, the Consortium of the Vigo Duty-Free Zone and private investors.

Galician Technology Park.

The Galician Technology Park, situated in Ourense, is an area with advanced services and infrastructures designed to group together highly technological and innovative companies and institutions.

The park has the following categories: technological, business-technological and services. The Business and Innovation Centre is an intelligent building housing the park's central services, technology transfer centre (Business Incubation Centre) and administration centre. The Business Incubation Centre presently has a "nest" occupation level of almost 100%, with a new building under construction in order to increase its supply.

The Galician Technology Park is a member of the International Park Association, the Network of Atlantic Arc Parks and the Spanish Association of Technology Parks. It has signed agreements with the three Galician universities, as well as European and Latin American universities and institutes.

Galician Technology Park. Ourense.

Business Reserve Parks (PRE).

These parks consist of large extensions of publicly-owned land that are reserved for future large-scale business initiatives. They come under the jurisdiction of the IGVS. There is a PRE in each province:

- Curtis PRE (A Coruña).
- O Porriño PRE (Pontevedra).
- A Pobra de Brollón PRE (Lugo).
- Xinzo de Limia PRE (Ourense).

Vigo Duty-Free Zone.

The Consortium of the Vigo Duty-Free Zone has undertaken an ambitious programme of industrial land creation, financing the completion of two industrial estates and a technology park, which will expand its initial area of one million square metres in the Balaídos district. Although the European Union reduced the privileges of such areas in 1988 by considering them as European territory, the initial conditions (tax benefits such as exemption from paying VAT, duties or special taxes) still apply in the case of non-member countries, which means that its industrial estate continues to be an attractive location.

The importance of the Vigo Duty-Free Zone is very significant, since the companies that are located there have an annual turnover of around 500,000 million pesetas.

BUSINESS-GALICIAN UNIVERSITY FOUNDATION (FEUGA).

The business world is fundamentally dynamic, which makes technological innovation indispensable. This implies the constant updating of personnel training, a command of the latest production techniques, the search for local resources and products in order to face such challenges in the most profitable and efficient way possible.

This situation led to the creation of the Business-Galician University Foundation (FEUGA), which is a private nonprofit institution; according to its statutes, "its objective is promoting and developing dialogue and communication between Galician universities and businesses; promoting, protecting and encouraging all kinds of studies and research about both sectors; seeking solutions to meet common needs, and acting as an information and coordination centre for all those businesses wishing to have a special relationship with the university sector in order to boost their development, promote social integration and improve Galicia's economy."

FEUGA is a mechanism linking Galician universities with businesses and public organisms, which shape our society's economic activities.

MUNICIPAL COMPANIES.

Municipal economic activities have filled a need that society had regarding the coverage of minimum services that, as of result of the important investments required and their scarce profitability, were not attractive for private investors. In this sense, the town councils assumed the role of businessmen in activities such as funeral service, water service, cleansing department and urban transport. They therefore created publicly-owned businesses, which play an important role in local economies.

At present, the need for improving such services and their administration have led to the majority of them being privatized. Their economic impact, as public driving forces, has thus been reduced since these services are now administered by the private sector.

LOCAL AND PROVINCIAL ECONOMIC DEVELOPMENT INSTITUTES.

In order to boost the provincial economies, the different provincial councils (except A Coruña's), created provincial development institutes, in order to correct inequalities within each province and stimulate business activities.

Thus, the following were established: INLUDE in Lugo, INORDE in Ourense and INDEPO in Pontevedra, all of which have human and financial resources that are included in each provincial council's budget.

VOCATIONAL TRAINING.

Vocational training is important for Galicia's youth, since it facilitates their incorporation into the job market.

In Galicia vocational training is divided into two basic branches: the *regulated* branch, which comes under the educational system, and the *vocational* branch, which is located in the workplace and, in turn, covers the continuous training of workers or the unemployed.

As of January 1, 1993, the Xunta de Galicia has been in charge of occupational training functions and services, which have the basic objectives of providing the unemployed with the professional qualifications required to enter the job market.

Vocational training provides extremely practical orientation and is closely linked to employment.

In order to develop and finance such training, the Galician government offers two alternatives, subsidizing, in both cases, the total cost of the courses provided by the collaborating institutions:

- The National Plan of Training and Professional Insertion, better known as the "FIP Plan", designed exclusively for unemployed workers.
- The European Social Fund, included in the European Union's support framework, by means of a system of co-financing, which, in the case of the 1996 programme was 25% for the Galician Autonomous Community and 75% for the European Union. It is directed at workers and the unemployed.

YOUTH EMPLOYMENT PLAN.

An obligatory reference point was the Commission of European Communities' 1993 "White Paper" entitled *Growth, competitiveness, employment.- Challenges and clues for entering the 21st century,* better known as the *Delors Report,* which proposed priority actions in the framework of lifelong education and training, labour flexibility, new work-related needs or the profound renewal of employment policies.

The Xunta de Galicia responded immediately to this concern and in 1983, bearing in mind, above all, the high unemployment rate among the Galician Autonomous Community's youth, designed the Youth Employment Plan (PEX), which was finally approved in 1994. It consists of several programmes and measures aimed at resolving the specific difficulties encountered by those under the age of 30 and basically divided into five main categories: occupational training and orientation, business promotion, hiring benefits, social economy and supplementary actions.

WORKING COMMUNITY: GALICIA-NORTH OF PORTUGAL.

In recent times there has been a growing tendency among the regions of European Union countries towards the development of common projects and objectives, as a result of the elimination of borders and greater rapprochement among them. With the single agreement, and in the wake of the Mastricht agreements, inter-regional collaboration is being promoted by European institutions by means of financial help, designed to construct a more socially, culturally, politically and economically united Europe. This tendency has also been followed by the neighbouring regions of Galician and the North of Portugal, which have been participating in intensive cooperation activities during the last few years, leading to the formation of the now fully consolidated Working Community.

Establishment and structure.

In 1986 the cooperation protocol between both regions was signed.

In 1991, under the European Framework Agreement on Trans-border Cooperation among the Council of Europe's territorial communities and authorities, with the backing of the European Union, Spanish and Portuguese administrations, and promoted by the Xunta de Galicia and the North of Portugal Region's Coordination Commission, the Galicia-North of Portugal Region Working Community was created.

The establishment of the Working Community consolidated a fruitful period of relations between Galicia and the North of Portugal.

Financing instruments.

The Working Community jointly selects the project proposals to be presented for financing by means of the structural funds set aside for objective number one regions, apart from coordinating the projects financed by the INTERREG I (1991-1993) and INTERREG II (1994-1999) European Initiatives.

Projects completed by means of the INTERREG I programme include the following:

- Communication infrastructures in the border area:
  - Tui-A Guarda road, sections I, II and III (Pontevedra)
  - Access to the Monçao international bridge.
  - Ferry between Caminha and A Guarda.
- Joint technical studies:
  - Collaboration between both region's vocational training centres.
  - Publishing of two guides to Portuguese pilgrimage routes to Santiago.

INTERREG II programmes include the following projects, among others:

- Modernization and improvement of transportation infrastructures in the border area: Vilanova da Cerveira-Caión Bridge.
- Conservation and improvement of the Baixa Limia-Serra do Xurés Park.
- Cattle inspection campaign in a radius of 50 km from the border.
- Maintaining collaboration between both region's vocational training centres.
- Establishment of optical-fibre cable between Tui and Valença.
- Development of rural tourism facilities.
- Creation of a joint capital-risk fund.
- Collaboration agreement between the Xunta de Galicia and the five North Region universities.
- Business gatherings.

Port of A Guarda.

XXIV

EDUCATION AND TRAINING

EDUCATION AND TRAINING.

Galicia was given complete authority on non-university educational issues in 1982. Responsibilities, functions and services, as well as the associated personnel, were transferred.

NON-UNIVERSITY EDUCATION.

The Organic Law of General Education System Regulation (LOGSE) of 1990 included important modifications in the educational system's content and structure.

The different kinds of education were established as follows:

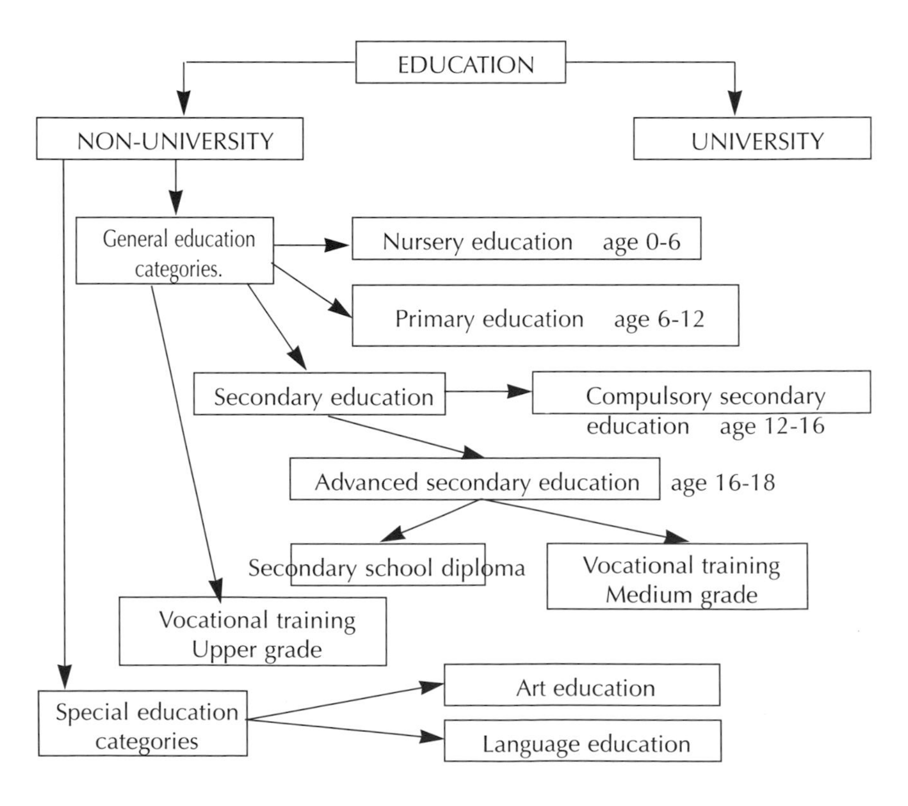

The reform began with the 1991-92 course and will have been completely introduced by the 1999-2000 course. In Galicia there is presently a coexistence of education regulated by the 1970 Education Law and the LOGSE. Thus, the 1996-97 course saw the introduction of the first year of Compulsory Secondary Education (ESO), which coexists with the former BUP secondary school diploma, which is being gradually phased out.

Network of centres.
Due to the LOGSE reform, Galicia's former network of centres will experience substantial modifications. The Network of Public Education Centres Project envisions the construction of new centres, as well as the extension and adaption of others.

The network of centres has been designed with Galicia's singular characteristics in mind and to guarantee a smooth transition to the new education system.

Budget.

Year 1997. 23.61 of every 100 pts included in the Xunta de Galicia's budget was spent on Education.

23.61% of the general budget is assigned to education and includes the educational agreements with almost all compulsory education centres, the agreements with some grades of vocational training (FP), the subsidization of some special education classes and the subsidization of nursery education classes for 4- and 5-year-olds.

There was a 31.1% increase in public centre investments (construction, repairs, extensions and improvements -RAM- as well as equipment), compared with 1996. The latest budget sum was 9,765 million pesetas.

Nursery education.
It has two levels (age 0-3, age 3-6). The second level began to be gradually introduced during the 1991-92 course. The Administration guarantees a sufficient number of places in order to meet the education demands. 82% of 3-year-olds and 100% of 4- and 5-year-olds attended school during the 1996-97 course. The pupils/class ratio established for this category is 25.

The *Preescolar na casa* (Preschooler at home) programme, created and run by the Lugo branch of Cáritas, organizes preventive and compensational measures in order to guarantee the most favourable conditions for providing schooling, during nursery education, for all those children who, due to their socio-economic conditions or any other reason, are at a disadvantage as regards education access and subsequent progress.

The programme centres on the family as the main educational instrument and is developed by means of orientation meetings, held once a fortnight, under the direction of travelling teachers, with the support of specific materials.

Primary education.

It aims at developing each pupil's capacities so that he may promote, in a critical and responsible way, freedom, tolerance and solidarity as part of a plural society.

It is divided into three levels (age 6-8, age 8-19 and age 10-12). It is compulsory and has already been fully introduced. This category provides personalized education, with continuous and global assessments.

Only pupils who have not attained the corresponding objectives may repeat a year within the same level. The pupils/class established for this category is 25.

The introduction of the LOGSE implies new specialities within this education category. The Education Administration is therefore offering its teaching staff, by means of university agreements, the possibility of obtaining specific degrees in order to give such classes.

Compulsory secondary education (ESO).

Objectives:

- Transmitting the basic elements of culture to all pupils.
- Preparing them to assume their duties and exercise their rights.
- Equipping them to find a job or access specialized, medium-grade vocational training.

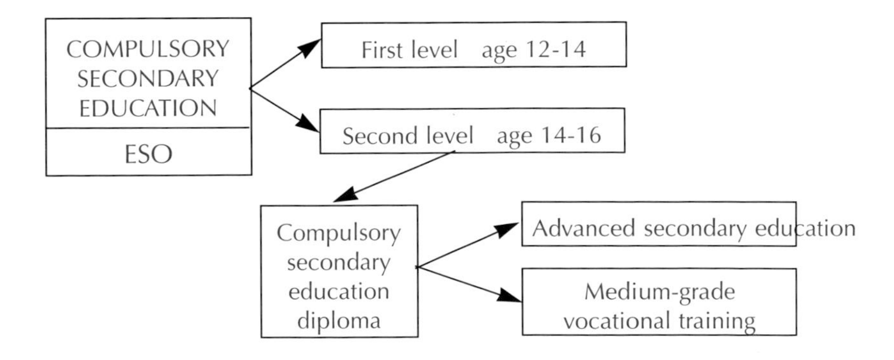

The established ratio is 30 pupils/class.

Diversified curriculum.
Due to ESO's comprehensive nature, integrating all pupils in a compulsory way, there is a need for diversity in order to satisfy the plurality of pupil needs, aptitudes and interests. Diversified curriculum programmes have therefore been established. Also aimed at adapting to pupils is the important role played by secondary school tutorials and orientation departments, in order to help them make the best choice as regards their professional future.

Advanced secondary education.
It consists of two courses and has a double objective: preparing for future studies and providing personal preparation for real life.

Advanced secondary education categories: Arts, Natural Sciences and Health, Humanities and Social Sciences, and Technology. The curriculums are organized into common subjects, each category's specialized subjects and optional subjects.

Advanced secondary education was introduced into the Galician Autonomous Community in advance. During the 1996-97 course, LOGSE advanced secondary education was functioning in 58 public and private schools with 6,175 pupils. The general introduction of the first course is planned for the 1998-99 course.

Education is a decisive factor in a community's development. Schools play an important role in providing such preparation.

Vocational training (FP).

Galicia's regulated Vocational Training Centres provide education for 60,000 pupils each year.

One of their main objectives at present is adapting professional training to production needs, forming closer links with companies. To that end around 600 new training classes will be established up to the year 2000. The number of registered students increased from 46,563 in 1989 to 54,533 in 1995.

- Agreements designed to form closer links between FP and companies are established to enable:
  - Students to gain practical experience in such companies.
  - The companies' workers to be retrained in the educational and vocational centres.
  - Qualified professionals to participate in the training provided by centres, as experts in their field.
- The following have been introduced: activities aimed at completing the training of technology teaching staff and work programmes with companies to provide practical experience.
- 1989-90 saw the gradual introduction of FP vocational modules, which, since 1995, have been substituted by the corresponding specific vocational training levels.
- Matriculation in the branches of Construction, Fashion and Clothing, Agriculture and Draughtsmanship is being promoted to meet the production system's demand for qualified technicians in such fields.
- The Galician Council of Vocational Technical Training was created as a consultation organ in the field of regulated and vocational training.
- In order to facilitate young people's access to the job market, the business training of students completing FP and ESO is being promoted. In order to monitor those with qualifications, some FP centres have joined the Galician Hiring Service network.
- Students who do not pass the ESO examinations may join social guarantee programmes in order to acquire basic vocational training enabling them to enter the job market.

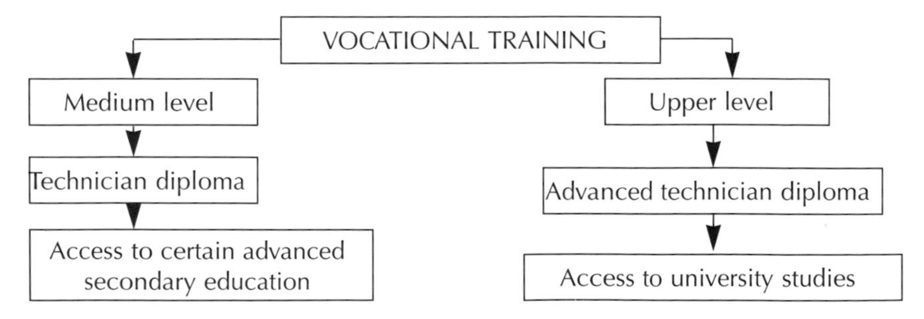

Special education.
In Galicia the education of pupils with special educational needs is regulated, as regards school incorporation conditions, the duration and promotion of education in normal schools, social guarantee programmes, as well as access to university studies and incorporation into special schools in the case of pupils who cannot be educated in ordinary schools.

The ordinary measures established by the LOGSE for such pupils are presently being introduced into the basic compulsory education system. The following special measures, when the aforementioned are not sufficient, are also planned: necessary curriculum adaption, adapting the duration of schooling and diversified curriculum programmes required, in such special cases, to obtain the secondary education diploma.

- The special education centres also perform other functions regarding early action, early stimulation, and pre-workshops and workshops.

- Psycho-pedagogic teams provide external support in order to advise, assess and collaborate with primary school teachers.

Continuous adult education.
The changing world of employment, incorporation into the international market, qualification and re-qualification needs of professionals, deficient basic training and knowledge of languages -all of these require a continuous education process.

- In order to fill such needs, the Galician Adult Education and Promotion Law of 1992 makes provision for academic, vocational and socio-cultural training.

- Activities are also programmed as regards adult literacy and training in order to obtain a school-leaving certificate, primary school diploma or auxiliary technician diploma.

- The Galician Council of Adult Education and Promotion advises about the coordination and monitoring of adult education and promotion programmes.

Special education categories.
The special education categories, according to the LOGSE, consist of art and language education.

In Galicia 268 music education classes have been created and a policy backing art education is being implemented.

Apart from the promotion of language education in schools, the Official Language Schools pay special attention to the study of European languages and co-official Spanish languages.

Complementary services.

1. *School transport.*

School transport is provided for pupils living more than 2 kilometres from the school they are assigned to.

The annual cost of this service, provided for 121,657 pupils and 844 schools, amounted to 8,561 million pesetas in 1997. Around 1,200 vocational training students use normal public transport with a free bus ticket paid for by the Education Administration.

2. *School dining halls.*

School dining halls provide meals for pupils living more than 10 km from school who do not have school transport at mid-day or do not have sufficient time to go home for lunch and come back to school for afternoon classes. The annual cost of this service amounts to 3,000 million pesetas.

Distance learning.

There is an important amount of distance learning opportunities. There are around 13 centres of this kind in the Galician Autonomous Community. The Autonomous Community's Adult Education has 2,081 registered students.

-BUP and COU secondary education. It is provided by means of the Galician Institute of Secondary Education Distance Learning (INGABAD), created in 1982 and based in Lugo, with 7 branches in different parts of Galicia, and collaborating centres (secondary schools) that provide distance learning. It has 7,027 students.

-Specific vocational training. It began with vocational training in branches related to services provided by the Galician Autonomous Community; however, its potentiality has led to the drawing up of plans to introduce various levels of training in different branches throughout Galicia.

-Languages. 1996-97 saw the beginning of a collaboration project with Galician Television as regards the distance teaching of English by means of the FROM-GALICIA programme.

Education agreements.
The Education Administration subsidizes private schools that, in general terms, teach compulsory education categories and satisfy a specific ratio, established by the Education Administration itself.

1996-97 COURSE	
- Total subsidy budget:	11,692,866,000 pts.
- No. of subsidized primary schools:	202
- No. of subsidized secondary schools:	4
- Module/class/primary school year:	4,780,748 pts.
- Module/class/secondary school year:	5,799,076 pts.

Resource Centres.
These were created in 1985 in order to provide the teaching staff of schools lacking didactic resources with materials and advise them as to their usage.

Teaching staff.
Galicia has more than 20,000 primary school teachers and more than 13,000 secondary school teachers.

CEFOCOP.
The Education Administration established a teacher training plan for the period 1990-1995. In order to implement it, 8 Centres of Continuous Teacher Training (CEFOCOP) were created, thus considerably increasing the training activities available to working teachers.

The introduction of new subjects into the education system requires specialized teaching staff. The use of new technologies in education, above all in specialized vocational training, makes it indispensable for teachers to be trained in such usage. Thus, in the case of primary school teachers, specialization courses are programmed in the fields of physical education, music, audition and language, and therapeutic pedagogy, in association with Galicia's universities.

Training leave will basically be centred on the promotion of studies abroad, to improve the training and updating of modern language teachers, and providing work experience in companies in the case of vocational training teachers.

Education inspection.
The specific mission of education inspection is controlling, supervising, assessing and advising public and private schools, as well as education programmes, activities and services.

UNIVERSITY EDUCATION.

The autonomous jurisdiction of the universities in academic, research, financial and administration matters is established by the University Reform Law, apart from the following capacities: drawing up their own curriculums and organizing their teaching systems, creating their own unofficial degrees (which are not valid nationally), bestowing official titles in the king's name, hiring teaching and research staff and proposing the introduction of new degrees by means of their Social Council.

The autonomous university system has the following powers:

a) General powers, established by state and autonomous legislation:

- Organizing, planning and implementing university and university education issues that come under the jurisdiction of the Autonomous Community, according to the aforementioned law, and state and autonomous regulations drawn up during its development.
- Organizing, planning and implementing the corresponding research promotion issues that come under the jurisdiction of the Autonomous Community, according to the 1986 Spanish Law of Research Promotion and General Coordination and the regulations drawn up during its development.

b) Powers specifically acknowledged in the decree transferring jurisdiction in university matters, namely:

- Administration, according to the criteria established by the State Administration, of university grants and financial help awarded by the Ministry of Education and Culture.
- Registering, recognising and ownership of university education foundations based in the Autonomous Community.

c) Powers specifically acknowledged by the LRU, the Spanish Law of Research Promotion and General Coordination and other basic legal regulations of the Autonomous Community, especially:

- Coordinating the universities within its autonomous community.
- Creating new universities, subject to the Council of Universities' report.
- Creating centres and authorizing studies, to the Council of Universities' report and the University Social Council's proposal.
- Fixing university fees for official degree studies, within the limits established by the Council of Universities.
- Financing the university system.

- Planning and coordinating the university system, taking the Community's University Council into account.
- Coordinating research resources in order to promote research, technological development and technology transfer within its Autonomous Community (state law of "research promotion and general coordination").

Galician university system.

The Galician university system is governed by the Galician University System Regulation Law (LOSUG) of July 20, 1989.

This law establishes a system composed of three universities, which were created by dividing up the material and human resources of what used to be, until the end of 1989, Galicia's only university: the five-hundred-year-old University of Santiago de Compostela. The system's basic function is that of coordination, respecting each university's autonomy in the terms established by law.

Palace of San Xerome, which houses the Santiago University chancellor's office.

The three universities and their campuses (Santiago de Compostela-Lugo; A Coruña-Ferrol; Vigo-Ourense-Pontevedra) have to work out their own character within a shared space, according to their own schemes and governed by the general principles established in the single-district LOSUG, totality of available degrees, complementarity of the campuses and correction of original imbalances.

The Galician university system has more than 4,000 teachers and 80,000 students in its own centres, distributed among more than 70 educational centres and 14 university institutes, with a built-up area of more than 500,000 square metres.

Science and technology incentives.

Research promotion is valuable per se, but it is also of strategic value due to its potential influence on industrial productivity, innovation and technological diffusion, advanced education, the improvement of citizen health and quality of life, and technological development in general.

The philosophy behind this tendency is summarized in the following general principles:

-Strategic value of Technological Research and Development (TRD).

-Modifying TRD financing as far as it contributes to innovation.

University of Santiago de Compostela. South Campus.

-Regionalizing TRD.
-Promoting technology transfer within small- and medium-sized companies (PYMES).

Galicia's Research and Technological Development Law of 1993 proposed the coordination of resources, according to priority fields, and the Autonomous Community's growth based on research and technological development.

Galicia contributes to Europe's regional development with the help of the scientific community -the Working Community of Galicia-North of Portugal, Galicia's situation in the Atlantic Arc regions and its presence in Europe's Committee of Regions, the Conference of Peripheral and Coastal Regions and Europe's Assembly of Regions are examples of this policy.

In the same line are the completed projects to generate infrastructures or Galicia's Network of Sciences and Technology (RECYTGA) in support of the university system, as well as the telecommunications network that is being set up.

Balanced development is aimed for by applying the principles of subsidiarity and cohesion throughout the Autonomous Community's territory, and that of historical brotherhood with the peoples who have welcomed Galicians abroad. University and research are two driving forces behind the new Galician reality that is being constructed, and their development provides us with a strategic instrument of innovation.

Authorized degrees in Galician university system

Total degrees per campus	Santiago	Lugo	Vigo	Pontevedra	Ourense	Coruña	Ferrol
	38	20	24	10	15	31	10

Total degrees in Galician university system: 148.
Total of different degrees: 85.

AUTHORIZED DEGREES IN GALICIAN UNIVERSITY SYSTEM HONOURS DEGREES							
Studies	**Santiago**	**Lugo**	**Vigo**	**Ourense**	**Pontevedra**	**A Coruña**	**Ferrol**
Business Administration and Management	x	x	x			x	
Fine Arts					x		
Biology	x		x			x	
Food Science and Technology (2nd level)		x		x			
Marine Sciences			x				
Political Science	x						
Law	x		x	x		x	
Economics	x		x			x	
Pharmacy	x						
German Philology	x						
Classical Philology	x						
French Philology	x						
Galician Philology	x				x		
Spanish Philology	x	x	x			x	
English Philology	x		x			x	
Italian Philology	x						
Portuguese Philology	x						
Romance Philology	x						
Philosophy	x						
Physics	x		x				
History	x		x				
History of Art	x						
Humanities		x					x
Naval Machinery (2nd level)						x	
Mathematics	x						
Medicine	x						

AUTHORIZED DEGREES IN GALICIAN UNIVERSITY SYSTEM

HONOURS DEGREES

Studies	Santiago	Lugo	Vigo	Ourense	Pontevedra	A Coruña	Ferrol
Marine Navigation and Transportation (2nd level)						x	
Odontology	x						
Pedagogy	x						
Journalism	x						
Advertising and Public Relations					x		
Psychology	x						
Psycho-pedagogy (2nd level)	x			x		x	
Chemistry	x		x			x	
Sociology						x	
Translation and Interpretation			x				
Veterinary Science		x					
Geography	x						
Physical Activity and Sports Science						x	
ORDINARY DEGREES							
Library and Documentation							x
Business Science		x	x	x		x	
Social Education	x			x		x	
Nursing	x	x	x	x	x	x	x
Physiotherapy					x	x	
Speech Therapy						x	
Naval Machinery						x	
Marine Navigation						x	
Optics and Optometry							
Labour Relations							
Occupational Therapy							
Social Work							

AUTHORIZED DEGREES IN GALICIAN UNIVERSITY SYSTEM

ORDINARY DEGREES

Studies	Santiago	Lugo	Vigo	Ourense	Pontevedra	A Coruña	Ferrol
Audition and Language Teacher						x	
Special Education Teacher				x			
Physical Education Teacher		x			x	x	
Nursery School Teacher	x	x	x	x	x	x	
Music Teacher	x				x		
Primary School Teacher	x	x	x	x	x	x	
Foreign Language Teacher	x	x		x			
ENGINEERING AND ARCHITECTURE (HONOURS DEGREES)							
Architecture						x	
Agronomy		x					
Car and Electronic Engineering (2nd level)							
Civil Engineering						x	
Industrial Engineering			x				x
Computer Engineering						x	
Mining Engineering			x				
Forestry Engineering		x					
Naval Architecture							x
Industrial Organic Engineering			x				
Chemical Engineering	x						
Telecommunications Engineering			x				

AUTHORIZED DEGREES IN GALICIAN UNIVERSITY SYSTEM

ENGINEERING AND ARCHITECTURE (ORDINARY DEGREES)

Studies	Santiago	Lugo	Vigo	Ourense	Pontevedra	A Coruña	Ferrol
Architecture						x	
Electrical Engineering							x
Industrial Electrical Engineering							x
Marine Structural Engineering							x
Fish Farming		x					
Forestry Engineering		x					
Horticulture and Gardening		x					
Food and Agriculture Industry		x		x			
Forestry Industry					x		
Administration Computing				x		x	
System Computing						x	
Mechanical Engineering			x				
Mechanical and Rural Construction Engineering		x					
Ship Structures and Services							x
Industrial Chemical Engineering		x	x				

XXV

TOURISM

- Introduction
- Eco-tourism, green tourism and nature tourism.
  - Scenery.
- Cultural and monumental tourism.
  - A tour of Galician art.
- Ethnographic tourism.
  - Feasts and customs.
  - Traditional art.
- Museums.
- Gastronomic tourism.
- Tourism policy.
- The future.

TOURISM.

Nature, history, art, customs, gastronomy...
an entire world of unending possibilities
for travellers coming to Galicia.

INTRODUCTION.

Tourist possibilities abound: visiting congresses and fairs; bathing in spas; playing river, sea and mountain sports; walking or cycling along unexplored paths; resting in rural tourism houses; visiting monasteries, castles, Romanesque chapels or palaces; enjoying yourself in museums, exhibitions and concerts; wandering around the old quarters of towns and cities; trying ecological agricultural and sea products; participating in feasts; discovering old traditional trades still in use; investigating traditional architectural styles; watching traditional dances and listening to folk music; being captivated by scenic views of inland valleys or rias; admiring a sunset over the Atlantic Ocean; horse riding; playing golf; fishing; chatting with women and men who still use the language of medieval poetry; becoming acquainted with the hospitable people of a mysterious Galicia, full of legends and singular traditions, always friendly...

You can see, experience and enjoy green, rural, active or nature tourism; cultural, monumental and religious tourism; health and thermal spa tourism; sports, beach and mountain tourism...

ECO-TOURISM, GREEN TOURISM AND NATURE TOURISM.

Galicia's multiple tourism possibilities do justice to the extraordinary boom experienced by tourism in recent years.

Scenery.

Galician scenery always has traces of human existence. It may be a hamlet, farm land, stone walls separating fields or bordering a path -they all reflect the Galician men and women who love and experience the land, who exult and suffer with it.

Inland, in the stockbreeding area, the scenery is full of fields, on hill slopes and in valley bottoms. Vineyards are common along the coast, especially the Rías Bajas area.

As a whole, agricultural landscapes are predominant, but with several exceptions. There are clear geographical contrasts: there is an abundance of vines and other Mediterranean species in the valleys of southern Galicia; birch trees populate the riverbanks of the central plains; there is a surprising association of species due to the variety found in valleys where box trees, olive trees and vines coexist with chestnut trees, pine trees and eucalyptus trees.

Galicia's vegetation landscape can be divided into three areas:

- *Coast*, with a landscape dominated by reforested pine trees, some eucalyptus trees and bushes. Agriculture, development and industry make up half of the area. It is the Galicia of corn and horticultural-fruit products.
- *Inland*, where deciduous trees and fields dominate. Higher up there are mixed forests of oak trees, birch trees, cork oaks, ash trees, hazel trees, strawberry trees, beech trees... Rye and potatoes are the most common crops.
- *South*, with Mediterranean species such as holm oaks and cork oaks. Higher up there is a dominance of shrubs, while varied agriculture is carried out on lower ground: corn, vines, potatoes... Reforested pine trees are also quite common.

CULTURAL AND MONUMENTAL TOURISM.

History and art join together in Galicia to offer visitors new paradigms in a land's end region. Understanding the life of Galician peoples also implies unique artistic interpretations, of both a cultured and traditional nature.

Let us therefore go on a diachronic tour of Galicia's immense artistic treasures.

A tour of Galicia's art.

The first artistic manifestations.

Magnificent open-air *rock carvings* date from the Bronze and Copper Ages. These *petroglyphs* represent different themes: pans, spirals, circular and abstract combinations, animal and human figures... They are distributed throughout numerous rocky outcrops in the north-west, especially in the Rías Bajas area.

Celtic era.

"Castros" (fortified Celtic settlements), situated in strategic locations, housed the inhabitants of the Iberian Peninsula's north-west during the Iron Age. Celtic art, characterized by curved lines, was used to decorate homes and gold articles. *Pendant earrings, torques, bracelets...* are beautiful pieces of jewellery made from gold, proof of the Celtic goldsmiths' handcrafted sensitivity.

**"Castro" of Santa Tecla, near the mouth of the River Miño.*

** Fortified celtic settlement*

Roman Galicia.
There are important traces of the Roman era throughout Galicia: walls, bridges, sculptures, ceramics, mosaics... The most outstanding public works include the Tower of Hercules in A Coruña, Lugo's ramparts, the bridge over the River Bibei and sections of roads.

Old drawing of the Tower of Hercules.

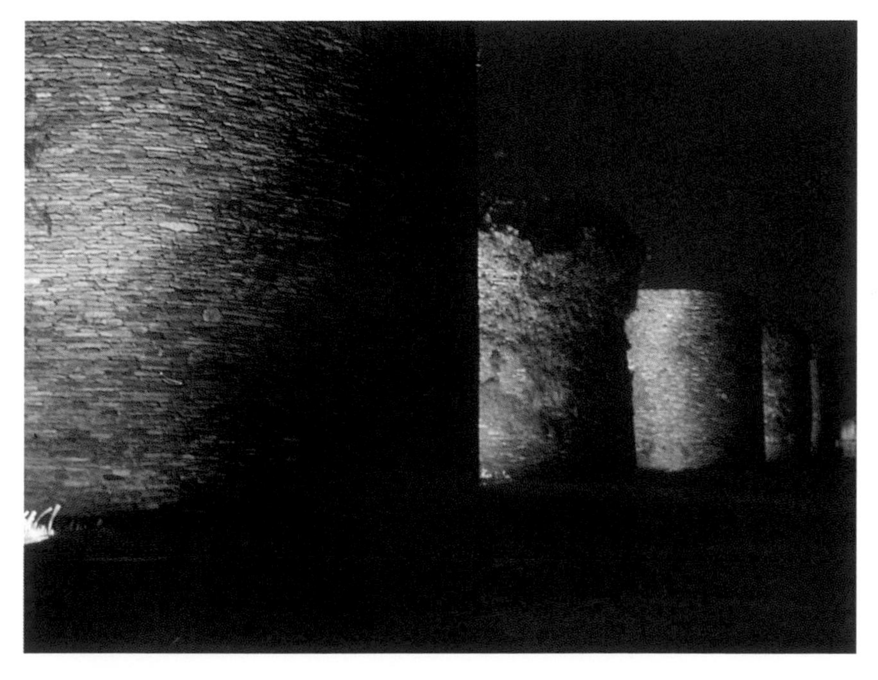

Lugo is the only city in the world whose surrounding ramparts are intact.

Montefurado.
The Romans bored through a hill to make a tunnel for the River Sil.
They hunted for gold nuggets in the former river bed.

Sigillate ceramic.

Paintings in Santa Baia de Bóveda, near Lugo.
Late-Roman construction, perhaps used later by followers of Priscillianism.

Pre-Romanesque art.
Coinciding with the arrival of Christianity, Galician culture was affected by oriental and North African influences, as can be seen in 4th-century sarcophaguses. During the 5th century the Swabians invaded the Iberian Peninsula and Galicia; under their dominium Galician art continued to develop in the form of tomb headstones and temples carved out of solid rock. The Visigoth period saw the arrival of Byzantine influences. When the Reconquest began, the Asturian monarchs imposed the Carolingian style, which was later altered by Arabian influences; the result was the *Mozarabic style.*

Romanesque art.
The 11th and 12th centuries were times of great political, religious and artistic intensity for Galicia. Transformations took place in harmony with the evolutionary tendencies experienced throughout Western Europe, as a consequence of the Crusades, pilgrimages and the establishment of new religious orders. In short, there was a predominance of religious sentiment.

Monasteries were centres of culture and Cluniac ideas gave way to the Cistercian principle of leading a simple life, based on work, poverty and prayer.

In this context a new style arose, *Romanesque*, the origin of which was linked to pre-Romanesque forms. In the mid-11th century, barrel and groin vaults were extended to the entire length of the nave, although in Galicia vaults were mainly used in the sanctuary. Walls were sturdy, with buttresses, and arcs were semi-circular.

Compostela's basilica was used as a model for numerous rural churches, which, using the genuinely Galician material of granite, copied the structural and decorative forms of what was later called a *pilgrimage church.*

King David in the Platerías facade of Compostela's cathedral. It is a typical example of Romanesque sculpture.

San Estebo de Ribas de Miño, in the Ribeira Sacra region.

Map of Romanesque art in Galicia.

Gothic art.

Recent studies show that Gothic art in Galicia was not only substantial per se but even included works that set new standards for the entire Iberian Peninsula. The usage of pointed arches, lancet vaults, flying buttresses... may not be considered as coincidental construction features. Their usage was due to a change of order. The Romanesque style was gradually abandoned and, by means of the pilgrimage route to Santiago, new European tendencies arrived.

The beginning of the Gothic style has its roots in constructions that were originally Romanesque, such as Compostela's basilica, and the figure of Master Mateo, whose work was centred on the second half of the 12th century, although his influence was felt in the centuries thereafter. His work on the crypt, which was done to overcome the difference in level between the square and the upper basilica, formed the basis for the second section of the Pórtico de la Gloria and acts as a transition between the Romanesque and Gothic styles. It dates from 1168, which makes it one of the new style's first constructions. The layout of this crypt, commonly called the old cathedral, includes an ambulatory and four naves, each with two sections. The real innovation is in its ribbed vaults, forming one of the first examples of this kind of roof in the Iberian Peninsula.

Map of Gothic art in Galicia.

Tomb of Fernán Pérez de Andrade. San Francisco church in Betanzos. Decorated with hunting scenes.

Santa Mariña church in Cambados. Ria of Arousa.

Octagonal cathedral dome in Ourense.

Gothic statue of the Virgin in Ansemil church.

Castles.

At the end of the Middle Ages Galicia was a land of castles. Many of them were destroyed during the *Irmandiños wars, although some were later rebuilt. Later on, the Catholic Monarchs, in order to guarantee the monarchy's power, ordered the destruction of the castles belonging to the Galician nobles who had not supported them during the successional wars.

However, some forts remain and stand out, high-standing, in strategic locations within the landscape.

*Brotherhood.

Map of Galician castles.

Monterrei castle.

Torres de Oeste, in Catoira. These towers were built as a defence against sea attacks from Normans and Arabs.

Tower in Viana do Bolo.

Vimianzo castle.

Monasteries.

During the Swabian era, San Martín Dumiense restructured the church in the north-west of the Iberian Peninsula. The foundation movement peaked during the 10th and 11th centuries, when the rule of St. Benedict guided the monks who "were Galicia's ploughmen, civilizers and educators, the creators of the new Galicia that was reborn in European style." Monasteries such as Samos, Celanova, Lourenzá and Mezonzo became permanent centres of culture.

Undoubtedly, this religious and cultural renewal was also fuelled by the discovery of the Apostle James' tomb and the support of the influx of pilgrimages to Santiago.

In later centuries the monasteries experienced architectural transformations, in harmony with the new Renaissance and baroque artistic tendencies.

Map of Galician monasteries.

Oseira monastery.

Armenteira monastery. This Romanesque facade is the only one in Galicia with a six-archivolt door.

San Martiño Pinario monastery.

Renaissance art.

The spread of *Renaissance art* throughout Galicia is due, above all, to a family linked to the culture and art of that time: the *Fonsecas*. Alonso III de Fonseca, archbishop of Santiago, was its main promoter. The new style developed three tendencies, each of which corresponds to a third of the 16th century:

- *Plateresque,* with a predominance of Italian decorative forms in buildings very similar structurally to the Gothic style.
- *Purist,* in the second third of the 16th century. The decoration was reduced and concentrated in very specific places.
- *Herrera-like,* in the final third of the 16th century, which followed manneristic guidelines and simplified ornamentation to an extreme. The structure of the buildings was superimposed onto the decorative forms.

Renaissance art in Galicia.

Cardinal School. Monforte de Lemos.

Fonseca School. Santiago de Compostela.

Royal Hospital. Santiago de Compostela.

Santa María Church. Pontevedra.

Baroque art.

In Galicia the baroque style represented a period full of artistic splendour. Streets and palaces acquired an architectural style full of vigour and fantasy, with movement and intense ornamentation. The majority of buildings are religious, since the church was the main sponsor during the 17th and 18th centuries. Compostela's Chapter, with its original Vega and Hangman figure, was the promoter of the construction work carried out during that period.

The monumentality of the construction work, the taste for movement, the superimposition of orders and the abundant decoration of large areas gave the new architecture a dynamic style, which extended its forms throughout the region, especially in the city of Santiago.

Map of baroque art in Galicia.

Compostela's baroque art.

Santa Clara Church.

Clock tower, Compostela Cathedral.

Bell tower of Santa María Salomé Church.

Dean's house.

"Pazos" (palaces).

"Pazos" are a frequent feature of Galicia's rural and urban landscape, with more than 400 buildings categorized as such due to their architectural characteristics.

"Pazos" were created for multiple reasons, but most of them were originally medieval forts. The economic-social relations of each "pazo" with its surroundings determined, in the rural environment, the intimate link between its dynamic structure, its daily activities, and the local farm workers. The architectural elements are harmoniously blended with the environment, both as regards the materials employed (wood, stone...) and functionality (construction elements characteristic of country life).

Fefiñáns "Pazo". Cambados. Large portals, walls, chimneys, balconies, arcades, sun terraces, chapels, gardens, courtyards, coats of arms... are genuine "pazo" characteristics.

Galician "pazos".

Oca "Pazo".
"Pazos" are ancestral homes in the country, which have been subject to different transformations and styles. They generally employ Renaissance or baroque elements, as well as medieval forms such as towers with battlements.

Bendaña "Pazo". Town "pazos", large houses with coats of arms, have their own characteristic features just like rural ones, although they blend well with the surrounding buildings.

19th-century art.

The 19th century was marked by the ideas of the Enlightenment. The town clergy, who were favourable to such ideas, tried to apply them to architecture, which constantly sought a style completely opposed to the baroque, as regards construction and decorative forms. This search for classicism was reflected in facades and ground plans, in ecclesiastical and civil buildings.

Compostela once more became a reference point bringing together the main architects of that time, who worked under the watchful eye of the Chapter, a defender of the new forms.

Collegiate Church in Vigo.

Raxoi Palace.

San Julían Church. Ferrol.

20th-century art.

The abandonment of 19th-century eclectic forms took place in Galicia at the beginning of the 20th century, based on *modernist* reactions. The architecture was adapted to the environment, respecting traditional buildings, and *balconies* were established as the main element. In the urban expansion areas buildings were constructed with iron, cement and glass being incorporated into the styles of the first half of the 20th century.

Caixa-Vigo Cultural Centre. Vigo and A Coruña were the first Galician cities to incorporate modernist influences.

In Compostela, Jenaro de la Fuente designed the student residence in the University's present-day South Campus. The buildings' grandiosity, of neo-baroque conception, is evident.

Expressionism was the style that was best suited to **plastic sculpture** during the first half the 20th century in Galicia. There was a predominance of traditional Galician themes, such as farmers and sailors. The stonemason tradition influenced the use of granite and the Romanesque-like forms.

Saint Joseph.

"Filliña" (Little Daughter).

Francisco Asorey, "the thoroughly Galician sculptor", reflects primitive and native themes. He covers the wood with fine polychromy. In other works he exalts the material by working stone.

Monument of St. Francis of Assisi. Santiago de Compostela.

Painting developed in the same direction as sculpture. The influence of expressionism revolutionized both forms and techniques.

Sotomayor, a painter of local customs.

Castelao, typical proponent of social realism.

Having overcome the effects of the Spanish Civil War, Galician art began to incorporate new tendencies from the sixties onwards. At present, a flowering of architects, sculptors, painters..., both Galician and foreign, are working on new and promising projects.

Congress Hall in A Coruña.

Neo-figurativeness, geometrical organicism, primitive expressionism... -any avant-garde tendency may be found in Galicia's present-day sculpture.

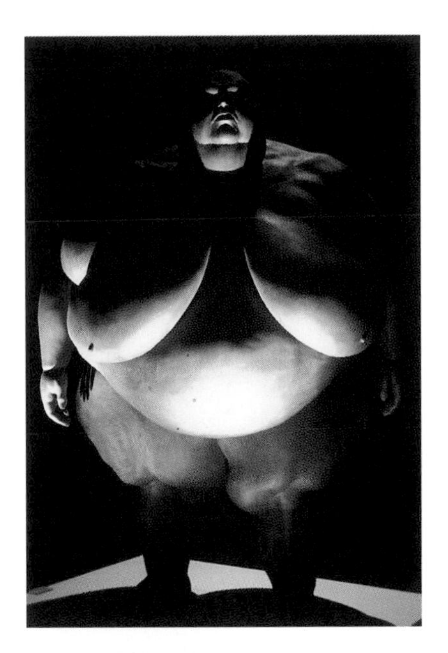

Cubist and expressionist influences affected the "novos", a group of painters that arose in the thirties. They had a less naturalist and academic vision, one that was a more genuine reflection of the Galician reality.

Manuel Colmeiro.

Galician painting changed direction starting in the forties. New dynamic tendencies of a cosmopolitan nature appeared, in harmony with the styles being followed in other countries.

Xaime Quessada.

Feasts and customs.

Traditional culture, i.e. living tradition transmitted through the centuries, is reflected in customs and feasts. In Galicia, the different climatological seasons, agricultural crops, beliefs, social behaviour, the way of understanding life and death... have resulted in singular traditions, folklore and celebrations.

Carnival celebration in Vilariño de Conso, in the O Bolo region.

Bagpipes are Galicia's most typical instrument. They are never lacking in any feast.

"Curro". A festival activity in which roaming horses are brought together to mark them and cut their manes.

Allegorical figures, giants and big-heads brighten up feasts in towns and cities.

"Romerías" are religious-secular feasts that are held in specific sanctuaries.

Spectacular view of Santiago's cathedral during the Apostle fireworks display on the night of July 24.

Traditional art.

Traditional art is perhaps one of the best collective expressions that characterizes a people and its cultural heritage.

Raw materials, domestic life, daily work, customs... all influenced, in Galicia, the birth and subsequent development of traditional craftsmanship that is passed down from generation to generation. Perfect functionality is not at odds with magnificent aesthetic results in the case of utensils, garments, pieces of jewellery..., which were and still are made in towns and villages.

Map of traditional Galician crafts.

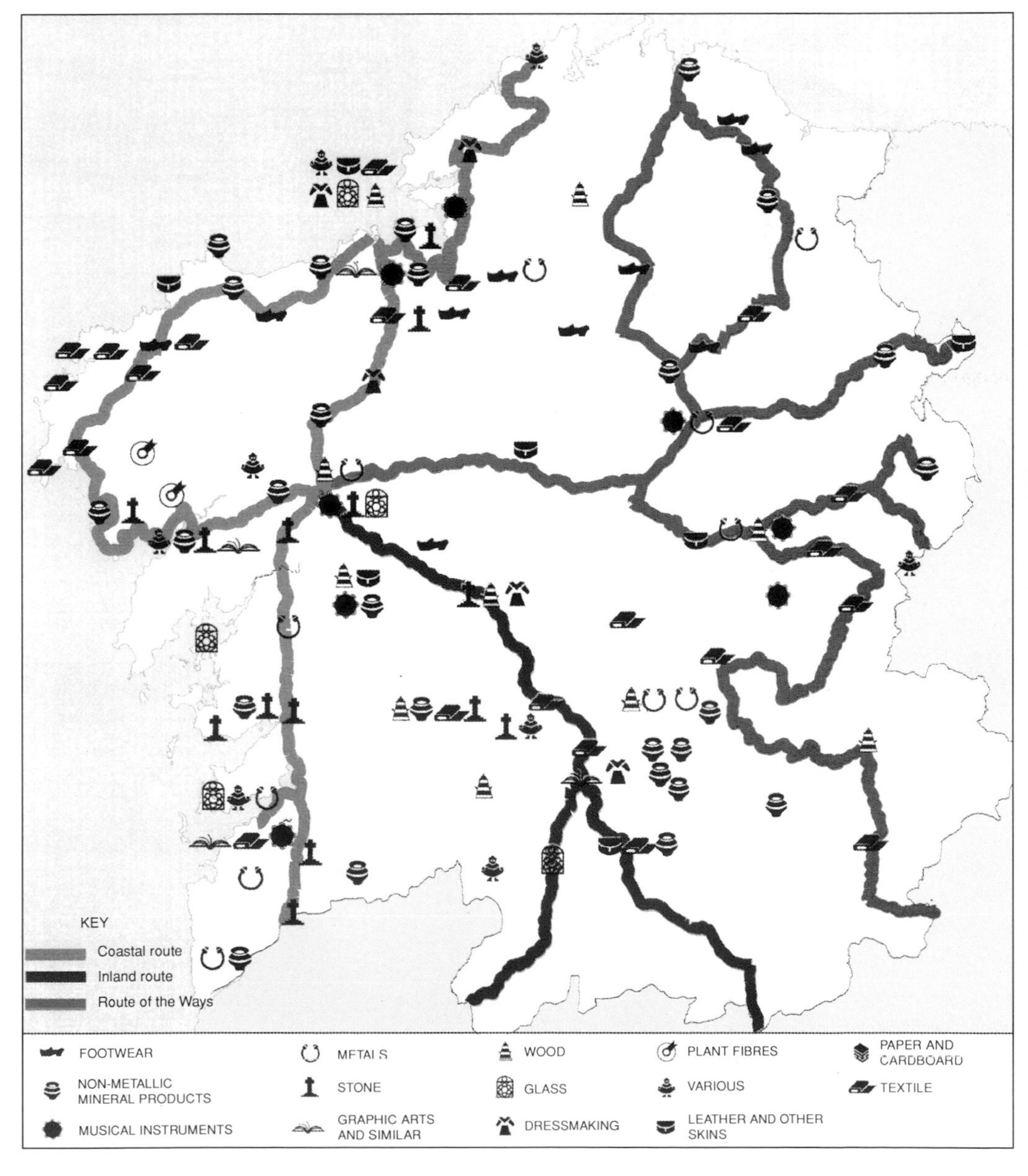

MUSEUMS.

History, geography, ethnography, art, science, technology... are well-suited to being didactically displayed in temporary or permanent exhibitions. Galicia's *museums,* some of which have impressive and extremely valuable collections, present visitors with significant examples of what our region was and is, and what its inhabitants have created and are creating.

Galician museums.

Museum of Pontevedra. It is one of the most important of its kind in Spain. Archaeology and art are combined in a beautiful building located in Pontevedra's old quarter.

GASTRONOMIC TOURISM.

Galician gastronomy still offers typical dishes from the end of the 19th century and beginning of the 20th century. Although the ingredients are the same: fish, shellfish, pork, beef and vegetables, there is a difference between town and country dishes, coastal and inland dishes, feast and daily dishes. There are also seasonal dishes.

Rye, corn or wheat bread, cow's milk, meat, potatoes, fruit and fish on the coast are the daily ingredients of Galician cooking. However, there are other dishes that add variety to its gastronomy: ham and turnip tops, tripe, cured ham, spicy sausages, "rixóns" (pork scratchings); pies of "raxo" (loin), eels, "xoubas" (small sardines), lamprey...; beef, kid, chicken, pigeon and, at Christmas, capons. There is also game (rabbit, partridge, boar...); cured meat, river and sea fish, of which sardine, cod, trout, octopus and shellfish deserve special mention. Omelettes, varied cheeses, different kinds of wine and eau-de-vie. Sweets include "Santiago" or almond cake, "rosquilla" doughnuts, "melindres"(aniseed-flavoured cake), "rosca" doughnuts, crepes with honey, "bicas" (sponge cake)...

Typical "empanadas" (pies), being offered to a medieval gentlemen by servants, are magnificently reproduced in the corbels of Compostela's 12th-century Gelmírez Palace.

Inland tourist promotion.

Correcting the imbalance between inland and coastal tourism development may be achieved by means of rural tourism, spa modernization, cultural tourism and the protection of areas of special touristic and scenic interest.

Rural tourism is one of the main categories to be developed, for the following reasons:

- Changes in demand, in relation to the desire to get back to nature.
- The extremely attractive image of Galicia's scenery.
- The urgent need to restore part of the patrimony formed by Galicia's "pazos".
- The income generated, which frequently complements income from other sources.
- It is an efficient way of attracting tourists to inland Galicia.

Excellent results are being achieved by means of the private promoters' quality restoration of old "pazos" and country houses, and the model of open development promoted by the Administration.

The modernization and touristic use of **spas** was implemented, along with rural tourism, by including them in an important programme financed by the European Union, via FEDER, in order to recuperate Europe's rural patrimony. This led to the exploitation of Galicia's abundant thermal and medicinal waters, and the promotion of this kind of health treatment, linked to a relaxing holiday, modern beauty care and fitness activities.

The services offered by newly built or reformed hotels and the availability of spa treatment facilities make up a competitive and modern tourism option.

A rural tourism establishment.

Cultural tourism is another instrument for attracting tourists to inland Galicia.

Monument restoration was also a factor in the promotion of inland sightseeing routes.

Promoting the Ribeira Sacra region began with the indispensable step of signposting the area's roads, which is essential for development.

The subsidized measures set out in the Programme of Tourism Development included the reconstruction of the old Portomarín "Parador", which the Xunta requested from the State and now provides accommodation as a "Pousada".

It also included the creation of a "Parador" providing accommodation in Monforte de Lemos, in order to attract tourists to a region, near the Ribeira Sacra area, with an abundance of monuments.

The Way of Saint James has been equipped with Pilgrim "Albergues" (hostels), which has stimulated the flow of visitors along this special route.

Pilgrim hostel.

Mountains and protected areas reflect all of nature's abundance and variety. Os Ancares, O Courel, the Manzaneda-Queixa-Invarnadeiro trilogy and the Trevinca massif are Galicia's most outstanding areas for mountain tourism. "White tourism" at the Manzaneda ski resort and "green tourism" are, along with rural tourism and hiking, the most attractive aspects of these mountains. Their flora, whose autochthonous vegetation is still intact, includes meadows with oak trees, yew trees, beech trees, hazel trees and holly trees. Trevinca, characterized by high-altitude tundra, includes the so-called Casaio "Teixidal", which is probably Southern Europe's best yew forest.

This rich flora provides a habitat and shelter for an interesting variety of fauna, some of whose species are especially protected, such as the capercaillie and brown bear in Os Ancares, whose National Hunting Reserve has an abundance of roe deer and boars.

These mountainous areas also offer unique lifestyles and anthropological aspects. Piornedo in Os Ancares has been declared a Historical-Artistic Site due to its "pallozas", prehistoric dwellings that have survived from the era of the "castros". The "palloza" is a combination of home, stable and storehouse, with all the elements of a primitive economy.

"Palloza" construction.

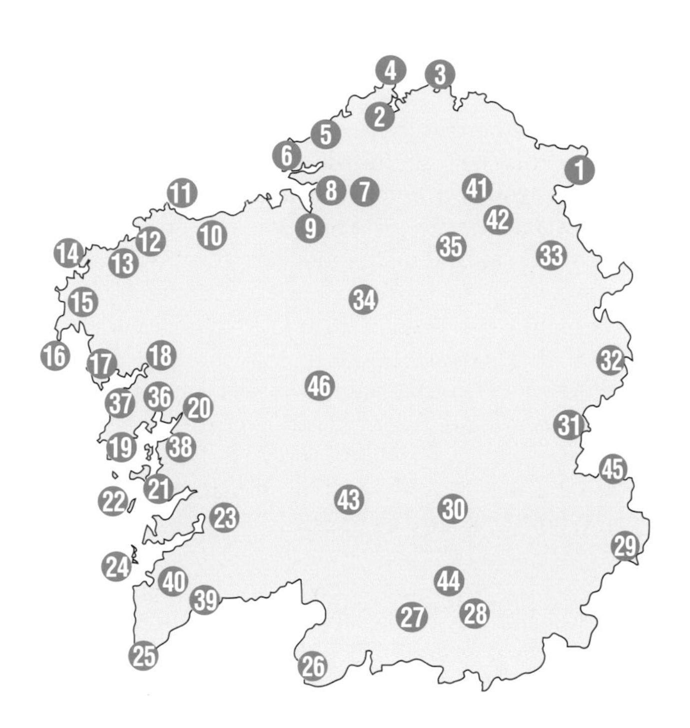

GALICIA'S PROTECTED NATURE AREAS

NATURE RESERVES

7 Fraga de Caaveiro
19 Corrubedo sand-dune system and Carregal and Vixán lagoons
24 Cíes Islands
26 Baixa Limia - Serra do Xurés
39 Monte Aloia

NATURE SITES OF NATIONAL INTEREST

3 Estaca de Bares
14 Cape Vilano
36 A Curotiña

RAMSAR AREAS
Protected by the RAMSAR agreement regarding international wetlands.

2 Ortigueira - Ladrido
5 Valdoviño
19 Corrubedo
21 Umia-O Grove-A Lanzada tidal system.

GALICIA'S AREAS OF NATURAL INTEREST

1 Eo Ria
2 Ortegueira and Ladrido Ria
3 Cape Estaca de Bares
4 Cape Ortegal and Sierra Capelada
5 Lagoa de Valdoviño
6 Lagoa de Doniños
7 Fraga de Caaveiro
8 Pontedeume Ria and tidal area
9 Betanzos Ria
10 Xuncal de Baldaio
11 Sisargas Islands
12 Corme-Ponteceso Ria
13 Lagoa de Traba
14 Cape Vilaño
15 Cape Touriñán
16 Cape Fisterra
17 Lagoa de Louro and Carnota beach
18 Mouth of River Tambre
19 Corrubedo lagoons and sand banks
20 Baixo Ulla (Dodro)
21 Umia-Grove system
22 Ons Islands
23 Vigo Ria (Rande)
24 Cíes Islands
25 Mouth of River Miño
26 Serra do Xurés
27 Lagoa de Antela (remains)
28 Serra do Invernadeiro
29 Pena Trevinca
30 Val do Sil (Ribeira Sacra)
31 Serra do Courel
32 Serra dos Ancares
33 Serra de Meira
34 Lagoa de Sobrado
35 Lagoa de Cospeito
36 A Curotiña
37 Lagoas de Xuño y Muro
38 Cortegada Island
39 Monte Aloia
40 Gándaras de Budiño
41 Serra do Xistral
42 Cova do Rei Cintolo (Mondoñedo)
43 Serra do Suído
44 Serra de Queixa
45 Serra da Enciña da Lastra
46 Lagoa Sacra. O Candán

Diversification of options.
Diversification is the best response to demand segmentation.

Apart from Galicia's classical tourism attractions (seaside, cultural and religious tourism), diversification is also offered by means of congresses and conventions, sailing and active tourism. In fact, a noticeable increase is taking place as regards the amount of congress and business tourism, recreational sailing and active tourism linked to sports participation.

Congresses and conventions: Galicia is competing for a share of this high-income market. The region's art and scenery provide magnificent sightseeing options, apart from its wonderful gastronomy. There is also a large number of Congress Halls, with the recent addition of Santiago de Compostela's Galician Congress and Exhibition Hall, including Caixa-Vigo's Cultural Centre, Santiago's Auditorium and A Toxa's Congress and Exhibition Hall, as well as plentiful hotel facilities for this kind of gatherings.

Bearing in mind that such events are held during tourism's low season, they provide a good solution for correcting seasonal imbalances, as well as adding to tourism diversification.

Galician Congress and Exhibition Hall. Santiago de Compostela.

Sailing is another means of diversification that attracts high-income tourism. Galicia's rias are the ideal setting for sailing, due to their safety conditions and strategic location in relation to Europe-America and Atlantic-Mediterranean routes. There are presently 23 fully-equipped marinas with 2,660 berths.

Since 1992 **active tourism** has been on the increase in Galicia. In 1996 Tur-Galicia published an Active Tourism Guide highlighting the travel companies and agencies that provide services and programmes with regard to mountain biking, horse riding and routes on horseback, climbing, potholing, skiing, bungee jumping, off-road driving, hiking, diving, sailing, wind-surfing, hot-air balloons, hang-gliding, ultra-light aircraft and catamaran or boat trips.

Training.
Galicia's Advanced Centre of Hostelry in Santiago de Compostela, with the help of Lausanne's prestigious École Hotelière, has filled the need for a hotel education system in Spain. The constant stream of applications is proof of the centre's success.

Organization of tourism promotion.
Tur-Galicia (Image and Tourism Promotion of Galicia) is a company with both public and private capital, which provides the necessary tourism promotion with the flexibility of a company.

Tur-Galicia employs modern promotion techniques: in its professional contacts and as regards the quality of its promotional materials and videos, in its participation in fairs, in which Galicia has been awarded prizes year after year. The proposal to open a tourism office in Madrid became a reality with the opening of "Casa de Galicia" (Galicia House), where tourist promotion and public information activities are carried out.

In 1996 Tur-Galicia participated in numerous international and national fairs. Its presentations of Galician tourist options to travel agents and the media were held in Latin American countries and Spain's main tourist sources, as well as workshops for company and convention organizers in Madrid and Barcelona. With regard to consumers, an important publicity campaign in the Galician and Spanish media was organized. Another technique was also widely used: promotional trips for journalists and travel agents to familiarize them with Galicia.

Two specialized programmes were also launched: "La Escapada Gallega" (The Galician Break) and "Galicia, aprender a divertirse" (Galicia, learn to enjoy yourself), for schoolchildren. Along with the other northern Autonomous Communities, the "Green Spain" programme was re-launched and well-received in Spain and Europe.

Galicia's Advanced Centre of Hostelry

Tourism infrastructures.
In recent years there has been a progressive increase in the accommodation capacity, despite the decrease in the number of cheap hotels and boarding houses. This indicates that there are now more hotel beds

available, which reflects an improvement in tourism quality. This tendency is expected to continue thanks to the end-of-millennium cultural landmarks.

The monasteries of Samos, Sobrado dos Monxes, Oseira and Poio also offer accommodation. The massive influx of tourists to Galicia's beaches makes summer the high season. Hygiene and health improvements and the establishment of services resulted in the awarding of European Union Blue Flags to 31 beaches and 4 ports.

Galician beach.

Tourism and trade balance.

Tourism is reinvigorating Galicia's economy. Galicia is in seventh place as regards the number of visitors, after the classical "sun and beach" resorts (Balearic Islands, Canary Islands, Andalusia, Catalonia and Valencia) and Madrid, the state capital. As regards the Bay of Biscay coast, it is in first place.

Tourist income amounts to 5.5% of the Gross Domestic Product. The tourist sector accounts for 12.7% of total employment.

THE FUTURE.

There is every indication that Galician tourism will experience a second development phase at the end of the nineties, as a continuation of the one that began in 1990. Such expansion will be boosted by the completion of dual carriageways linking Galicia with the centre of Spain, Santiago's "1999 Xacobeo Holy Year" and "Santiago de Compostela, European City of Culture in the Year 2000".

Compostela, World Heritage City, is the destination of the Way of Saint James, declared as the "First European Cultural Itinerary" by UNESCO.

Auditorium of Galicia. Santiago de Compostela. All Galicia and especially Santiago de Compostela are preparing for the 1999 Holy Year and its status as a European City of Culture in the yea 2000. Galicia will be one of Europe's tourism centres. This Auditorium holds wonderful concerts and extraordinary exhibitions.

XXVI

CULTURE AND SPORTS

- Culture. Galician arts and culture.
  - -Books.
  - -Libraries.
  - -Stage arts.
  - -Cultural diffusion.
  - -Audiovisual.
  - -Plastic arts.
- Infrastructures.
- "Galicia, Terra Única."
- The Way of Saint James.
- Sports and leisure facilities.
- Sports policy.
- Sports promotion..
- Galicia's participation in top-class sports.

CULTURE AND SPORTS.

The number of books published in Galicia has gone from less than 300 in 1982 to more than 1,000 in 1996.

GALICIAN ARTS AND CULTURE.

Books.

While twenty years ago mainly literary (poetry and fiction) books were published, today all kinds of books are being published in Galicia. An important percentage of titles are school or children's books, accounting for almost 40% of all published books.

An incipient publishing industry is beginning to develop, with the participation of large publishing groups that offer permanent collections of Galician-language books. Galician-owned companies have become more professional and now compete qualitatively with Spanish ones, almost exclusively in the school-book market.

Some publishers, such as Galaxia or Edicións Xerais de Galicia, have a total collection of more than 1,000 titles.

Booksellers, publishers and the Xunta de Galicia organize 15 book fairs in Galicia's main towns and cities in order to present potential readers with a variety of books.

Galicia has a long writing tradition and is the home of two prestigious Spanish-language writers: Gonzalo Torrente Ballester and Camilo José Cela, Noble Prizewinner for Literature.

As regards Galician-language writers, Xabier Puente Docampo and Fina Casalderrey won the National Children's Literature Prize in 1995 and 1996, respectively. Manuel Rivas was awarded the National Fiction Prize in 1996. Previous national prizes were obtained by Alfredo Conde, Teresa Barro, Valentín Arias, Raquel Villanueva or Antón Santamarina. The books of many Galician writers have been translated into other Spanish or European languages.

Bust of Camilo José Cela in Iria Flavia, Padrón.

Book illustration, despite the difficulty of publishing in colour, has advanced noticeably and some artists are beginning to receive international recognition, such as López Domínguez, who has been selected several times for the Bologna Fair (Italy) and won prizes at the Bratislava Fair. Miguelanxo Prado, an internationally renowned artist, publishes his comics worldwide. In 1997 he participated in a project with the cinema director Steven Spielberg.

The literary journals *A trabe de ouro, Anuario de estudios literarios galegos, Boletín Galego de Literatura* and *Grial* enjoy prestige in the literature world. *Grial* is the longest running, with more than 130 issues published.

Libraries.

Galicia has a network of public municipal libraries and reading agencies with more than 300 centres; every town with a population of more than 2,000 inhabitants is equipped with a reading centre.

The Galician library network's nodal libraries situated in A Coruña, Lugo, Ourense, Pontevedra and Vigo, which are run by the Autonomous Administration, have considerably improved the services they offer.

The head of the library system is the Department of Culture and Social Communication's *Advanced Library Centre of Galicia,* which coordinates the libraries and creates bibliographic databases with the *Joint Catalogue of Bibliographic Patrimony,* in collaboration with the central administration and other autonomous communities. The project of digitalizing Galicia's press and periodicals, which began in 1997, is worth mentioning.

Stage arts.

Theatre, music and dance have a long tradition. The *Theatre, music and dance guide* of 1997 contains information about more than 1,300 groups. According to it, Galicia has 116 theatre groups, between professional and amateur ones, more than 1,000 musical associations and more than 200 classical and traditional dance groups.
This richness of artistic manifestations goes back a long time and includes the participation of numerous children and young people. Milladoiro and Carlos Núñez are internationally well-known and give concerts in the United States and Japan.

In summer Galicia is full of feasts, most of which have a long tradition. They include the participation of music bands, groups of bagpipes and dance or theatre groups.

Street theatre, one of the most popular artistic manifestations.

Different production, promotion and diffusion projects regarding all kinds of theatre, dance and music are undertaken by the *Galician Institute of Stage and Musical Arts,* which runs the following three entities: the *Galician Dramatic Centre,* the *Rey de Viana Galician Ballet* and the *Autonomous Community's Group of Bagpipes.*

In the field of classical music, the *Real Filharmonía* philharmonic orchestra, conducted by Helmuth Rilling and Maximino Zumalave, stands out. It runs the *School of Advanced Music Studies* and the *Young Orchestra of Galicia.* The *Symphony Orchestra of Galicia* is run by the A Coruña City Council.

Cultural diffusion.

There are more than 3,000 registered cultural associations whose cultural objectives are specifically mentioned in their charters. They carry out multiple activities with regard to cultural diffusion, such as congresses, conferences, recitals or competitions.

The following associations stand out:

Cultural associations	
- Otero Pedrayo Foundation. - Rosalía de Castro Foundation. - Alfredo Brañas Foundation. - Foundation of Galician Art Criticism Prizes. - Cánovas del Castillo Foundation. - Pedrón de Ouro Trust. - Royal Sargadelos Trust. - Camilo José Cela Foundation.	- Castelao Foundation. - Vicente Risco Foundation. - Celso Emilio Ferreiro Foundation. - Jorge Castillo Foundation. - Mario Granell Foundation. - Prieto Nespereira Foundation. - Associations of plastic artists. - Music in Compostela.

Professional and amateur associations	
- Galician Choir Federation. - Federation of Galician Booksellers. - Galician Association of Publishers. - Association of Galician-Language Writers. - Pen Club. - Galician Association for Children's and Young People's Books.	- Galician Federation of Traditional Music Bands. - Galician Federation of Dance Groups. - Galician Association of Bagpipe Bands. - Association of Galician Bagpipers. - Association of Galician Theatre Companies.

Among the prizes awarded in recognition of creative talent, in its broadest sense, the Prize of Galician Literature and Art stands out. It has been awarded to Antón Fraguas (1995), José Filgueira Valverde (1996) and Francisco Fernández del Riego (1997) for their contribution to the development of cultural expansion in Galicia.

Castelao.

The *Galician Centre of Cultural* plays an important role in the diffusion of culture. It provides the latest information about exhibitions, congresses, courses, recently published books, cultural activities in the fields of theatre, music and dance, as well as other cultural news.

Audiovisual.

Although Galicia played a leading role in the appearance of films, it was only recently that an incipient audiovisual industry was created. A public Galician television company and, above all, the initiative of artists and technicians who are becoming more and more professionalised, are the main factors behind the growth of Galicia's audiovisual sector, which consists of 80 companies with a wide-ranging audiovisual production: industrial videos, advertising, television programmes, documentaries, films and, more recently, multimedia productions.

As regards film productions, there is an annual average of between one and three full-length feature films. In 1997 three full-length films were premiered and a similar number began to be produced. Since 1995 there has been a noticeable increase in the production of short-length films, especially due to the work of the *Image and Sound School.*

The Department of Culture and Social Communication runs a specialized organism in this sector: the *Galician Centre of Visual Arts* (CGAI), which has the following objectives:

- Recuperating and conserving Galicia's audiovisual patrimony.
- The diffusion of visual arts.
- Promoting the audiovisual sector, collaborating directly with professionals in the European field who are involved in the business development of productions.

Casa de la Parra.

Plastic arts.

Artistic activity, in its multiple manifestations, has a deep-rooted tradition in Galicia. Almost all Galician towns and cities, and many villages, have exhibition facilities, which have traditionally been supported by savings banks, foundations, recreational societies, businesses and the different public administrations. The private art galleries are grouped together in the *Association of Gallery Owners,* which organizes diffusion projects in Galicia, the rest of Spain and the North of Portugal, such as the Atlantic Forum held in A Coruña in 1997.

Places such as the Casa de la Parra and Pazo de Bendaña in Santiago de Compostela, the Kiosko Alfonso in A Coruña or the Caixa-Vigo Cultural Centre in Vigo are obligatory reference points as regards the artistic activities of recent years.

INFRASTRUCTURES.

There are 139 municipal districts with cultural centres. Another 35 were being created during 1997. The network is completed by the Congress and Exhibition Hall, the Auditorium of Galicia and the Principal Theatre in Santiago de Compostela, the Congress Hall and Coliseum in A Coruña, the Principal Theatre in Ourense, the Gustavo Freire Auditorium in Lugo, the Auditorium and Congress and Exhibition Hall in Pontevedra, the Caixa-Vigo Cultural Centre in Vigo and the Joffre Theatre in Ferrol.

Auditorium of Galicia.

"GALICIA, TERRA ÚNICA"

During 1997 the "Galicia, Terra Única" (Galicia, Unique Land) project was developed, with the aim of being Spain's most important cultural event. It included the celebration of 25 exhibitions and 250 shows, with a diversified proposal of artistic and socio-cultural activities throughout all Galicia.

By means of this project the Galician Government aims at gauging and transmitting the cultural force of a millenniums-old people that is alive and in constant development. This initiative will provide valuable experience as regards the preparation of two important events to be held in Galicia in the near future: the 1999 Xacobeo Holy Year and the celebration in Santiago, in the year 2,000, of its status as a European Capital of Culture.

All of Galicia's main cities held a thematic exhibition as a central reference point, complemented by activities aimed at highlighting Galicia's history and identity. These central exhibitions evoked the periods of Galician history that were most closely associated with each city:

- The city of Lugo, an old Roman town, was chosen as the project's starting point with the exhibition *Celtic and Roman Galicia.*
- Ourense, by means of its cathedral, presented *Romanesque and Gothic Galicia.*
- Santiago, due to the fundamental presence in its streets of Renaissance, baroque and neoclassical styles, held an exhibition on Galician history between 1500 and 1800.
- Pontevedra centred its proposal on 19th-century Galicia.
- Vigo was the venue of the exhibition about *Galicia abroad.*
- Ferrol displayed Galician artistic creations from 1900 to 1990.
- A Coruña presented *Galicia today.*

The *Galicia, Terra Única* programme also included different stage and musical manifestations in a total of 89 municipal districts. Cities and towns held concerts, recitals, children's events, theatre and dance productions and monographic shows about Galician cultural themes. These activities, complementing the large exhibitions, made up the programme of events between May and October, 1997.

THE WAY OF SAINT JAMES.

A long tradition, backed by ancient writings, associates the first evangelization of Spain with the preaching of the Apostle James. This tradition, supported by ancient accounts, before the discovery of the Apostle's tomb, is linked to that of the "traslatio" and the Apostle's burial in Spain, after being martyred in Jerusalem.

The Apostle's tomb was discovered at the beginning of the 9th century and news soon spread throughout Europe. Backed by the church, protected by kings and rooted in popular devotion, a stream of pilgrims converted Europe's main roads into pilgrimage routes to Santiago: the small village of S. Fiz de Solovio, at the foot of the Libredón forest, was transformed into Compostela and the final destination of the West's most important route. The Way of Saint James is a spiritual and cultural route and a "communication space" that, eleven centuries later, is as popular as ever, having been catalogued as the **First European Cultural Itinerary** by the Council of Europe, declared as *World Heritage* by UNESCO and described as "one of the pillars of the historical construction and formation of European cultural identity."

The French Way of Saint James.

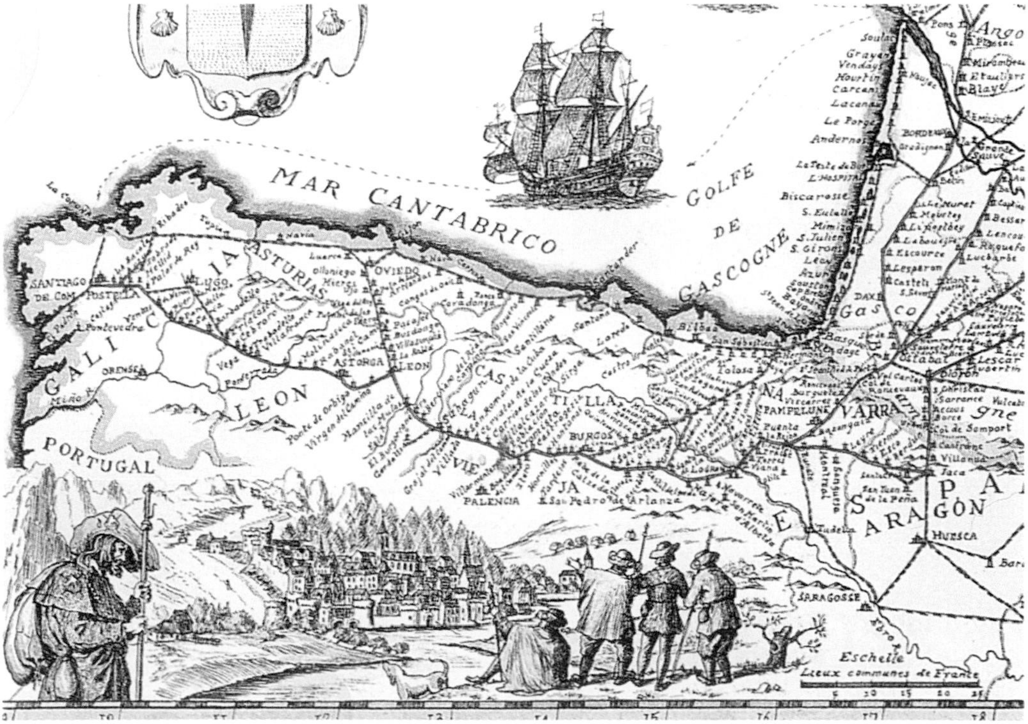

The Santiago pilgrimage is a highly significant theme with different dimensions:

- Geographical-territorial dimension that, in the form of a network or system of routes, covers a large part of Europe, with manifestations in distant places.
- Cultural dimension, which makes the Way an important space of creation and cultural communication.
- European dimension, highlighted by important international organisms.
- Socioeconomic dimension, which is presently being encouraged by means of Jacobean Plans, the first of which formed the basis for preparing and promoting the 1993 Holy Year.

During the Middle Ages, the Way of Saint James was the backbone of the spirituality, culture and economy of all of the North of Spain. It was not a spontaneous phenomenon, separate from the period's social life and politics. Under the direction of Sancho the Great and his successors in Navarre and that of Alfonso VI, Alfonso VII, Fernando II and Alfonso IX, some of whom where buried in Compostela, the Way's route and physical improvement were organized, including fords and bridges and its network of monasteries, hospitals, hostels and inns, the repopulating and establishment of new settlements, support for arts, craftsmanship and trade, the construction of cathedrals and churches, and legal protection for new settlers and pilgrims.

In 1999, the next Holy Year, a new cultural project will be set in motion: Xacobeo 99, whose most recent predecessor was the one held in 1993.

The most outstanding aspects of Xacobeo 1993 were its seven million visitors, who accounted for 38 million stays, its wide-ranging popular support, new specialized infrastructures (150 km of pilgrim routes rehabilitated, 16 hostels, Monte del Gozo reception complex), urbanistic construction work in localities and towns along the French Way and the creation of cultural infrastructures in Santiago de Compostela (Congress Hall, Sar Sports Centre, etc), the wide-ranging parallel cultural programme and the extremely important recognition and support of prestigious international organisms: UNESCO, "Euoropa Nostra" Prize.

The activities for 1999 are in harmony with the Council of Europe's Declaration of Santiago de Compostela, divided into the following seven sections:

- Identification and demarcation of the different Ways and their cataloguing and legal protection.
- Information and signposting.

- Conservation and study of cultural, historical-artistic, archaeological, ethnographic and natural patrimony.
- Socioeconomic and cultural promotion.
- Foreign promotion and transregional and transnational exchange and cooperation programmes.
- Support for artistic creation regarding the Santiago pilgrimage: music, theatre, poetry, plastic arts...
- Special programmes in relation to support activities, safety, civil protection, health, volunteer service, etc.

"Galicia, Terra Única" is the forerunner of the second millennium's last Xacobeo Holy Year. Xacobeo 1999 will also include two unique aspects:

- The relationship with Jerusalem and Rome, Western Christianity's other two main pilgrimage centres.
- The subsequent celebration in the year 2000 of the Roman Holy Year and the fact that Santiago de Compostela will be a European Capital of Culture in the same year.

Fontes de Sar Sports Centre.

SPORTS AND LEISURE FACILITIES. SPORTS POLICY.

Sports have also become an important part of the transformation process being experienced by Galician society, thereby becoming another indicator of the improvement in the quality of life. The creation in 1989 of the General Secretariat for Sports led to important changes in the sports scene, infrastructures, and the promotion of and support for sports.

The *Comprehensive Sports Facilities Plan* was designed to correct the imbalances between rural and urban Galicia, and the historical delay that had been experienced in this sector. Galicia's sports infrastructures are now on a level with those of the most advanced communities.

The first objective of the basic plans to create sports facilities was providing all of Galicia's municipal districts with a covered sports centre.

Furthermore, the infrastructure plan also established that municipal districts with more than 10,000 inhabitants should be equipped with a second covered sports centre, and that those with more than 16,000 inhabitants should have covered, heated swimming-pools.

This programme also includes the construction of athletic tracks in municipal districts and regions where such sports are popular, and equipping large population centres with a complete range of sports facilities: neighbourhood sports centres, heated swimming pools and large sports and leisure grounds.

SPORTS PROMOTION.

This is carried out by subsidizing sports federations and clubs with a policy of encouraging sports in collaboration with federations, clubs and other sports entities.

The first objective is attained by means of requirements that are negotiated and annually updated with Galicia's 56 federations. Thus, the subsidies are applied automatically, without having to apply for them.

School sports activities are directly promoted by means of campaigns such as "Sports at School Age" and the Technical Training Programme, designed to prepare trainers in different sports, who thereafter promote and extend them.

Sports modernization is also being developed by means of the *Pontevedra Centre,* the *INEF of Galicia* and the *Galician Sports School,* in collaboration with the top-class federations and clubs of each sector.

GALICIA'S PARTICIPATION IN TOP-CLASS SPORTS.

Galician sports have obtained important achievements. In athletics, Julia Vaquero and Alejandro Gómez are the main representatives of a generation of athletes that have won international victories for Spanish sports. In handball, three Galician clubs play in the Asobal league. Volleyball has several teams at top-class national level. In rowing, Galician competitors often finish in the leading positions.

Galician canoeing is the best in Spain, which explains why 50% of the canoeists in the national team are from Galicia. In sailing, Galicia has international champions in ocean classes such as Javier de la Gándara,

José María Lastra or Pedro Campos; in Atlanta, three Galicians were included in the national team.

Other sports such as swimming, cycling, martial arts or wrestling also contribute to the consolidation of Galician sports.

In short, the Xunta de Galicia's policy is to bring sports and society closer together and improve the quality of life. The continuous increase in the number of sports licences, clubs, entities and associations, of professionals in the fields of physical education and sports technique, as well as in the number of participants in school competitions, is a reflection of the excellent state of Galician sports.

Index

GALLICIA.
OCEANUS OCCIDENTALIS.
C. de Bellem
C. Coriane
C. de Finisterre
C de Prior
Sisarga ysla
Coruña
Cayon
Malpico
Mons
Ançobre
Terrio
Val de la Veyga
Camelle
Laxe
Camarinnas
Tinis
Lamas
Penela
Villar d' Francos
Encobra
Carral
Travies[a]
Brives
Mongia
Viniancο
Finisterre
Saas
Vergantin-os
Figueroa
Buscas
Montas
Polo
Villa dabao
Bacariza
Corcalion
Cea
Mojinno
Xallos
Port de Portomouro
P. Signeyro
Baynas
P. Brandomil
Rio Lezaro
P. Alvar
Barcala
Dos casas
P. Maceyras
Altamira
Muros
R. Tambre
Luáña
Alquoidos
Compostella
Nota
Nebra
Docon
Villa major
Puebla del Dean
Agoeyro
Rianio
R. Bucacos
Franços
Tabeiros
Padron
Chapa
Carril
Torres do Este
P. Valga
Villa Garcia
Vanueua
Caldas
Daroca
Groba Ysla
Cambados
P. de Combarro
R. Leria
Pontevedra
Bldones
P. de Marin
Soto maior
Campo de
Redondela
Cagias
Vigo
Boneas
Mos
Yslas d'Bayon
Mosente
Porrino
Gondomar
Entenca
Bayona
Tuy
Salvat[ierra]
Forcadella
Valencia
Barca
Guardia
PORT
Leucæ Hispanicæ
Septentr
Merid